Meaning-making Methods for Coping with Serious Illness

This book provides an alternative, complementary approach to the existing conventional approaches to religious and spiritually oriented coping. By focusing on the role of culture, the authors take into account the methods employed by a vast number of people who do not directly identify themselves as religious. The empirical data used in this book derive from studies conducted in several countries; Sweden, China, South Korea, Turkey and Malaysia, across which religion plays a different role in the social and cultural life of individuals. This approach and these empirical data are unique and allow comparisons to be made between different cultural settings.

By introducing the concept of meaning-making coping, the authors explore the influence of culture on choice of coping methods, be they purely religious, spiritual or secular. The term "meaning-making coping" is used to describe secular coping methods that are related to existential questions; these methods include religious, spiritual and secular existential coping methods.

Meaning-making Methods for Coping with Serious Illness contributes to new approaches and theoretical models of coping. As such it is an invaluable resource for health care, medical, public health and sociology students and researchers. It will also be of interest to educators and policy-makers working in the area of health.

Fereshteh Ahmadi, PhD, Full Professor of Sociology, Faculty of Health and Occupational Studies, University of Gävle, Sweden. Professor Ahmadi is presently specializing in issues related to health, religion and spirituality. In addition, she has conducted research on *gerontology, international migration,* Islamic Feminism and Music and Coping at Uppsala University. She is responsible for a research on Diversity Barometer. She is also responsible for an international project on Meaning-Making Coping. The project involves researchers from Sweden, South Korea, China, Japan, Malaysia, Philippines, Brazil, Turkey, Portugal and Iran.

Nader Ahmadi, PhD, Full Professor of Sociology and pro vice-chancellor of the University of Gävle, Sweden. His research has mainly focused on areas such as welfare and social policy, international social work, identity and youth problems, coping strategies among cancer patients, socio-cultural perceptions of the self and gender roles. Professor Ahmadi has extensive experience of international research and development projects in more than 15 countries, from Eastern Europe to Central and South-East Asia. He has been a consultant for UNICEF, the UN, the World Bank, and the European Union.

Routledge Advances in the Medical Humanities

Collaborative Arts-based Research for Social Justice
Victoria Foster

Person-centred Health Care
Balancing the Welfare of Clinicians and Patients
Stephen Buetow

Digital Storytelling in Health and Social Policy
Listening to Marginalized Voices
Nicole Matthews and Naomi Sunderland

Bodies and Suffering
Emotions and Relations of Care
Ana Dragojlovic and Alex Broom

Thinking with Metaphors in Medicine
The State of the Art
Alan Bleakley

Medicine, Health and Being Human
Edited by Lesa Scholl

Meaning-making Methods for Coping with Serious Illness
Fereshteh Ahmadi and Nader Ahmadi

A Visual History of HIV/AIDS
Exploring The Face of AIDS film archive
Edited by Elisabet Björklund and Mariah Larsson

https://www.routledge.com/Routledge-Advances-in-Disability-Studies/book-series/RADS

Meaning-making Methods for Coping with Serious Illness

Fereshteh Ahmadi and Nader Ahmadi

LONDON AND NEW YORK

First published 2018
by Routledge
2 Park Square, Milton Park, Abingdon, Oxon OX14 4RN

and by Routledge
711 Third Avenue, New York, NY 10017

Routledge is an imprint of the Taylor & Francis Group, an informa business

© 2018 Fereshteh Ahmadi and Nader Ahmadi

The right of Fereshteh Ahmadi and Nader Ahmadi to be identified as authors of this work has been asserted by them in accordance with sections 77 and 78 of the Copyright, Designs and Patents Act 1988.

All rights reserved. No part of this book may be reprinted or reproduced or utilised in any form or by any electronic, mechanical, or other means, now known or hereafter invented, including photocopying and recording, or in any information storage or retrieval system, without permission in writing from the publishers.

Trademark notice: Product or corporate names may be trademarks or registered trademarks, and are used only for identification and explanation without intent to infringe.

British Library Cataloguing-in-Publication Data
A catalogue record for this book is available from the British Library

Library of Congress Cataloging-in-Publication Data
A catalog record for this book has been applied for

ISBN: 978-1-138-29936-8 (hbk)
ISBN: 978-1-315-09803-6 (ebk)

Typeset in Times New Roman
by Apex CoVantage, LLC

Contents

List of figures vii
List of tables viii
Contributor ix
Foreword x
Acknowledgments xvii

1 Introduction 1
Objectives and the scope of the book 2
The structure of the book 2

2 Theoretical framework 8
Religion/religiousness, spirituality, and transcendence 8
Definitions of religiosity and spirituality in meaning-making coping studies 15
Definition of coping 17
The many methods of religious coping: RCOPE 21
References 25

3 Western Protestant culture Swedish culture and coping 28
Introduction 28
Religious coping methods (RCOPE) 29
Existential secular coping methods 36
What do the statistics have to say? 41
The Swedish studies on coping from a cultural perspective 52
Notes 56
References 57

4 The study in East Asia 60
The study in South Korea 60
The study in China 65
Culture and meaning-making coping in East Asia 70
References 73

5 The study in Muslim countries 77
The study in Turkey 77
What do the statistics say? 82
The study in Malaysia 89
Culture and meaning-making coping in Turkey and Malaysia 93
Notes 97
References 97

6 The relationship between culture and health 101
Health 101
A macro-sociological perspective 102
Globalization, health, and culture 105
The relationship between religion and health 107
Sanctification in coping from a cultural perspective 120
Religious struggles and culture 132
Summary 136
Notes 138
References 138

Index 142

List of figures

0.1	Cultural dimensions in healthcare contexts	xiii
5.1	Description of the sample – age – Turkey	83
6.1	Sacred core and ring (Pargament et al., 2017: 3)	123
6.2	Alternative sacred core and ring	130
6.3	Relation of existential meaning-making domains (La Cour & Hvidt, 2010: 1294)	135
6.4	Alternative relation of existential meaning-making domains	136

List of tables

3.1	Sample	29
3.2	Coping methods	43
4.1	Demographic characteristics of the participants, South Korea	60
5.1	Demographic characteristics of the participants, Turkey	77
5.2	Demographic characteristics of the participants, Malaysia	90

Contributor

Valerie DeMarinis, Ph.D., Psychologist. Full Professor in Psychology of Religion and Cultural Psychology. She holds three professorships in Sweden and Norway in the areas of psychology of religion and cultural psychology, public health promotion, and public mental health. In the clinical context, she is responsible for developing the meaning-making assessment framework, including existential meaning, used in mapping patient worldviews. Her clinical work and research in these areas include international experience in Sweden, Norway, the United States, Brazil, Syria and Japan.

Foreword

Health, existential information, and culture

It is a privilege to be invited to prepare the Foreword to this volume, *Meaning-making Methods for Coping with Serious Illness*. In so many respects, the volume contributes to one of the most important topics in healthcare today, across the globe in different cultural contexts, and in the new cultural formations brought about through globalization processes, involving movement of persons and groups by choice or due to forced circumstances.

My hope and intention in this Foreword is to provide a perspective for approaching the integrated concerns of health, existential information, and culture, which are also among the key concerns undergirding this volume. Naturally, this perspective emerges from the research, clinical consultation, and clinical work I have done particularly in the areas of mental health, addiction treatment, migration health, and mental health and well-being in palliative care. The name of the perspective is public mental health promotion, and the central question guiding us is: 'Why is meaning-making essential for promoting mental health and well-being in coping processes during serious illness?'

Perspective of Public Mental Health Promotion

In 1980, the World Health Organization (WHO) through the initiative of the European office and the Ottawa Charter for Health Promotion (1986), developed a renewed understanding of the term, health promotion. Central to this understanding was a shift in perspective beginning with the definition of health as the ability to realize aspirations and satisfy needs and to change or cope with the environment. This third revolution in public health, as summarized by Kickbush (1986, 2003), sees health promotion as built on the following principles: 1) involve the population as a whole in the context of everyday lives; 2) be directed towards action on the determinants of health; 3) combine diverse but complementary methods or approaches; 4) aim for effective and concrete public participation; and, 5) involve health professionals. Areas covered by health promotion activities (Kickbush 1986, 2003) need to include: 1) access to health; 2) development of an environment conductive to health; 3) strengthening of social networks and social supports; 4) promoting positive health behavior and appropriate coping strategies; and. 5) increasing knowledge and disseminating information.

The public health promotion framework involves an important reorienting process in health policy priorities from a risk factor approach to strategies that address the determinants of health and empower people to participate in improving the health of their communities. The focus is shifted toward health determinants rather than health behaviors.

In examining these public health promotion principles, it becomes clear that public health promotion needs to incorporate fully public mental health and public mental health promotion. The summarizing principles from the WHO mental health webpage (2016) provide the logic behind this need for the fundamental role of public mental health in public health:

- Mental health is more than the absence of mental disorders.
- Mental health is an integral part of health; indeed, there is no health without mental health.
- Mental health is determined by a range of socioeconomic, biological and environmental factors.
- Cost-effective public health and intersectoral strategies and interventions exist to promote, protect, and restore mental health.

Public mental health promotion involves actions to create living conditions and environments that support mental health and allow people to adopt and maintain a level of mental health and well-being throughout the lifecycle.

Understanding the role of public mental health in a larger public health promotion research agenda is exemplified in the priority research areas of the ROAMER (Roadmap for Mental Health Research in Europe) project. It aimed to develop a comprehensive and integrated mental health research agenda within the perspective of the European Union (EU) Horizon 2020 program, with a translational goal, covering basic, clinical, and public health research.

In the initial listing of 20 areas presented in a ranked listing (Forsman et al., 2015) the first three ranked priority areas include:

1 Positive mental health and well-being and protective factors should be increasingly addressed in public mental health research.
2 Public mental health research should build on interdisciplinary perspectives in order to understand the complexity of mental health.
3 To strengthen the understanding of the cultural factors (i.e., ethnicity, religion and value systems and nationality), relevant for public mental health.

Clearly, concerns for public mental health and well-being are concerns for all human beings. Public mental health promotion involves the societal level and not only the individual or group treatment level of understanding the importance of meaning-making and existential meaning strategies. This is emphasized in the WHO and ROAMER points and principles, as health promotion involves coordination at the inter-sectorial levels. In the macro (national), meso (community), and micro (group and individual) level plans for public mental health promotion, research at the meso level needs to be prioritized (Kickbush, 2003).

As this current volume is focused on meaning-making coping methods in relation to serious illness, attention to mental health and well-being aspects are essential. The need for attention to these areas is supported by statistics concerning the growing number of older adults (WHO, 2017), many of whom will develop serious illness conditions, conditions not infrequently involving multiple conditions of serious illness, related to both mental health and somatic diagnoses. The situation of multiple conditions is not limited to older adults, but may result in other populations struggling with severe illness as well. And, even if there is not a diagnosis of mental ill-health involved, certainly finding strategies to deal with decreased well-being through social isolation, perceived stigma, psychological distress, and existential anguish, are of primary importance. Critically important for the work of public mental health, and especially through a health promotion perspective, as noted in the third priority area, understanding cultural factors is essential.

Approaching culture and meaning-making

Central to a public mental health promotion approach is an understanding of meaning-making. Meaning-making takes place within cultural contexts. Here culture is understood as an open, dynamic system of practices, rules, and knowledge that "includes language, religion and spirituality, family structures, life-cycle stages, ceremonial rituals, and customs, as well as moral and legal systems" (American Psychiatric Association, DSM-5, 2013: 749).

Before examining how meaning-making is approached here, let us look at a model of the cultural dimensions, developed originally by the medical anthropologist and psychiatrist Arthur Kleinman (1980, see also DeMarinis, 2003) for understanding the types of information needed from patients to understand and work with them throughout their illness (See Figure 0.1).

Examining the figure, the five dimensions in the model are connected through arrows going in both directions indicating that the dimensions are connected and a change in one can bring about changes in the others. The dimensions include: existential/symbolic meaning; biological-physical; psychological; social; and ecological. The biological-physical dimension is focused on the body's ways of functioning. This dimension includes both the body's biochemical/neurological processes as well as the body's way of reacting to and approaching its surroundings (DeMarinis 2003: 44–45). The psychological dimension includes aspects of the personality, intra-personal and inter-personal coping strategies, memory processing, etc. (DeMarinis 2003: 44–45). The social dimension focuses on the relational world including social structures, networks, society, and also the institutions that function as normative and meaning-giving systems as well as the power system they present (DeMarinis 2003: 44–45). The ecological dimension refers to the interactions with the environment including both natural and constructed structures and spaces (DeMarinis 2003: 44–45). The existential/symbolic

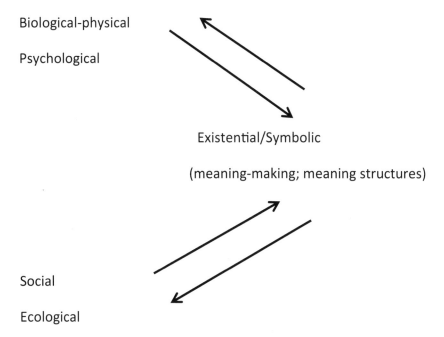

Figure 0.1 Cultural dimensions in healthcare contexts
(DeMarinis, 2003, 2010; adaption of Kleninman, 1980)

meaning dimension focuses on the information contained in the primary stories, beliefs, rituals, symbols of deepest meaning for understanding life, death, health, ill-health (disease), illness, and coping (DeMarinis 2003: 44–45). As changes happen through the illness experience, on any of the dimensions, they will need to be processed through the existential/symbolic meaning dimension. In this way, new or modified information can be added, deleted, or adjusted. The existential/symbolic meaning dimension can be understood, therefore, ss coordinating the adjustment and coping processes. This is why access to information in this dimension is so very important. This entire model could well be renamed, and will so be for future publications, the "Meaning-making model of cultural dimensions in health care contexts", as both the larger meaning-making process (including all the dimensions and their interactions) as well as the specific existential/symbolic meaning dimension's function are included.

Being able to access information on all of these dimensions from the patient, the person, in a safe and trusted environment is essential for the treatment process and for maximizing the mental health and well-being aspects of care. The American Psychiatric Association's guidelines for the Culture Formulation Interview (CFI) (American Psychiatric Association, 2013) state that: "Understanding the cultural context of illness experience is essential for effective diagnostic assessment and clinical management" (American Psychiatric Association 2013: 749), and note that "all forms of distress are locally shaped" (American Psychiatric Association 2013: 758). The 16-question CFI covers the following areas of information:

- Cultural definition of the problem;
- Cultural perceptions of cause, context, and support;
- Stressors and supports;
- Role of cultural identity;
- Cultural factors affecting self-coping and past help seeking; and
- Cultural factors affecting current help seeking.

It is for use with every patient, and though developed in mental health, it is now being used in somatic contexts as well.

Understanding the role of culture in how people make meaning has been given considerable attention in terms of refugee, immigrant, and minority group acculturation processes and the importance of this information for the clinical diagnostic process not in the least in mental health research (Lewis-Fernández et al., 2014). Research with clinical groups within the majority population also highlights the importance of cultural assessment for understanding differences in meaning-making processes at the individual patient level (DeMarinis et al., 2009; Haug et al., 2015). The DSM-5 inclusion of the "Cultural Formulation Interview" (CFI) has been described as a meaning-making tool for use with all patients (Lewis-Fernández et al., 2016). Gaining access to a patient's way of making meaning is essential to a person-centered approach (Mezzich & Salloum, 2008; DeMarinis, 2014), strengthens the therapeutic alliance and medical communication (Lewis-Fernández, 2016) and increases the empowerment, resilience, and involvement of patients in the therapeutic process (DeMarinis, 2014).

Worldview analysis in psychiatry (Josephson & Peteet, 2004) and the growing tradition of meaning-making assessment of global and local patterns in clinical therapeutic contexts (such as Schnell, 2011) has focused special attention to spiritual or existential meaning components as central to the larger meaning-making process. In the more secularized and multi-cultural Scandinavian context a means of approaching the complex "religious/spiritual" or other system (nature, atheist) dimension of meaning-making in clinical work and research is frequently referred to in a broader framework of meaning-making processes (DeMarinis et al., 2011; Ulland & DeMarinis; Lloyd et al., 2015). Within many Swedish and Norwegian clinical contexts existential meaning, as a focused dimension of the larger meaning-making process, is understood as a category of information that every patient has, though the content and function may vary widely. Existential information here includes both larger life questions AND daily life concerns, AND the function of such (DeMarinis, 2014). Identifying existing existential meaning strategies, and working with individuals and groups to strengthen or build new strategies that contribute to well-being and support resilience are public mental health promotion aims. Gaining access to existential meaning information, existential meaning strategies, and to meaning-making more generally means gaining access to and assessing the patient's sources of meaning. Meaning-making, especially in clinical contexts, is not a static process. Inclusion of health promoting cultural and meaning-making information in the clinical context is essential for proper diagnosing and for development of treatment strategies in the clinical context (Lewis-Fernández, 2016). Not including this information may not only lead to incorrect diagnosis, but may also have a negative effect for patients' mental health (Lilja et al., 2016; DeMarinis, 2014).

Concluding note

In the opening paragraph I noted that this volume makes contributions in many respects to this very important topic. It is a complex volume that takes very seriously the need for critical thinking, clear definitions, culturally-situated and culturally-informed knowledge, and a multi-disciplinary approach that always anchors the reader in the primary discipline, approach, or framework that is being used. It adds both explicitly and implicitly to critical reflection on the development of theoretical insights as well as highlights methodological challenges. The country chapters provide intricate case studies reflecting insightful research team work, teams entrusted with the precious meaning-making stories, coping strategies, and existential information of patients in the context of culture, persons in the midst of living and coping with serious illness.

Returning to our guiding question: "Why is meaning-making essential for promoting mental health and well-being in coping processes during serious illness?" Meaning-making is essential in addressing all of life situations, and all the more so when addressing the challenges brought on by serious illness. The paradigm presented here has, it is hoped, provided an initial foundation for understanding how important mental health and well-being aspects are in relation to all illness situations. As a clinician and public mental health promotion researcher and strategist, gaining access to a person's way of making meaning provides essential information needed for person-centered and responsive best practice care. From a public mental health promotion perspective, built from a cultural dimensions model, the knowledge that ALL persons have this information yet that the content of the information will vary greatly across and often within cultures, pushes us to understand that this is a type of information we cannot get elsewhere. Using broad categories, such as meaning-making, and an inclusive category for the existential/symbolic meaning dimension (as in Figure 0.1), are essential strategies that are used in public health and public mental health research. Using these broad and inclusive categories does not mean that we are making the claim that there is no difference between types of content and how they actually function for the person. Here is where societal cultural-knowledge, community/group knowledge, and individual/family knowledge becomes essential. But without the more broad and inclusive categorization it is quite possible to mislabel or exclude persons from being able to provide this essential information in the clinical context.

Valerie DeMarinis

References

DeMarinis, V. (2003). *Pastoral care, existential health, and Existential Epidemiology. A Swedish postmodern case study.* Stockholm: Verbum Förlag.

DeMarinis, V. (2008). The impact of postmodernization on existential health in Sweden: Psychology of religion's function in existential public health analysis. *Archive for the Psychology of Religion*, 30: 57–74.

DeMarinis, V. (2014) Public mental health promotion, meaning-making and existential meaning: Challenges for person-centered care of refugees in a secular, pluralistic context. In G. Overland, E. Guribye, & B. Lie (Eds.), *Nordic work with traumatised refugees: Do we really care?* (pp. 316–324). Newcastle upon Tyne: Cambridge Scholars.

DeMarinis V., Scheffel-Birath C., & Hansagi H. (2009) Cultural analysis as a perspective for gender-informed alcohol treatment research in a Swedish context. *Alcohol and Alcoholism*, 44(6):615–619.

DeMarinis, V., Ulland, D., & Karlsen, K. E. (2011). Philosophy's role for guiding theory and practice in clinical contexts grounded in a cultural psychiatry focus: A case study illustration from southern Norway. *World Cultural Psychiatry Research Review*, 6(1): 47–56.

Forsman, A. et al. (2015) Research priorities for public mental health in Europe: Recommendations of the ROAMER project. *European Journal of Public Health*, 25 (2): 249–254.

Haug, S. H. K., DeMarinis, V., Danbolt, L. J., & Kvigne. K. (2016) The illness reframing process in an ethnic-majority population of older people with incurable cancer: Variations of cultural- and existential meaning-making adjustment.- *Mental Health, Religion & Culture,* 19(2):150–163, DOI: 10.1080/13674676.2015.1126705.

Kleinman, A. (1980). *Patients and healers in the context of culture.* Berkeley: University of California Press.

Lewis-Fernández, R., Aggarwal, N. K., Bäärnhielm, S. et al. (2014). Culture and psychiatric evaluation: Operationalizing cultural formulation for DSM-5. *Psychiatry*, 77: 130–154.

Lewis-Fernández R., Krishan Aggarwal, N., Hinton, L., et al. (Red., 2016). *DSM-5 Handbook on the cultural formulation interview.* Washington, DC: American Psychiatric Publishing.

Lloyd, C. S., af Klinteberg, B., & DeMarinis, V. (2017). An assessment of existential worldview function among young women at risk for depression and anxiety – a multi-method study. *Archive for the Psychology of Religion,* 39(2): 165–203.

Mezzich J. E. & Salloum I. M. (2008). Clinical complexity and person-centered integrative diagnosis. *World Psychiatry,* 7: 1–2.

Schnell, T. (2011). Individual differences in meaning-making: Considering the variety of sources of meaning, their density and diversity. *Personality and Individual Differences,* 51: 667–673.

Other sources

American Psychiatric Association. (2013). Diagnostic and statistical manual of mental disorders (5th ed.) (DSM-5). Washington: Author.

Ottawa Charter for Health Promotion (1986). In Health Promotion, l. 1. Geneva, Switzerland: World Health Organization, iii–v.

WHO (2016). Mental health: strengthening our response. Retrieved 13 January 2017 from http://www.who.int/mediacentre/factsheets/fs220/en/.

WHO (2017). Mental Health of Older Adults. Retrieved 15 September 2017 from http://www.who.int/mediacentre/factsheets/fs381/en/

Acknowledgments

We are first of all grateful to our informants in different countries. We would like to express our very great appreciation to our colleges in the project Meaning-making Coping in different countries, Dr. Kyung Mee Kim (Soongsil University, South Korea), Dr. Jisung Park (Retirement Research Center, South Korea), Dr. Chen Weijia (Chinese Academy of Social Science, China), Dr. Pelin Erbil (Oncology Clinic, Humanity Psychiatry, Turkey), Dr. Önver, A. Cetrez (Uppsala University, Sweden), Mrs. Asli Ortakmac (Cancer Survivors Association, Turkey), Dr. Nur Atikah Mohamed Hussin (Sains Malaysia University, Malaysia), Dr. Mohd Taufik Mohammad (Sains Malaysia University, Malaysia) and Fariba Mousavi, Master in Psychology (Stockholm University). We are particularly grateful to the University of Gävle for the financial support for this research project. We would like to thank Riksbankens Jubeleumsfond (The Swedish Foundation for the Humanities and Social Sciences) for its grant and also the Swedish Research Institute in Istanbul; without these organizations' help the study in Turkey would be difficult. We wish also to acknowledge the help provided by Karen Williams in editing the book.

The project on the basis of which this book is written was supported by grants from the University of Gävle and Riksbankens Jubeleumsfond and the Swedish Foundation for the Humanities and Social Sciences.

1 Introduction

Each year, millions of people die of cancer. WHO estimates that by 2030 the cause of death for one in five men and one in six women will be cancer. It is, thus, not surprising that cancer causes tremendous feelings of anxiety, fear, despair, and powerlessness among those hit by these disease. Patients, all around the world, grab hold of what is within their reach to lessen the burden they are carrying and to cope with cancer. Depending on the historic, socioeconomic, and cultural contexts in which they live, individuals choose or adhere to different coping methods.

Although there is a large body of literature examining how people cope with different serious illnesses, the effects of contextual parameters, among others culture, have largely been neglected. This lack of attention exists despite a strong body of research studying the effect of religious attitudes and beliefs, as well as spiritual feelings, on help-seeking behavior. Traditionally, researchers have found significant relations (both negative and positive) between religious and spiritual variables and mental health. Some researchers have showed greater sensitivity to, and integration of religion and spirituality in their research. Much of this research, however, has been conducted in the United States, where religion is an integrated part of a large number of individuals' lives. Studies on religious and spiritually oriented coping in other countries have also mainly been conducted among religious people. There are, however, many individuals who are either non-believers or, if believers, do not consider themselves religious people, i.e., religion is not an important part of their life. We also find societies in which the dominant culture and ways of thinking do not leave much scope for religion to play an important role in people's lives. This issue is rarely taken into consideration in the research area focused on coping. An important question to pose here is, thus: What role does culture play in coping? And what is the role of culture and ways of thinking in the choice of religious and spiritually oriented coping methods? To answer these questions, there is a need for sociologically and clinically relevant theoretical frameworks to advance research in this area by focusing on the cultural perspective. This book attempts, within the framework of a sociological study, to meet such a need.

The fact that individuals cope with different illnesses in a number of different ways has been a major topic of interest in health research during recent decades. This book will hopefully promote a clearer understanding of the roles culture and social context play in the coping process. In addition, the study may help us better understand the needs and challenges faced by ailing people and provide creative ideas concerning how their psychological well-being can be enhanced. What we are facing is the lack of a cultural approach to the study of religious and spiritual coping. This has paved the way for an increased tendency toward generalization of results obtained from research conducted among religious people, especially in the United States, to other people. To get beyond the above-mentioned problem, we have turned our focus to studying the meaning-making coping methods (religious, spiritual, and secular existential coping methods) used by people facing a serious crisis.

Objectives and the scope of the book

This book, thus proceeding from a contextual approach to coping and health, is based on an international research project aimed at identifying culturally bound coping methods used by cancer patients in several different countries, namely Sweden, China, South Korea, Malaysia, and Turkey. The empirical data for the book were collected using both qualitative (semi-structured and in-depth interviews) and quantitative (surveys) methods.

In our studies, we have tried to answer the following questions: What role do religion and spirituality play in coping when non-theists or non-religious people face difficult life events? Are there other coping methods that focus on existential questions, but that are not related to the religious and spiritual coping methods usually called RCOPE?[1] And what is the role of culture and ways of thinking in the choice of religious and spiritually oriented coping methods?

One important aim of the international project "Meaning-Making Coping and Culture" has been to conduct international studies on meaning-making coping (i.e., existential secular, spiritual, and religious) among people who have been affected by cancer and who live in a secular society. In this respect, studies have been conducted in South Korea (qualitative) and China (qualitative) as well as in Sweden (both qualitative and quantitative). Turkey and Malaysia were studied to help us discover possible variations in coping strategies in religious countries. In most of the previous studies on coping, the dominant religions were Christianity and/or Buddhism. For this reason, we have looked in particular at two Islamic countries, because Islamic culture is completely different from Christian and Buddhist culture regarding views on health and disease. The cancer patients' socialization in either an individual or collectivist cultural setting was another factor in choosing these countries.

The structure of the book

Chapter 1: In Chapter 1, the background, objectives and the structure of the book are presented.

Chapter 2: Because the book focuses on meaning-making coping, which includes religious and spiritually oriented coping methods, and against the background of existing controversies and disagreements surrounding definitions in the field of health, religion, and spirituality, we present our own working definition of the terms religion and spirituality in the first part of Chapter 2. Later on in this chapter, we deepen the definition to include notions of religiosity, inwardly and outwardly oriented transcendence, coping and coping strategies, RCOPE and, finally, we present our notion of meaning-making coping. According to our definition, meaning-making coping goes beyond the scope of religious and spirituality oriented coping and embraces other coping strategies, e.g., connectedness to nature, connectedness to the Self and to others. These kinds of coping strategies are all related to individuals' search for meaning without any correspondence whatsoever to religion or religious symbols. Rather, these strategies concern individuals' endeavors to find a source – in nature, in themselves or in others to help them cope with problems that have caused an existential vacuum – a disorder that requires elaboration of the old order into a new order and that, thus, helps them fill this vacuum. This means that we define meaning, not in relation to the "divine," but as something of cognitive origin. According to this perspective, if individuals are to avoid falling into meaninglessness, they should find some kind of contrasting rational (meaning) that can play an essential role in restructuring their "worldview." These new experiences are then assimilated, and life becomes more comprehensible and predictable, and thus filled with trust. We conclude therefore that using the term "meaning-making coping" prevents the misunderstandings found in the previously predominant definitions focused on religious coping and semi-/non-religious coping methods. Meaning-making coping is thus used in this book, and in all parts of our international project, to address the entire spectrum of religious, spiritual, and existential secular meaning-making coping methods.

Chapter 3: In Chapter 3, we present two sociological studies on individuals stricken by cancer in Sweden – a society where religion is not an integrated part of the social life of individuals. In these studies, we aimed to examine meaning-making coping with cancer from a cultural perspective. One of the studies was carried out using a qualitative and the other a quantitative research methodology. The first study investigated the assumed prevalence of religious and spiritually oriented coping methods among cancer patients in Sweden. It showed, however, the existence of a strong tendency among Swedes to rely primarily on themselves for solving problems related to their disease, rather than on other sources, such as God. Another important finding of this study was that nature-related coping methods were prevalent among participants, illustrating the impact of culture on coping. The subsequent quantitative study examined the extent to which the results obtained in the qualitative study among cancer patients were applicable to a wider population of cancer patients in Sweden. The results showed that the three most important coping methods used by the informants were related to nature.

The study showed that, in a given community, some dominant cultural traits may affect how patients deal with difficult diseases. In other words, although the choice of coping strategies is undeniably individual, it is influenced by the culture in which the person has been socialized. For instance, research on religion and health has shown that the negative or positive impact of religion on older people's well-being, as well as the matter of using religion as a coping strategy, may depend on factors such as gender, ethnicity, culture, income, education level and marital status. Chapter 3 illustrates the effect of culture on meaning-making coping methods among people who had been hit by cancer and had been socialized in Sweden and Swedish culture, with its Protestant background, although this does not imply that the informants were necessarily Christians. None of the informants was chosen based on their interest or lack of interest in religion or spirituality. One of the main conclusions presented in this chapter is that the value system of the people in the Protestant northern European countries (including Sweden) is marked by a high degree of secular-rational rationality as well as a postmodern view on individual identity and integrity. Some results from the study underlying this chapter reveal that nature has replaced the church and, likewise, that oneness with nature has replaced unity with the holy. Thus, the chapter maintains that the possibilities for coping that spending time in and relating to nature offer cancer patients should be taken more seriously by healthcare providers, particularly by therapists trying to address the psychological problems cancer patients face in different phases, such as diagnosis, treatment, and post-treatment. Generally speaking, there should be more focus on developing less conventional therapeutic methods, such as creating opportunities for patients to come into contact with nature. For example, well-designed, health-promoting gardens within clinics would allow patients to engage in gardening, meditation, or just give them an opportunity to feel the earth.

Chapter 4: This chapter focuses on the characteristics of coping with cancer in secular societies and non-religious segments of the populations, e.g., patients who either are uninterested in institutional religiosity, but have their own individual approaches to spirituality, or who express no interest in spirituality and religiosity. China, South Korea, and Japan were selected as the sites for this study, because according to WIN-Gallup International 2015 – in Scandinavia and East Asia, particularly in China – atheists and non-religious people make up the majority. In South Korea and China, the majority of people do not self-identify as religious, but instead spirituality (what some researchers call "secular spirituality") is prevalent among the populations.

We discuss in this chapter the four coping resources most frequently employed by the Korean informants: belief in the healing power of nature; mind-body connection; relying on a transcendent power; finding oneself in relationships with others. Furthermore, we observed one shared meaning derived from the Korean experiences, namely cancer as "a turning point in life." Fighting cancer had been a great ordeal for all of them, but the outcome of their struggles included positive aspects. Experiences of struggling with cancer gave the Korean participants a chance to appreciate the small things in life, to stop worrying about what others think, to realize the futility of petty arguments, and to find themselves in relationships with family and friends they love.

The study in China also showed no use of any religious coping methods besides visiting church and praying. Regarding "spiritual" coping methods, none of the conventional spiritual meaning-making coping methods could be found among our Chinese informants, despite the fact that some reported believing to some extent in a mysterious spiritual power, without being able to explain this belief clearly. The existential secular meaning-making coping methods were, as it seems, prevalent among the informants. These methods are family, inner peace, and listening to music to ease the pain.

When it comes to family relationships, there is a considerable difference between Chinese and Korean society. Although participants in both countries were afraid of death and worried about family members who would be left behind, the Korean participants had a more critical attitude toward their relation to family.

The studies in the two East Asian countries indicated that the relation between body and soul has an impact on the use of meaning-making coping strategies among cancer patients. Development of the idea of body-mind-spirit in the ways of thinking of people in East Asia is primarily influenced by a holistic system of thought advocated by Eastern philosophers, particularly the Chinese. Chinese civilization has greatly influenced other cultures in East Asia, including Japan and Korea as well as Southern Asia. Use of various body-mind-spirit techniques to ease pain or to cope with illnesses is an old traditional cultural practice among people in East Asia. Among both Chinese and Korean informants, we found the use of meaning-making coping methods related to the doctrine of a body-mind-spirit relation: inner peace among the Chinese and peaceful mental attitude among South Koreans.

Chapter 5: This chapter presents the results of the studies carried out in Turkey and Malaysia. In Turkey, despite the important role played by religion in social and cultural life, many people do not self-identify as religious. In fact, Turkish society has strong features of both religiosity and secularism that affect social as well as cultural life. In addition, most people have been socialized into a society where Islam is the dominant religion. Malaysia provides an example of a Muslim country where ethnicity and religion coincide; it is a multi-religious society. In Malaysia, there are different ethnic groups, especially Chinese and Indians, whose cultures have historically strongly influenced the social and cultural life of people in Malaysia. People in Malaysia are strongly influenced by the characteristics of the pre-Islamic cultures of Shamanism, Hinduism, and Buddhism. Many customs, the dress code, and the language bear witness to the fact that people in Malaysia have been greatly influenced by the Indian/Hindu and Chinese cultures. Even after conversion to Islam in the 14th century, many of these influences on their culture still remain; this may explain why although Islam is widely practiced in Malaysia, its presence is subtler and more downplayed in everyday life compared to in Turkey, where Islam plays a greater role in society.

In Chapter 5, our point of departure was that Islamic culture is completely different from Christian and Buddhist culture regarding views on health and disease. Two Muslim countries in very different cultural contexts, namely Turkey and Malaysia, were chosen for this part of our international study. The Turkish study reveals that several religious coping methods found to be prevalent in other countries – such as Spiritual Discontent, Seeking Support from Clergy or Members, Punishing God Reappraisal, and Demonic Reappraisal or Self-Directing Religious Coping – were not applied by the Turkish informants. Nor were the non-religious coping methods highly prevalent among these informants. The most important coping methods used by cancer patients in Turkey were the RCOPE methods, especially Spiritual Connection, Active Religious Surrender, Passive Religious Deferral, and Pleading for Direct Intercession. The Malaysian study indicates that informants used several RCOPE methods, both passive and active. It also shows that shamanism – although it is in opposition to the religion of our informants (all of whom were Muslims) – played a role in how they coped with cancer. The study highlights the important role of culture in the choice of coping methods. It is convenient to maintain that the reason people in Turkey and Malaysia turn to religion in times of crisis is that religion has a prominent position in people's ways of thinking. Yet there are certain differences between the two countries.

Furthermore, based on results from the studies in Turkey and Malaysia, the chapter concludes that, in both countries, the notion of being patient (Sabr) was important among the informants when they were coping with the psychological problems caused by cancer. The notion of Sabr implies that the problems of this world are meant to test people and the thought of having patience is highly influential among people in Muslim countries, including Turkey and Malaysia.

Chapter 6: Focusing on the relation between religious, spiritual, and existential secular meaning-making coping, in Chapter 6, we discuss globalization, health, and culture and underline the importance of taking cultural differences into consideration when studying the meaning-making coping methods used by people who are facing a serious crisis. We emphasize that culture affects the selection of strategies that an individual uses in any given situation. Cancer patients use a multitude of meaning-making coping methods, be they spiritual, religious, or existential. The strategies people employ when they are stricken by disease, accidents, misfortune, etc., are cultural and historical constructions. When discussing the issue of health and culture, we should remember that we are not talking solely about different cultural settings that are geographically separate. These settings are not islands. In a world that is becoming more and more linked to international trade, immigration, and electronic communication, health issues are increasingly affected by both global and local forces and cultures are becoming more and more connected. In many societies, the populace consists of people with different cultural and ethnic backgrounds. Therefore, healthcare systems should take into consideration the distinct cultural characteristics of the population they serve.

Regardless of the employed strategies or the secular or religious characteristics of these strategies, coping is about consoling. The coping methods individuals choose depend on where and when they live – on what trends dominate their life context. In secular societies, religious or spiritual coping methods do not have the same ability to console as they do in religious societies. Nevertheless, in secular societies, too, some people try to find a meaning in what is happening and to put it into a larger framework. However, secular individuals' quest for meaning does not necessarily involve a belief in God or religion. Similar to spiritual and religious coping strategies, secular coping strategies are often employed to console the individual with the belief that she/he is part of a greater or supreme project – a small cog in bigger machine. The individual tries to look at her/his problems from above, from the perspective of a greater whole, and see how small and unimportant she/he and her/his maladies are in relation to this whole. In this chapter, we describe how Protestantism, Catholicism, Judaism, Islam, and Buddhism look at health and illness.

Our studies show clearly that, in secular societies, religion is not the only available resource in individuals' orientation system. Religion would seem to play an important role as a coping resource for those with limited options. In cultures with large non-religious resources and where religion is less a part of individuals' everyday life, religion plays a minor role in the coping process. To "turn to religion in coping," is primarily a question of religion's position in the culture in which the individual has been socialized. In societies where religion is less prominent in the orientation system, and less relevant to life experiences, it loses its importance for coping, while other existential meaning-making coping methods related to nature or an inner "force" or positive solitude are the kinds of resources that provide meaning and comfort to individuals facing a serious crisis.

Note

1 We are going to explain in more detail about Pargament's measurement instrument RCOPE in Chapter 2.

2 Theoretical framework

Religion/religiousness, spirituality, and transcendence

In the first part of this chapter, after presenting some relevant approaches to the definitions of religion/religiousness, spirituality, and transcendence, we will put forward our own working definitions of religion and spirituality used in our project on meaning-making coping, which is presented in this book.

For the past 150 years, work conducted in the social sciences has examined the phenomena of religion and spirituality. Early inquiries were also conducted within the field of psychology by scholars such as William James (1902/1961), Edwin Starbuck (1899), G. Stanley Hall (1904) and George Coe (1916). Particularly at the turn of the 21st century, the relationship between religion, spirituality, and health has been taken seriously into consideration.

During recent decades, the number of publications in books and journals focused on religion, spirituality and health has increased. Yet despite the growing knowledge in this field, there is still no real consensus among scientists regarding the definition of religion and spirituality.

Because this book focuses on meaning-making coping, which includes religious and spiritually oriented coping methods, it is necessary to define these two terms. Before doing so, we introduce some of the most important classical definitions of religion and spirituality.

It should be mentioned that there is a great deal of controversy and disagreement surrounding definitions in the field of health, of religion and spirituality, and there is not sufficient space here to pursue a full discussion of these complex issues. We therefore confined ourselves to some issues we found interesting for our project on the role of culture in meaning-making coping.

Approaches to religion

The classical definitions of religion have ranged from "a system of beliefs in a divine or superhuman power, and practices of worship" (Argyle & Beit-Hallahmi, 1975) to "Feelings, acts and experiences of individual men in their solitude, so far as they apprehend themselves to stand in relation to whatever they may consider the divine" (James 1961: 42). In a study conducted by Jenkins and Pargament (1995: 52), religion refers to an "organized system of belief and practice such as those found in formal denominations (e.g., Catholic, Jewish, Protestant, Moslem, Buddhist) or recognized systems of theological ideas (e.g., Calvinistic, Protestant, Evangelical Christian)."

Although religion is usually described as a framework for a system of beliefs and as being the external practice of spiritual knowledge, there are certain central definitions of religion intended to characterize it in accordance with the intrinsic qualities that religious experiences have for those who practice religion. Proceeding from this perspective, religion is defined as the claimed experiences that individuals perceive to be extraordinary, transcendent, and clearly different from the everyday reality perceived most of the time. However, some scholars, e.g., Berger (1974), have suggested that experience in these circumstances is undeniable and more real than what is perceived in daily life. Berger (1974: 130–131) writes:

> In the context of religious experience, the reality of daily life loses in dramatic form its status as supreme reality. It appears, to the contrary, as the anteroom of another reality, one of a drastically different nature and nevertheless of immense importance for the individual. Through this change in this perception of reality all worldly activity of quotidian reality is seen as radically reduced in importance, trivialized – in the words of Ecclesiastes, reduced to vanity.

In the contemporary social sciences, religion is defined in an analytic manner, that is, religion is characterized by the different ways in which it manifests itself. From this perspective, it is supposed that there is considerable consensus among all religions regarding the forms through which the religious person may express her/his religiosity. Based on such a consensus, it becomes possible to establish the aspects that constitute such religiosity. These aspects include:

- Sharing the beliefs that constitute the body of doctrine of the group;
- Participating in rituals and acts of devotion;
- Experiencing direct contact with ultimate reality;
- Acquiring religious information;
- Experiencing changes or results in everyday life derived from the other aspects of religiosity.

Some researchers have approached a definition of religion that distinguishes it from other systems of meaning. For instance, Glock and Stark (1965) differentiate between the "humanist perspectives" and religions. In their view, humanist perspectives attempt to make significant the life of man. Religions, in contrast, assert that they have identified or established paths that lead to discovery of the true meaning of life. Actually, regarding the humanist perspectives, the aim is to give life a meaning that is agreed upon and based on a relatively free will. In the case of religions, however, it is presumed that life has a meaning that pre-exists any meaning individuals may wish to give it. On this subject, Bibby (1983: 103) suggests the following:

> Religious perspectives imply the possibility that our existence has a meaning which precedes that which we as human beings decide to give it. By contrast,

the humanist perspective leaves to one side the search for the meaning of existence in favor of a new preoccupation with giving meaning to existence. Religion is a complex phenomenon that can be defined in different ways and from different perspectives. One of the problems involved in introducing religion as a factor in medical and sociological research concerns the way in which it is operationalized.

There are, however, certain methods that have allowed socio-medical researchers to operationalize religion. There are both one-dimensional and multidimensional measures of religion. Here we have confined ourselves to the multidimensional measures.

There are different types of multidimensional measures of religious involvement. The Index of Religiousness and Glock's multidimensional measurement model of religion are among the most important ones.

The Index of Religiousness (Zuckerman et al., 1984) contains a three-item measure covering the frequency of attendance at services, perceived religiousness, and the degree to which religion is a source of comfort.

Glock's multidimensional measurement model of religion (Glock & Stark, 1965) is another multidimensional measure. Glock and Stark (1965) devised a scale for measuring religiosity based on five dimensions of religion: experiential (religious feelings), ritualistic (religious practice), ideological (religious beliefs), intellectual (religious knowledge) and a fifth dimension called consequential (generalized effects of religion on an individual's life). The latter dimension examines how the first four are applied in real life.

King et al. (1994: 632) describe religion as the external practice of spiritual knowledge and/or the framework for a system of beliefs, values, codes of conduct, and rituals. Thus, some may regard religion as synonymous with spirituality, while for others spirituality may be a broader term including the behavioral, cognitive and organizational elements of religion, but encompassing broader, more mystical experiences as well. In the following, we discuss how spirituality is conceptualized in the field of religion and health.

Approaches to spirituality

The term "spiritual" may be considered to relate to the search for the existential meaning of any life experience (Hungelmann et al., 1996; Burkhardt, 1993; Emblen, 1992). Spirituality may also refer, on the other hand, to belief in a "higher power" outside oneself that can influence one's life. This higher power may or may not be referred to using the word God (Hungelmann et al., 1996; Foley et al., 1998). Emphasizing this distinction is important in an inquiry into the religious and spiritually oriented coping methods used in societies where people are more spiritual than religious. People who are spiritual do not always describe themselves as religious.

Spirituality points to an element of transcendence, of meaning in life and a concept of self that goes beyond societal expectations or definitions. Dudley and

Helfgott (1990: 287) speak of the spiritual dimension as "[encompassing] the need to find satisfactory answers to the meaning of life, illness, and death, as well as seeking a deeper relationship with God, others, and self." Seen in this light, spirituality is different from religion, which is related to a particular social institution. Spirituality, as Pastorello and Wright (1997) stress, does not necessitate association with a formal religion.

Summing up, definitions of spirituality are diverse. According to Moffitt (1997), spirituality can be understood as a search for the meaning of life, and religion as one way of conducting this search. Generally, spirituality is conceptualized as an orientation to life and death, as that which provides meaning in life. In other words, religion can be seen as "the doing and spirituality as the being" (ibid.). Seen in this light, the difference between religiously directed individuals and spiritually directed individuals is that while the first group "use their religion" (i.e., are extrinsically oriented), the second group "live their religion" (are intrinsically oriented) (Allport & Ross, 1967: 434). Although the distinction between spiritual and religious is vague, it is generally supposed that spirituality has been likened to intrinsic, as opposed to extrinsic religiosity, assuming some sort of continuum. Allport's distinction between intrinsic and extrinsic religious orientation is grounded on the Weberian approach to religion. According to Weber (1964), what makes religion consequential for human behavior is the meaning provided by religious ideas. In this regard, he distinguished conceptions of the supernatural based on taboo from those based on religious ethics. While the former focus on the perception and proscription of behavior, the latter involve a more general orientation toward all aspects of life and social relationships.

Approaches to transcendence

One of the major concepts used when defining religion and spirituality and the differences between them is transcendence. The concept of transcendence also plays an essential role when studying meaning-making coping. This concept has featured in debates about religion and spirituality and health as a core defining feature of how we can consider religion and spirituality, and also as a significant point of disagreement between scholars. It is for these reasons that reviewing the divergent approaches to the concept of transcendence seems worthy of particular attention. Transcendence is a keyword not only in definitions of religion and spirituality, but also regarding the role of religion and spirituality in health research; it is therefore important to shed light on how it is viewed from different perspectives. Below, we present some approaches to the concept of transcendence, its relation to religion, on the one hand, and spirituality, on the other.

Outwardly directed transcendence

The field of mental health, religion, and spirituality often focuses on a transcendent relationship (i.e., with God) as being at the heart of the ability of spirituality to offer resilience to and better recovery from mental disorders (Cook 2013: 142).

12 Theoretical framework

Cook, in an interesting discussion on the role of transcendence in defining religion and spirituality, focuses on how religion and spirituality are defined in the *Handbook of Religion and Health* (Koenig et al., 2012). Religion, according to Koenig et al. (2012: 45):

> Involves beliefs, practices, and rituals related to the transcendent, where the transcendent is God, Allah, Hashem, or a Higher Power in Western religious traditions, or to Brahman, manifestations of Brahman, Buddha, Dao, or ultimate truth/reality in Eastern traditions. This often involves the mystical or supernatural. Religions usually have specific beliefs about life after death and rules about conduct within a social group. Religion is a multidimensional construct that includes beliefs, behaviors, rituals, and ceremonies that may be held or practiced in private or public settings, but are in some way derived from established traditions that developed over time within a community. Religion is also an organized system of beliefs, practices, and symbols designed (a) to facilitate closeness to the transcendent, and (b) to foster an understanding of one's relationship and responsibility to others in living together in a community.

With regard to spirituality, Koenig et al., write (2012: 46):

> Spirituality is distinguished from all other things – humanism, values, morals, and mental health – by its connection to that which is sacred, the transcendent. The transcendent is that which is outside of the self, and yet also within the self – and in Western traditions is called God, Allah, Hashem, or a Higher Power, and in Eastern traditions may be called Brahman, manifestations of Brahman, Buddha, Dao, or ultimate truth/reality. Spirituality is intimately connected to the supernatural, the mystical, and to organized religion, although also extends beyond organized religion (and begins before it). Spirituality includes both a search for the transcendent and the discovery of the transcendent and so involves traveling along the path that leads from nonconsideration to questioning to either staunch nonbelief or belief, and if belief, then ultimately to devotion and finally, surrender. Thus, our definition of spirituality is very similar to religion and there is clearly overlap.

Koenig concludes that "for the sake of conceptual clarity researchers not include personal beliefs that have nothing to do with the transcendent under the term spirituality" (Cook 2013: 143). Therefore, it is neither necessary nor helpful to extend the concept of spirituality to physiological states and beliefs if they are not concerned with the transcendent.

This way of relating spirituality to the transcendent limits spirituality to the realm of religiosity; transcendent is "out of the self" and is defined as GOD or whatever the divine entity is called in different religious traditions. In this view, if people find meaning and purpose in life from what according to him is spirituality, the term transcendent should not be used to explain these experiences.

Psychological language and concepts are adequate for such things, according to Koenig (Cook 2013: 144).

Some researchers do not share Koenig's view. These "other things," which are often regarded as spiritual according to these researchers, are related in one form or another to the transcendent. Kenneth I. Pargament is one of these researchers, whose views we will discuss later in the chapter; here it is enough to mention that, according to Cook (2013: 144), in his view, these "other things" are part of what he refers to as the "sacred ring," "that is, a realm of life within which things become sacred (we might say here, transcendent or spiritual) through association with a sacred 'core'" (Pargament, 2011).

Richard Sloan has a completely different view on the matter in question. He generally opposes the use of spirituality and religion within healthcare, because he believes it trivializes the transcendent. He writes: "By implementing the approach of scientific reductionism, the transcendent aspects of the religious experience are diminished if not lost altogether" (Sloan 2006: 241).

Cook (2013: 144) mentions another view of the transcendent, which regards it as a point of contention. He refers to Rob Poole who states that "The insistence that even nonbelievers have a spiritual life shows a lack of respect for those who find meaning within beliefs that reject the transcendent and the supernatural" (Poole et al., 2008). Cook is of opinion that "It is not necessarily the case, although it might be a reasonable assumption, that the assertion that "nonbelievers have a spiritual life" means that those who do not self-identify as spiritual nonetheless (in the eyes of those who do) have a life in relation to transcendent reality" (Cook 2013: 144).

Summing up, we are dealing with two groups of scholars in relation to views on the transcendent and its place in health research: 1) those who consider that the "transcendent dimension will cause offence to those who deny it, or that it will somehow be degraded for those who value it, the clear implication is that transcendence should be kept out of clinical practice" and 2) those who "affirm the place of spirituality in research and clinical practice," thus who seemingly affirm the transcendent (ibid.).

Both Poole et al. (2008) and Koenig et al. (2012) consider the transcendent, spirituality and the supernatural to be related, and their definition of transcendence is limited within the framework of religiosity. We call this "*Outwardly directed transcendence,*" which means seeing the transcendent as God or as whatever the given religious tradition calls its divine being – as *something out of self.*

Inwardly directed transcendence

We call perspectives that do not regard the transcendent as God or any transcendent order external to worldly life "inwardly directed transcendence."

There are different approaches here, one of which is called "self-transcendence." Cook (2013: 146) emphasizes that there are researchers for whom "transcendence is primarily concerned with *self*-transcendence of a kind that reaches out intrapersonally and interpersonally but not necessarily transpersonally."

Actually, self-transcendence does not refer to any transcendent order external to the self.

Craigie's understanding of transcendence, which differs almost radically from Koenig's and Pool's, considers transcendence an important issue for psychologists. He views transcendence as the transcendence of suffering (Craigie, 2008). According to Cook (2013: 145), a similar understanding can be also found in *Howden's Spirituality Assessment Scale*. Here, transcendence is understood as "The ability to reach or go beyond the limits of usual experience; the capacity, willingness, or experience of rising above or overcoming body or psychic conditions; or the capacity for achieving wellness or self-healing" (Burkhardt and Nagai-Jacobson 2005: 155). Here, transcendence – which is addressed as self-transcendence – "is about facing pain and suffering, accepting that some things are unchangeable and finding a meaningful way through life that acknowledges these realities." These realities are "letting go," acceptance, mindfulness, non-attachment, serenity, spiritual surrender, gratitude, and forgiveness (Cook 2013: 145). All these realities except spiritual surrender, which "more or less, requires some kind of understanding of the transcendent as God or a Higher Power," "employ a psychological kind of self-transcendence that requires no concept of the supernatural, God or any Higher Power external to the self" (ibid.).

The other definition of transcendence that can be regarded as actually defining self-transcendence, according to Cook, is that of Ellermann and Reed. They define self-transcendence in terms of "the person's capacity to expand self-boundaries intrapersonally, interpersonally and transpersonally, to acquire a perspective that exceeds ordinary boundaries and limitations" (Ellermann and Reed, 2001). What is at stake here is "a personal capacity to 'expand self-boundaries', thus a capacity for a certain sort of self-understanding" (Cook, 2013: 146).

Another approach, in the realm of self-transcendence, is advocated by Polly Young-Eisendrath. She identifies psychotherapy as a kind of "ordinary transcendence." This kind of transcendence, as Cook (2013: 415) explains, "provides evidence and insight that being human means being dependent, and that the life space we inhabit is one of interdependence, not independence. It also shows us that self-protectiveness, isolation, and the ubiquitous human desire for omnipotence produce great suffering" (Young-Eisendrath, 2000: 133). "Ordinary transcendence, again, is a kind of transcendence that does not require reference to a transcendent other in any supernatural or theological sense. It is a form of self-transcendence, a transcendence of self-protectiveness and of the lust for power."

In our studies within the framework of the project "Meaning-making coping," we have found coping methods, such as "Sanctification of Nature," which brought forth a new understanding of transcendence (Ahmadi, 2006). Here too, the transcendent neither refers to God, or the corresponding entity in different religious traditions, nor to the self, as we saw in self-transcendence. It refers to something external to the self, but not external to the realm of worldly life. It is *an inwardly directed transcendence*, out of self. We will return to this in another chapter when we explain existential secular meaning-making coping. Here it suffices to mention that there are, besides the self, other objects that can be also referred to as transcendent without relating to any Outwardly directed realm.

One of the researchers whose views on transcendence seem to float between inwardly directed and Outwardly directed is Pargament. In our project, we have used Pargament's measurement instrument RCOPE and in our definition of religion and spirituality, we have made considerable changes to his definitions. Because he is one of the most influential scholars in the field of religious and spiritual coping, we devote a special section to discussing his views on religion, spirituality, and transcendence.

Definitions of religiosity and spirituality in meaning-making coping studies

Kenneth I. Pargament is among the most important researchers in the field of religious coping. His measurement instrument – RCOPE – is one of the most important instruments in this area. It is for this reason RCOPE has been applied in designing the qualitative and quantitative studies presented in our project. Because one of the purposes of the conducted studies has been to investigate the use of meaning-making coping strategies in cultural contexts where religion is not an integrated part of people's life, the RCOPE items were modified for use in these studies (see Appendix 1). Moreover, it was necessary to critically review the definitions of religion and spirituality used in formulating the RCOPE items. This was essential if the cultural aspect was to be in focus and if new "meaning-making coping" methods were to be identified. It is for this reason the definitions of religion and spirituality presented by Zinnbauer and Pargament (2005) are critically examined, and new definitions – more applicable to studying meaning-making coping in secular societies – are presented (Ahmadi, 2006). In the following, we present these definitions.

Religiosity

Zinnbauer and Pargament emphasize two alternative definitions of religion and spirituality. Both researchers criticize modern approaches that polarize religion and spirituality. They also believe that definitions of both religion and spirituality should be embedded in a context, and that the context can be used to distinguish between these two constructs. Both researchers view the search for the sacred to be an important component of religion and spirituality. However, while Zinnbauer considers spirituality the broader construct, Pargament sees religiosity as the broader one (Zinnbauer & Pargament, 2005). Pargament views spirituality as a search for sanctity, whereas religiosity constitutes a search for meaning in relation to the holy (Zinnbauer et al., 1999: 909). Zinnbauer defines spirituality as a personal or collective search for holiness, whereas religiosity is defined as a personal or collective quest for the sacred that manifests itself within a traditional sacred context (Zinnbauer & Pargament 2005: 35).

When studying meaning-making coping in secular societies like Sweden, Ahmadi found these definitions problematic (Ahmadi 2006: 56–71) and put forward another definition, partly based on the work of Jenkins and Pargament (1995: 52). According to this definition, religion is *a search for significance that unfolds within a traditional sacred context. It is then related to an organized system of belief and practice relating to a sacred source that includes individual and institutional expressions, serves a variety of purposes, and may play potentially helpful and/or harmful roles in people's lives* (Ahmadi 2006: 72).

This definition of religion differs from Zinnbauer's, because it sees religiosity not only as a search for the sacred, but also as a search for significance, in accordance with Pargament's definition. This definition encompasses a broader goal of individual and collective seekers. It corresponds to the many purposes religion may serve in people's lives, because significance involves the sense of satisfaction, value, and importance associated with the search and achievement of the goal. The definition also includes issues related to sanctity. The latter aspect indicates that Ahmadi regards religion differently from those who ignore the fact that one the greatest tasks of religion involves the individual as well as collective search for the sacred.

On the other hand, Ahmadi's definition limited the search for the sacred to a traditional sacred context, as seen in Zinnbauer's definition. This was done to reflect the spirit of our times, which takes exception to traditional authority and institutional expressions of faith. This definition, as opposed to Pargament's, facilitates communication with the public, in that it is sensitive to how people self-identify in a cultural environment that is more spiritual than religious.

Spirituality

Spirituality is more difficult to define and cannot be put into a box. But we need an operational definition if we are to conduct studies on coping in which religion and spirituality are involved. We use Ahmadi's definition, which is partly based on her own study and partly on the ideas of Jenkins and Pargament. Spirituality is defined as *a search for connectedness with a sacred source that is related or not related to God or any religious holy sources. Spirituality involves efforts to consider metaphysical or transcendent aspects of everyday life as they relate to forces, transcendent and otherwise. Spirituality encompasses then religion as well as many beliefs and practices from outside the normally defined religious sphere* (Ahmadi 2006: 72–73).

Spirituality, as defined here, can be experienced without having any faith, without myths, legends, and fictional super-personalities, and without superstition. It can be applied in a religious context, but also outside that context. It is understandable that people who have been socialized in a secular and rational society like Sweden have difficulty believing in many aspects of traditional religions. We mean that because many aspects of life have been established rationally and logically outside the context of religious thought, individuals who lack a strong faith will find it difficult to accept traditional religion. Therefore, we have chosen a definition focused on spirituality both in religious and non-religious contexts. Our definition focuses on the higher aspects of human life and is aimed at individuals who rise above the banality of everyday life and experience a transcendent view of life.

Definition of coping

What is coping?

The concept of coping has been essential in psychology for over 60 years. Generally, coping is regarded as the means people use to combat or prevent stress. It can be defined as a process of managing the discrepancy between the demands of the situation and the available resources – a process that can alter the stressful problem or regulate the emotional response. According to Lazarus and Folkman (1984: 141), prominent scholars in the field, coping constitutes the changing cognitive and behavioral efforts made to manage specific external and/or internal demands that are appraised as taxing or as exceeding the individual's resources. These cognitive and behavioral efforts are, as they write in a later work, "constantly changing as a function of continuous appraisals and reappraisals of the person-environment relationship, which is also always changing" (Folkman & Lazarus 1991: 210).

Lazarus and Launier (1978) define coping as efforts, both action-oriented and intrapsychic, a person makes to manage (that is, master, tolerate, reduce, minimize) the environmental and internal demands, and the conflicts between them, that tax or exceed his/her resources.

Coping may also be defined as the process through which individuals try to understand and deal with significant demands in their lives (Ganzevoort 1998: 260) or as a search for significance in times of stress (Pargament 1997: 90). By significance, Pargament means "what is important to the individual, institution, or culture – those things we care about" (1997: 31). Significance, according to Pargament (ibid.), includes "life's ultimate concerns – death, tragedy, inequity." It encompasses other possibilities as well, "possibilities that are far from universal, possibilities that may be good or bad" (ibid.). The concept of significance is important in Pargament's theory of coping, especially with regard to religious coping.

According to Hobfoll (1988: 16), coping constitutes behaviors employed in order to reduce strain in the face of stressors.

Coping is regarded (Folkman & Lazarus 1980: 148; Pargament 1997: 89) as a multilayered contextual phenomenon that has several basic qualities. In this regard, Pargament (1997: 89) stresses that coping "involves an encounter between an individual and a situation; it is multidimensional; it is multilayered and contextual; it involves possibilities and choices; and it is diverse." Another dimension of coping is that it constitutes a process that evolves and changes over time.

Several components are important in coping: coping strategies, coping style, coping resources and burdens of coping.

Coping strategies

Generally speaking, coping strategies constitute those efforts, both behavioral and psychological, that people facing a difficult situation make in order to master, reduce or minimize stressful events. Coping strategies mediate evaluation of the significance of a stressor or threatening event as well as evaluation of the controllability of the stressor and a person's coping resources.

Two general types of coping strategies are recognized: problem-solving strategies and emotion-focused strategies.

Problem-solving strategies are efforts that actively ease stressful circumstances. In emotion-focused coping strategies, efforts are aimed at regulating the emotional consequences of stressful events. Research (Lazarus & Folkman, 1980) has shown that people use both types of strategies when dealing with stressful events. Different factors play a role in choice of one type of strategy over the other; personal characteristics and type of stressful event are among the most important factors. When dealing with potentially controllable problems, such as those occurring with the family, people tend to employ the problem-solving style, whereas when facing less controllable situations, such as serious physical health problems, people tend to employ emotion-focused coping.

Two overall goals of coping strategies are recognized: changing the relationship between the self and the environment and reducing emotional pain and distress. Different individuals have different ways of approaching these goals. Researchers (Lazarus & Launier, 1978; Billings & Moos, 1981) have divided coping strategies into the categories active and avoidant (or passive) on the basis of how people face stress, illness, or loss. Active coping means doing something to affect the stressor, while avoidant coping implies an escapist and passive approach.

Active coping strategies are behavioral and psychological responses that can change the nature of the stressor itself or influence a person's attitude toward the stressor. Active coping strategies enable the patient to assume responsibility for management of the physical as well as psychological effects of illness. Active coping may include different ways of involving the patient in physical therapy or other exercise, using various forms of relaxation to reduce mental strain, and diverting the patient's attention away from the stress and pain.

When using avoidant coping strategies, the patient shifts responsibility for management of his/her stress and/or pain to someone else or allows other areas of life to be adversely affected by this stress and/or pain. Some researchers, such as Holahan and Moos (1987), feel that active coping is a better approach to dealing with stressful events, while avoidant coping constitutes an adverse response to stressful life events.

Other researchers, such as Pargament, believe that there are no truly passive coping strategies, because:

> Even if a passive, avoidant, or reactive stance is taken toward problems, this does not erase that, at some level, the stance was chosen. In this very basic sense, coping is an active process involving difficult choices in times of trouble.
>
> (Pargament, 1997: 87)

Like Pargament, we have difficulty categorizing the behavior of a person who chooses to react passively to her/his problem, thus who uses a passive coping strategy, particularly if we consider that avoidant coping strategies often lead to activities (e.g., alcohol use) or mental states (e.g., withdrawal) that keep the patient from thinking directly about the stressful event. Thus, the patient is not actually passive when facing the problem her/his illness causes, but has chosen passivity.

Coping styles

Coping styles may be defined as generalized ways of behaving. These styles may affect a person's emotional or functional reaction to a stressor and are relatively stable over time and across situations. Different styles have been identified that represent the patterns of thought, feeling, and behavior a person may display when facing a serious illness. Greer and Watson (1987) have identified five adjustment styles among cancer patients:

Fighting spirit: "This is a challenge. I will win." When this style is used, the patient regards the illness as a challenge. This usually leads to a positive attitude with regard to the outcome. The patient often tries to actively influence the process of treatment by seeking information from, for example, local information centers, the Internet and by making full use of the medical and alternative options available.

Avoidance or denial: "It is not that serious." Here the patient denies the threat inherent in the diagnosis. Sometimes this style is useful, but only if it does not interfere with acceptance of treatment. This style is regarded as a form of distraction, in that it allows the patient to get on with life and maintain a positive attitude.

Fatalism: "It.s out of my hands" or "what will be will be." When this style is used, the patient's attitude is passive acceptance. The patient rarely tries to gather information or challenge the situation. She/he has trust in the doctors and accepts the treatments offered. Although this passive style may be frustrating for friends and relatives, it is effective at keeping darker and more difficult emotions at bay.

Helplessness and hopelessness: "There is nothing I can do. What is the point of going on?" Here, the patient simply "gives up". Trying to tackle the problem is seen as useless. Feelings of helplessness and hopelessness are often predominant.

Anxious preoccupation: "I'm so worried about everything all the time." When using this style, the patient spends a great deal of time worrying about the cancer. She/he assumes that all physical symptoms are part of the disease. Excessive information-seeking feeds the fear, which can sometimes be unbearable and lead to panic. When waiting for test results and appointments, the patient often becomes impatient and panicky.

Each of the five styles briefly explained above gives the person a way of dealing with the uncomfortable thoughts and feelings caused by her/his illness. Some patients use all or only some of these five coping style categories at different times during the initial adjustment period. There are certainly many factors that affect choice of coping style. Among these factors are the specific coping resources and burdens of coping the patient brings to the coping situation.

Coping resources and burdens of coping

Coping resources: as Pargament (1997: 101) stresses, the resources individuals bring to coping may be material (e.g., money), physical (e.g., vitality), psychological (e.g., competence), social (e.g., interpersonal skills), or spiritual (e.g., feeling close to God). A number of coping resources have been identified and examined through research. Problem-solving skills constitute one such resource. It is thought (Dubow & Tisak, 1989) that people with good problem-solving skills have fewer behavior problems than do those with less developed skills. According to some researchers (Norris & Murrell, 1988), prior experience with a stressor is an effective coping resource. Social support is another possible resource in times of stress (Cohen & Wills, 1985), and still another is having a tendency toward pursuing goals tenaciously as well as adjusting goals (Pargament 1997: 101). An additional effective coping resource is believed to be religion, but it can also be a burden (we will return to this issue when we discuss the positive and negative patterns of religious coping).

Burdens of coping: like coping resources, burdens of coping may be material, physical, psychological, social or spiritual. Examples of such burdens are having a history of failure, a physical handicap, a destructive family, a personality problem, financial debt or dysfunctional beliefs about oneself or others (Pargament 1997: 101). Several studies have tried to determine the effects of burdens of coping. For instance, one longitude study of the relationship between pessimism and physical health (Peterson et al., 1988) showed that having a pessimistic explanatory style predicted poorer physical health among certain sub-groups of the study population. A study by Wheaton (1983) suggests that fatalistic beliefs and inflexibility in coping may function as a burden.

Both the resources and burdens people bring with them to a coping situation help to form their orienting system (Kohn, 1972), which may be "defined as a general way of viewing and dealing with the world. One's orienting system consists of habits, values, relationships, generalized beliefs, and personality. It is a frame of reference, a blueprint of oneself and the world, that is used to anticipate and come to terms with events in life. The orienting system directs us to some life events and away from others" (Pargament 1997: 99–100).

Clearly, an orienting system that guides and grounds individuals faced with a crisis serves as a (material, biological, psychological, social, and spiritual) frame of reference for thinking about and dealing with life situations. Some orienting systems may be stronger and more comprehensive than others. Still, any system has its weak points and limitations (Pargament 1997: 102). An orienting system is not static, but changes over time. Thus, coping resources are not only used, but also developed – and burdens are not only taken on, but also lightened (Pargament 1997: 104).

An orienting system represents the way in which culture impacts on the individual's life and, therefore, the way in which she/he copes with stress when facing disturbing circumstances. As mentioned above, one of the qualities of coping is that it is a multilayered contextual phenomenon. Pargament points out (1997: 85) that it is not possible to remove individuals from the layers of social relationships

– family, organizational, institutional, community, societal and cultural – in which they find themselves. One of the most important layers of social relationships is culture. However, in coping studies, the fabric of culture – the cultural rules, roles, standards and morals that were once part of the background of life – are rarely noticed (Pargament 1997: 73). As Aldwin (2000: 191) stresses, in the research field of coping there is consensus around the notion that the situational context affects coping (Eckenrode, 1991; Moos, 1984), but acceptance of the effects of sociocultural context on the coping process is not widespread. Given that the main objective of the present study is to investigate the role of culture in the use of religious and spiritually oriented coping methods, we will now begin a more detailed discussion of the role of culture in coping.

The many methods of religious coping: RCOPE

Although identifying new and unknown religious and spiritually oriented coping methods has been the primary focus of the project Meaning-making Coping, it was still necessary to consider the established religious and spiritually oriented methods found in previous studies – qualitative as well as quantitative. In this connection, we have compared the results of our studies in different countries with what is called "the Many Methods of Religious Coping" or RCOPE. Our reason for choosing RCOPE was not only that it is based on theoretical as well as empirical studies, but also that it includes many of the religious coping methods identified in different studies and that it has been tested on a large sample of different groups.

One of our aims was to examine whether cancer patients in different cultural settings have used any of the religious coping methods in RCOPE and whether culture has played a role in their use or non-use of RCOPE methods.

Naturally, we have not confined ourselves to the RCOPE methods and, thus, RCOPE has not guided our study. We have taken RCOPE into consideration when structuring our interview guide and then used it, after analyzing our interviews, to examine whether there are any similarities between the coping methods found in our studies in different countries and the methods in RCOPE.

What is RCOPE?

RCOPE, as mentioned, is a relatively new "theoretically based measure that would assess the full range of religious coping methods, including potentially helpful and harmful religious expressions" (Pargament et al. 2000: 521). The measure is based not only on global indicators of religiousness (e.g., frequency of prayer, service attendance), but also on how the individual uses religion to try to understand and deal with stressors. Moreover, RCOPE reflects coping's non-static nature. Pargament (1997: 89) sees coping is a process. According to Ekedahl (2002: 90), Pargament's theory of religious coping is based on stress and coping research that derives from the psychology of self, with an emphasis on cognition. This psychology tradition, formed by Lazarus and Folkman (1984), is process oriented. However, this process orientation takes the form of an end-oriented effort in Pargament's theory. Thus, Pargament is primarily interested in evaluating the coping process.

One of the advantages of RCOPE is that it focuses not only on the positive dimension of religious coping, but also considers the potentially dysfunctional forms of religious coping – as required by a spirit of comprehensiveness and scientific openness. This means that even methods that may be ineffective or harmful in dealing with stressful situations are also taken into consideration.

RCOPE was designed to assess five religious coping functions: meaning, control, comfort, intimacy and life transformation. Specific religious coping methods were defined for each of these functions, and subscales were created. These five key religious functions form the basis of RCOPE (Pargament et al. 2000: 521). Because we use these key functions in our study, we describe them briefly below.

1. Meaning. According to some theorists, such as Clifford Geertz (1966), religion plays a key role in the search for meaning. When people face suffering and baffling life experiences, religion can offer frameworks for understanding and interpretation.
2. Control. Other theorists, such as Erich Fromm (1950), have stressed the role of religion in the search for control. When people are confronted with events that require more resources than they actually have, religion offers many avenues for achieving a sense of mastery and control.
3. Comfort/Spirituality. In the classic Freudian (1927/1961) view, religion is designed to reduce the individual's apprehension about living in a world where disaster can strike at any time. It is challenging, however, to differentiate comfort-oriented religious coping strategies from methods that may be genuinely spiritual in function. From a religious perspective, spirituality – the desire to connect with a force that transcends the individual – is the most basic function of religion (Johnson, 1959).
4. Intimacy/Spirituality. Sociologists, such as Durkheim (1915), have generally emphasized the role religion plays in facilitating social cohesion. Religion is thought to be a mechanism for fostering social solidarity and social identity. Intimacy with others, using spiritual methods, is often encouraged. This may involve offering spiritual help to others or receiving spiritual support from clergy or members. Thus, again, it is difficult to differentiate many of the methods that foster intimacy from those that foster closeness with a higher power (Buber, 1970).
5. Life Transformation. Theorists have traditionally seen religion as being conservational in nature – helping people maintain meaning, control, comfort, intimacy, and closeness with God. However, religion also may help people make major life transformations by enabling them to give up old objects of value and find new sources of significance (Pargament, 1997).

The definitions and items in RCOPE were mainly designed for use in quantitative studies. Given the aim of our study, we have chosen a qualitative data collection method. Thus, we needed to "reconstruct" the RCOPE methods for use in a qualitative study.

We created a shorter list (see Table 2.1) of the definitions and items for the various religious and spiritually oriented coping methods in RCOPE. Our "reconstruction" tackled the major drawback – for researchers and counselors – which the originators of RCOPE pointed out, namely that RCOPE is very long. However, researchers interested in studying the role of religion in coping with specific life stressors can choose RCOPE subscales that have theoretical ties to their subject of interest (Pargament et al., 2000: 540).

Investigating whether our informants reported having used any of the RCOPE methods enabled us to examine the five key religious functions described by Pargament et al., in the context of cultures where people tend not to practice their "religion" in a organizational way, but in a subjective and non-organizational way. Such a culture is the Swedish one.

Besides the five key religious functions, other factors have proven to be important in categorizing RCOPE methods, i.e., the positive and negative outcomes of the methods in questions. RCOPE methods can be divided into two categories: positive and negative (Pargament et al., 1998). Positive religious coping methods are an expression of "a sense of spirituality, a secure relationship with God, a belief that there is meaning to be found in life, and a sense of spiritual connectedness with others" (Pargament et al. 1998: 712). Benevolent religious reappraisals, collaborative religious coping, and seeking spiritual support are examples of coping methods in this category. Negative religious coping is an expression of "a less secure relationship with God, a tenuous and ominous view of the world, and a religious struggle in the search for significance" (ibid.). This category includes punitive religious reappraisals, demonic religious reappraisals, reappraisals of God's powers and spiritual discontent. In the list of RCOPE, we used both the positive and negative coping methods.

In addition to religious coping methods similar to the methods in RCOPE, in our study we have also found religious and spiritually oriented coping methods that are not among the RCOPE methods. In following chapters, we will present these methods.

Meaning-making coping

In the study we carried out earlier among Swedes, we mainly employed terms such as religious and spiritual coping when addressing coping methods that principally involve existential issues. Nevertheless, the results of the studies conducted among cancer patients in Sweden (Ahmadi, 2006; Ahmadi & Ahmadi, 2013) indicate the prevalence of other coping strategies – e.g., strategies connected to nature – that can hardly be regarded as religious or spiritual. These kinds of coping strategies can be defined as being existential in nature, thus as related to people's search for meaning without any correspondence whatsoever to religion or religious symbols. When the results of the qualitative study carried by Ahmadi (2006) were analyzed, it became clear that certain coping methods could hardly

24 Theoretical framework

be categorized either as religious coping (RCOPE) or as spiritual coping (SCOPE) (see Chapter 5). To address this problem, we defined a third category: "New Spiritually Oriented Coping Methods Dissimilar to RCOPE." These new methods included Spiritual Connection with Oneself, Spiritual Sanctification of Nature, Positive Solitude, Empathy/Altruism, Search for Meaning, Visualization, Healing Therapy, Spiritual Music and Meditation. Analyses of these methods showed clearly that they had much more to do with *connectedness to nature, to self, and to others than to something vertical (God or any spiritual power).*

The weakness of our analysis in the Swedish study lay in not being sufficiently responsive to the data from our own interviewees. We fell into the same traps we had shown that other researchers, such as Pargament, had fallen into before us (Ahmadi 2006: 58–71). Although our interviewees described for us how they had coped with their crisis using methods that – although touching upon existential questions – had nothing to do with religion or spirituality, we interpreted their coping methods as a kind of "secular" spiritual coping. We even lost contact with our own definition, which maintained that spirituality involves searching for connectedness with a sacred source that is related or not related to God or any other religious holy source (Ahmadi). Spirituality involves efforts to consider metaphysical or transcendent aspects of everyday life as they relate to forces, transcendent and otherwise. Thus, spirituality encompasses religion as well as many beliefs and practices that fall outside the religious sphere, as it is normally defined (Jenkins & Pargament 1995: 52–53).

As mentioned, none of the methods employed by our interviewees had an obvious connection to a sacred source; nonetheless we interpreted them as being connected to a sacred source and were thus influenced by Pargament's Sanctification theory (Ahmadi, 2006). We could have used the term existential secular coping, because these methods concern individuals' endeavors to find a source – in nature, in themselves or in others. This source helps them cope with problems that have caused an existential vacuum – a disorder that requires elaboration of the old order into a new order and that, thus, helps them fill this vacuum.

What we failed to realize was that Pargament was trying to keep spirituality – as well as all endeavors in people's existential search for meaning or understanding of the life situation – within the realm of religiosity and transcendentally. In hindsight, we know now that it would have been more appropriate to employ secular theories such as attribution theory (Fölsterling, 2001). Salander (2015) touches on this issue when explaining Frankl's perspective on meaning, in which meaning is not of "divine," but of cognitive origin. According to this perspective, if individuals are to avoid falling into meaninglessness, they should find some kind of contrasting rational (meaning) that can play an essential role in restructuring their "worldview." These new experiences are then assimilated, and life becomes more comprehensible and predictable, and thus more trustful. According to Salander (2015: 18):

> In more secular terms, the process of giving a special meaning to objects may well be encompassed by Winnicott's (1971) intermediate area as well

as attribution theory (Fölsterling, 2001). According to Winnicott and object-relational theory, people are, from early childhood to death, able to "play with reality" (Salander, 2012). The intermediate area is the mental area of human creation: in childhood in the doll's house or sandpit, in adulthood in the area of art and culture. It is the mental space between the internal world and external reality and it is thus both subjective and objective. Being human is being in between and thus being able to elaborate with facts, especially when confronted with unexpected negative facts such as a cancer disease.

This explains why we have decided to use the term "meaning-making coping." This term prevents misunderstandings of the nature of the non-religious coping methods we discuss. Meaning-making coping is thus used in our quantitative study in Sweden, as well in studies conducted in the countries within the project Meaning-making Coping, to address the entire spectrum of religious, spiritual and existential secular meaning-making coping methods.

References

Ahmadi, F. (2006). *Culture, religion and spirituality in Coping: The example of cancer patients in Sweden.* Acta Universitatis Upsaliensis.Studia sociologica Upsaliensia 53. Uppsala: Uppsala University.

Ahmadi, F. & Ahmadi, N. (2013). Nature as the most important coping strategy among cancer patients: A Swedish survey. *Journal of Religion and Health*, 52(4): 1177–1190.

Aldwin, C. M. (2000). *Stress, coping and development.* New York: Guilford Press.

Allport, G. & Ross, J. M. (1967). Personal religious orientation and prejudice. *Journal of Personality and Social Psychology*, 5: 423–443.

Argyle, M., & Beit-Hallahmi. B. (1975). *The social psychology of religion.* London: Routledge & Kegan Paul.

Berger, P. L. (1974). Some second thoughts on substantive versus functional definitions of religion. *Journal for the Scientific Study of Religion*, 13:125–134.

Bibby, R. W. (1983). Searching for invisible thread: Meaning systems in contemporary Canada. *Journal for the Scientific Study of Religion*, 22(2): 101–119.

Billings A. G. & Moos R. H. (1981). The role of coping response in attenuating the impact of stressful life events. *Journal of Behavioural Medicine*, 4: 157–189.

Buber, M. (1970). *I and thou.* New York: Charles Scribner's Sons.

Burkhardt M. A. (1993). Characteristics of spirituality in the lives of women in rural Appalachina community. *Journal of Transcultural Nursing*, 4: 212–218.

Burkhardt, M. A. & Nagai-Jacobson, M. G. (2005). Spirituality and health. In B. M. Dossey, L. Keegan. & C. E. Guzzetta (Eds.), *Holistic nursing: A handbook for practice* (4th ed., pp. 137–172). Sudbury: Jones & Bartlett.

Coe, G. A. (1916). *The psychology of religion.* Chicago: University of Chicago Press.

Cohen, S. & Wills, T. A. (1985). Stress, social support, and the buffering hypothesis. *Psychological Bulletin*, 98: 310–357.

Cook, C. C. H. (2013). Transcendence, immanence, and mental health. In *Spirituality, theology and mental health: interdisciplinary perspectives* (pp. 141–159). London: SCM Press.

Craigie, F. C. (2008). *Positive spirituality in health care*. Minneapolis MN: Mill City.

Dubow, E. F. & Tisak, J. (1989). The relation between stressful life events adjustment in elementary school children: The role of social support and social problem-solving skills. *Child Development*, 60: 1412–1423.

Dudley, J. R. & Helfgott, C. (1990). Exploring a place for spirituality in the social work curriculum. *Journal of Social Work Education*, 26(3): 287–294.

Durkheim, É. (1915). *The elementary forms of religious life*. New York: Free Press.

Eckenrode, J. (Ed.). (1991). *The social context of coping*. New York: Plenum Press.

Ekedahl, M. A. (2002). *Hur Orkar Man i Det Svåraste?: Copingprocesser Hos Sjukhussjälavårdare i Möte Med Existentiell Problematik: En Religionspsykologisk Studie (How can you bear the challenge of working at the edges of life and death? Coping processes with hospital chaplains encountering existential confrontation: A study in psychology of religion)*. Uppsala: Acta Universitatis.

Ellermann, C. R. & Reed, P. G. (2001). Self-transcendence and depression in middle aged adults. *Western Journal of Nursing Research*, 23(7): 698–713.

Emblen, J. (1992). Religion and spirituality defined according to current use in nursing literature. *Journal of Preofessional Nursing*, 8: 41–47.

Foley, L. S., Wagner, J., & Waskel S. A. (1998). Spirituality in the lives of older women. *Journal of Women & Aging*, 10(2): 85–91.

Folkman, S. & Lazarus, R. S. (1980). An analysis of coping in a middle-aged community sample. Journal of Health and Social Behavior, 21: 219–*239*.

Folkman, S. & Lazarus, R. S. (1991). Coping and emotion. In A. Monat & R. S. Lazarus (Eds.), *Stress and coping: An anthology* (pp. 207–227). New York: Columbia University Press.

Fölsterling, F. (2001). *Attribution – an introduction to theory, research and application*. Philadelphia: Psychology Press.

Freud, S. (1961). *The future of an illusion*. New York: Norton.

Fromm, E. (1950). *Psychoanalysis and religion*. New Haven, CT: Yale University Press.

Ganzevoort, R. R. (1998). Religious coping reconsidered (part two): A narrative reformulation. *Journal of Psychology and Theology*, 26(3): 276–286.

Geertz, C. (1966). Religion as a cultural system. In M. Banton (Ed.), *Anthropological approaches to the study of religion* (pp. 1–48). London: Tavistock.

Glock, C. Y. & Stark, R. (1965). *Religion and society in tension*. New York: Rand McNally.

Greer, S. A. & Watson, M. (1987). Mental adjustment to cancer: Its measurement and prognostic importance. *Cancer Surveys*, 6(3): 439–53.

Hall, G. S. (1904). *Adolescence: Its psychology and its relations to physiology, anthropology, sociology, sex, crime, religion, and education* (2 vols). New York: Appleton.

Hobfoll, S. E. (1988). *The ecology of stress*. Washington, DC: Hemisphere.

Holahan, C. J. & Moos, R. H. (1987). Risk, resistance, and psychological distress: A longitudinal analysis with adults and children. Journal of Abnormal Psychology, 96: 3–13.

Hungelmann, J., Kenkel-Rossi, E., Klassen, L., & Stollenwerk, R. (1996). Focus on spiritual well-being: Harmonious interconnectedness of mind-body-spirit-use of the JARL spiritual well-being scale. *Geriatric Nursing*, 17: 262–266.

James, W. (1902/1961). *The varieties of religious experience*. New York: Collier.

Jenkins, R. A. & Pargament, K. I. (1995). Religion and spirituality as sources for coping with cancer. *Journal of Psychosocial Ontology*, 13(1–2): 51–74.

Johnson, P. E. (1959). *Psychology of religion*. Nashville, TN: Abingdon Press.

King, M., Speck, P., & Thomas, A. (1994). Spiritual and religious beliefs in acute illness – is this a feasible area for study? *Social Science & Medicine*, 38(4): 631–636.

Koenig, H. G., King, D. E., & Carson, V. B. (2012). *Handbook of religion and health*. New York: Oxford University Press.

Kohn, M. L. 1972. Class, family, and schizophrenia. *Social Forces*, 50: 295–302.
Lazarus, R. S. & Folkman, S. (1984). *Stress, appraisal, and coping.* New York: Springer.
Lazarus, R. S. & Launier, R. (1978). Stress-related transactions between person and environment. In L. Pervin & M. Lewis (Eds.), *Perspectives in interactional psychology* (pp. 287–327). New York: Plenum Press.
Moffitt, L. C. (1997). *Religiosity: A propensity of the human phenotype.* Commack, NY: Nova Science.
Moos, R. H. (1984). Context and coping: Towards a unifying conceptual framework. *American Journal of community Psychology*, 12(5): 5–25.
Norris, F. H. & Murrell, S. A. (1988). Prior experience as a moderator disaster impact on anxiety symptoms in older adults. *American Journal of Community Psychology*, 16: 665–683.
Pargament, K. I. (1997). *The psychology of religion and coping.* New York: Guilford Press.
Pargament, K. I. (2011), *Spiritually integrated psychotherapy*, New York: Guilford.
Pargament, K. I., Koenig, H. G., & Perez, L. M. (2000). The many methods of religious coping: Development and initial variation of the RCOPE. *Journal of Clinical Psychology*, 56: 519–543.
Pargament, K. I., Zinnbauer, B. J., Scott, A. B., Butter, E. M., Zerowin, J. & Stanik, P. (1998). Red flags and religious coping: Identifying some religious warning signs among people in crisis. *Journal of Clinical Psychology*, 54: 77–89.
Pastorello, T. & Wright E. (1997). *Spirituality, social work and aging.* Paper presented at the Association for Gerontology in Higher Education (AGHE) conference, Boston, MA.
Peterson, C., Seligman, M. E. P., & Vaillant, G. E. (1988). Pessimistic explanatory style is a risk factor for physical illness: A thirty-five year longitudinal study. *Journal of Personality and Social Psychology*, 55: 23–27.
Poole, R., Higgo, R., Strong, G., Kennedy, G., Ruben, S., Barnes, R., Lepping, P., & Mitchell, P. (2008). Religion, psychiatry and professional boundaries. *Psychiatric Bulletin*, 32(9): 356–357.
Salander, P. (2012). Cancer and 'playing' with reality: Clinical guidance with the help of the intermediate area and disavowal. *Acta Oncologica*, 51(4): 541–560.
Salander, P. (2015). Introduction: A critical discussion on the concept of spirituality in research on health. In F. Ahmadi (Ed.), *Coping with cancer in Sweden: A search for meaning* (pp. 13–27). Uppsala: Uppsala University.
Sloan, R. P. (2006). *Blind faith: The unholy alliance of religion and medicine.* New York: St Martin's Press.
Starbuck, E. D. (1899). *The psychology of teligion.* New York: Scribner.
Weber, M. (1964). *The dociology of religion.* Boston: Beacon Press.
Wheaton, B. (1983). Stress, personal coping resources, and psychiatric symptoms: An investigation of interactive models. *Journal of Health and Social Behavior*, 24: 208–229.
Winnicott, D. (1971). *Playing and reality.* London: Tavistock Publications.
Young-Eisendrath. & M. E. Miller (Eds.). (2000). *The psychology of mature spirituality* (pp. 133–144). London: Routledge,.
Zinnbauer, B. J. & Pargament, K. I. (2005). Religiousness and Spirituality. In R. F. Paloutzian & C. L. Parks (Eds.), *Handbook of Psychology and Religion* (pp. 21–42). New York: The Guilford Press.
Zinnbauer, B. J., Pargamnet, K. I., & Scott, A. B. (1999). The emerging meaning of religiousness and spirituality: Problems and prospects. *Journal for Personality*, 67(6): 889–919.
Zuckerman, D. M., Kasl, S. V., & Ostfield A. M. (1984). Psychosocial predictors of mortality among the elderly poor. *American Journal of Epidemiology*, 119: 410–423.

3 Western Protestant culture Swedish culture and coping[1]

Introduction

A previous interview study by Ahmadi (2006) studied how the Swedish culture and mentality affect the choice of meaning-making coping strategies. This was the first study in Scandinavia to focus on the role culture plays in religious and spiritual coping. It showed that, in a community, some dominant cultural traits may affect how patients deal with difficult diseases. In other words, although the choice of coping strategies is undeniably individual, it is influenced by the culture in which the person has been socialized. As mentioned in Chapter 2, we are critical of how the term "spirituality" was used, in the above-mentioned study, to explain several of the coping methods found there. Here, we present the study as it has been presented in previous texts without taking into consideration our current critique.

The aim of the study was to detect the religious and spiritually oriented coping methods used by cancer patients in Sweden. To address the study aim, semi-structured interviews were conducted with 51 cancer patients. All of the interviewees had been socialized in the Swedish cultural environment. Because the topic had not previously been investigated, by focusing on the importance of culture for coping in non-religious societies, a qualitative approach was chosen.

We attempted to understand how the informants had dealt with their illness, not to generalize the results quantitatively. For this reason, we chose purposive sampling.

Religious and spiritual coping strategies constitute a project that is highly personal. Previous studies have revealed the importance of the social and cultural aspects of these strategies. For instance, research on religion and health has shown that the negative or positive impact of religion on older people's well-being, as well as the matter of using religion as a coping strategy, may depend on factors such as gender, ethnicity, culture, income, education level and marital status. Owing to the study's qualitative nature, all of these factors could not be taken into consideration. Some of them however, such as gender and age, were focused on. Thus, informant selection was strategic, because including a number of background and location factors was important.

Given that the effect of culture on meaning-making coping methods was broad, the focus was limited to informants – people who had been hit by cancer – who had been socialized in Sweden and Swedish culture, with its Protestant background.

Table 3.1 Sample

Sex	Age			Age at diagnosis			Outlook on life		
	18–40	*41–64*	*65+*	*18–40*	*41–64*	*65+*	*Theist*	*Non-theist*	*Atheist*
M	0	10	8	2	12	4	6	5	7
F	10	21	2	14	18	1	8	22	3

M: Male; F: Female

This background does not imply that the informants were necessarily Christians. None of the informants was chosen based on their interest or lack of interest in religion or spirituality.

The sample consisted of 51 people (18 men and 33 women) between the age of 25 and 83 years. Based on their responses, the informants were divided into one of three groups: atheists (who did not believe in God), theists (who believed in a personal God) and non-theists (who did not believe in a personal god, but in a force that could influence events). No respondents could be categorized, based on their responses, as agnostic. More detailed information is provided in Table 3.1. The informants were recruited through the Swedish Cancer Society and several other organizations.

The focus was on three main questions: Which of the religious and spiritually oriented coping methods used by cancer patients can be categorized as religious coping (as defined by the Many Religious Coping Methods: RCOPE)? In addition to RCOPE methods, what new religious and spiritually oriented coping methods have the cancer patients used? What role has culture played in the choice of religious and spiritually oriented coping methods?

An analysis of the results shows that some religious coping methods can be classified as RCOPE. Moreover, some spiritually oriented coping methods are found that are similar to RCOPE. All of these methods are categorized using the five overarching methods of religious coping presented below:

- Group 1: Religious Methods of Coping to Find Meaning;
- Group 2: Religious Methods of Coping to Gain Control;
- Group 3: Religious Methods of Coping to Achieve Comfort and Closeness to God;
- Group 4: Religious Methods of Coping to Achieve Intimacy with Others and Closeness to God;
- Group 5: Religious Methods of Coping to Achieve a Life Transformation.

Religious coping methods (RCOPE)

Benevolent Religious Reappraisal, Punishing God Reappraisal, Demonic Reappraisal and Reappraisal of God's Powers. In the Swedish study, Benevolent Religious Reappraisal was the only method some informants from the "theist group" reported having used to cope with their cancer. There were no reports of use of the other approaches to Religious Methods of Coping to Find Meaning – e.g., Punishing God Reappraisal, Demonic Reappraisal, and Reappraisal of God's Powers (Ahmadi 2006: 106).

According to Ahmadi (2006: 106),

> applying Punishing God Reappraisal, Demonic Reappraisal and Reappraisal of God's Powers as coping methods presumably requires a belief in a God or Devil who can determine the course of individuals' lives: a God who not only created man, but also continually controls man's deeds and his destiny, or in the same vein, a Devil who has the power to change man's life. The prevalent view of God among Protestant Swedes is, however, a God who, although having created man, has left him to determine his own destiny and make his own history.

Ahmadi suggested this as one of the possible reasons why Punishing God Reappraisal, Demonic Reappraisal, and Reappraisal of God's Powers, three ways of coping to find meaning, were not found among the informants.

Concerning *Religious Methods of Coping to Gain Control*, informants from all three groups – the "theist group," the "non-theist groupm" and the "atheists group" – chose to rely on their own initiative rather than God's help to gain control over the difficult situation they were facing (Ahmadi 2006: 109). Informants revealed their inclination to trust in their own problem-solving ability more than they trusted in other sources of power, such as God or a religious authority. This result is thought to be, to some extent, an effect of the strong individualism that characterizes Swedish culture.[2] According to Ahmadi (2006: 110).

> the question of who turns to God and who relies on herself/himself in a critical situation is too complicated to be answered by solely referring to the extent to which individuals are committed. One of the most important factors in this regard, besides background and situational factors, is the culture within which the individuals are socialized. . . . culture influences the ways in which people cope with crises and consequently impacts on whether or not people turn to religion and whether, as believers, individuals choose to get help from God or to face the crisis alone.

Concerning *Religious Methods of Coping to Achieve Comfort and Closeness to God*, thinking about spiritual matters, developing a sense of spirituality and seeking spiritual help seem to have been more prevalent among informants than was engaging in religious activities or in any religious ritual (Ahmadi 2006: 114).

In the study, none of the informants reported having used any of the methods belonging to the group *Religious Methods of Coping to Achieve Intimacy with Others and Closeness to God*, i.e., Seeking Support from Clergy or Members, Religious Helping, Interpersonal Religious Discontent, where the relation is with others: the first involves searching for comfort with the help of congregation members and clergy; the second concerns gaining comfort by praying or giving strength to other persons and the third stresses dissatisfaction with the clergy (Ahmadi 2006: 115). Ahmadi (ibid.) suggests that one possible explanation for informants not using any of these methods is Swedes' tendency toward being self-reliant and disengaging with other people when confronted with a difficult situation.

As the study (Ahmadi 2006: 115) shows, none of the three methods in the group *Religious Methods of Coping to Achieve Life Transformation*, i.e., Seeking Religious Direction, Religious Conversion and Religious Forgiving, were observed among the informants, even though some reported that cancer did have an impact on their outlook on life and led to a life transformation. However, no one referred to the role of religion in this respect. Ahmadi (ibid.) hypothesizes that

> the strong position of secularism and rationalism in Swedes' ways of thinking has probably prevented religion from playing an important role in bringing about a life transformation that could result in a complete change in their present way of life and lead them to a new path, God's path.

The above findings concern the various RCOPE methods. In the following, the results on new spiritually oriented coping methods, similar to RCOPE, will be discussed. We refer to them as SRCOPE methods.

As mentioned, none of the informants reported having redefined the stressor as a punishment from God for her/his sins. Some informants, who reported not believing in God or not regarding their cancer as God's punishment, still thought of their illness as a kind of penalty, simply not a religious one. Ahmadi (2006: 118) labels this method SRCOPE-*Punishment*. She found two patterns connected to this method. According to her (ibid.), some informants saw their illness as punishment inflicted on them by an unknown or incomprehensible power for their "bad" deeds, but not for their sins. Others believed their illness was their body punishing them for their unhealthy lives.

In Ahmadi's (ibid.) view, by reframing their illness as well-deserved punishment, the informants sought to gain a sense of control over the situation, which helped them cope with their illness.

Even when seeing coping from a functional perspective, reframing negative events may jeopardize the individual's psychological or physical well-being, or lead to reconstruction of a new view on life from a new perspective. Ahmadi (2006: 120) found that, generally speaking, informants' reframing of negative events resulted in positive rather than negative outcomes.

According to Ahmadi (ibid.), culture can be considered one of the factors determining whether the outcome of reframing will be negative or positive. In her view, two characteristics of Swedish culture seem to contribute to positive outcomes of reframing. One is pragmatism. The other involves long-term planning, which involves an exaggerated belief that we can plan all aspects of life. This belief in planning, in turn, gives rise to a kind of optimism about individuals' ability to control the course of their own life.

As we saw above, some informants did use one of the RCOPE methods: Benevolent Religious Reappraisal. This method involves using religion to redefine the stressor as benevolent and potentially beneficial (Ahmadi 2006: 120). There were some informants who did not believe in God and who stressed that they did not get any benefit from religion; they also reported having tried to determine how their situation could be spiritually beneficial or to find a lesson. Ahmadi (ibid.) labels this method SRCOPE-*Benevolent spiritual reappraisal.*

Ahmadi () found two patterns in this regard: the first shows that informants reinterpreted the situation to make it spiritually beneficial, the second that informants attempted to learn a lesson from it.

As regards the first pattern, facing the dark side of life can make people question the meaning of life and attempt to understand the purpose of life and death. By redefining the situation, the informants tried to imbue it with spiritual meaning. Through their illness, they tried to interpret life in a spiritual manner, which could help them cope with the illness.

Concerning the second pattern, Ahmadi stresses (ibid.) that because the informants believed everything has meaning, they wished to gain life experience through the situation and come to understand the meaning of life. Their central idea was as follows: In the end, everything would improve, because it is the result of a meaningful life process. This process, in turn, would give them a spiritual feeling, which would become their coping strategy. Ahmadi (ibid.) suggests that

> One factor that may have caused informants to try to gain a spiritual benefit from their illness is the strong tendency in Swedish culture toward spirituality, on the one hand, and plan-oriented optimism, on the other . . . Swedes are more likely to describe their "sacred" feelings and lives in spiritual terms than in religious ones, and it seems there exists a rather strong tendency toward spirituality among Swedes. On the other hand, it is pointed out that Swedes are generally regarded as optimists and pragmatists. Given these cultural characteristics, it is not difficult to understand why informants who stressed that they were neither religious nor had faith in God have tried to benefit spiritually from the situation of facing cancer.

As previously explained, some informants used a partnership with God to seek control in solving their problem. In both the "theist group" and the "non-theist group," there were informants who sought a partnership with a kind of non-God power – at times without being able to describe the nature of this power. Ahmadi (2006: 122) called this search SRCOPE-*Collaborative Spiritual Coping* and recognized two patterns. In the first pattern, the informants sought partnership with some kind of Spiritual Being, while in the second, they believed in collaboration between the individual and destiny.

The first pattern reveals how informants wanted to not be left alone in their struggles and needed a spiritual power – some entity they could lean on and that could be a partner on their difficult journey. Here, their search for control through partnership with a spiritual power is seen as a method of coping with their cancer.

The second pattern shows how informants reframed negative events using a positive outcome. Here, they accepted their illness as part of their life cycle and destiny. This acceptance, however, did not mean giving up or being passive. By considering cancer as part of their destiny, the informants tried to create a collaboration of some kind between themselves and their destiny (Ahmadi 2006: 123).

Note that with regard to both patterns, the informants used a coping strategy that involved getting encouragement and strength from a "power" – not waiting for God to perform a miracle that would make things better. In this behavior, Ahmadi recognizes a tendency among Swedes toward talking about their sacred experiences and feelings in spiritual as opposed to religious terms (ibid.)

Note that such a tendency toward receiving help from an otherworldly power was not observed among informants from the "atheist group," some of whom reported relying only on themselves, while others reported relying on themselves as well as on science.

Spiritual discontent is considered a manifestation of confusion and discontent with God's relationship to the individual in a traumatic situation. In Ahmadi's (2006: 124) view, among informants who do not believe in God, SRCOPE-*Spiritual Discontent* concerns, in contrast, an expression of confusion regarding the existence of or the relationship to a Spiritual Being/beings.

There are different approaches to the very idea of seeing God and His power. In the study, among informants who reported not believing in God, different ways of approaching the Spiritual Being were found. Ahmadi (2006: 124) explains the patterns found in these approaches as follows:

The first pattern is when informants reporting believing in a higher power that could change events, but not in the power depicted by religions.

The second pattern is when informants professed belief in a power that once created the cosmos unintentionally and then left it alone – thus a power unable to exercise any control over the life of its creatures.

The third pattern concerns those who reported believing in there being a spiritual force in every individual – the notion of the Unity of Existence. Members of this group showed an ambiguous attitude toward the Spiritual Being's ability to affect outcomes. As Ahmadi (2006: 124–125) writes:

> The demarcating lines between these three categories were not, however, clear. It happened that, on different occasions, one and the same informant gave different pictures of this higher power. Facing a serious life crisis may affect individuals' attitudes toward God/a higher power and his/its ability to impact the situation. Being socialized in a society with a high degree of secularism and rationalism augments the risk that a person will lose her/his belief in God or a higher power who can change events or her/his faith in all things sacred, as we saw in the case of the above-mentioned woman.

The coping method SRCOPE-*Spiritual Prayer* was found in the study and is similar to one of the RCOPE methods, i.e., Pleading for Direct Intercession. SRCOPE-*Spiritual Prayer* refers to searching for inner harmony through prayer. Here, the informants used prayer as a means of relaxing or achieving calm. This kind of praying differs from the conventional pleading to God for a miracle or divine intercession to make things better, as we see in Pleading for Direct Intercession.

Two patterns were observed in the study. The first pattern involves praying as a relaxation method, actually as meditation. The second involves praying as a deep-seated habit, where praying functions as a coping method that helps the individual feel safe and peaceful (Ahmadi 2006: 125).

According to Ahmadi, whereas praying is seen as a religious coping strategy, meditation is typically considered non-religious coping. She identified informants who had used praying as meditation. Here she refers to the results of EVSS (European Values Study) from 1990, which show that, in the Nordic countries – particularly in Sweden – "fewer believe in the traditional dogma of the churches whereas more associated with a diffuse, spiritual world view" (Riis 1994: 107). Ahmadi (2006: 126) also points out the rise in a tendency toward "New-Age religiosity," "i.e., belief in re-incarnation, a soul, a spirit force, and practicing prayer or meditation" (ibid.), or as the study indicates, prayer as meditation.

When analyzing the interviews in relation to this method, Ahmadi started from Pargament's notion of the availability of religion in coping. As Pargament (1997: 149) points out, religion "is more likely to be accessed in coping when it is available to the individual, that is, when it is a larger part of the individual's orienting system for relating to the world."

With regard to the second pattern, i.e., prayer as a deep-seated habit functioning as a way to achieve safety and tranquility, Ahmadi (2006: 127) writes:

> we are facing the availability of religion in the orienting system. As both informants stressed, they have been used to praying since their childhood, and though as adults they no longer believe in God, they have used praying as a means of relaxation. These informants turn to prayer for relaxation because praying is an accessible tool in facing difficult situations in their orienting system.

Instead of relying on the help of God or someone else when trying to gain control over a difficult situation, several informants from all three groups – the "theist group," the "non-theist group" and the "atheists group" – reported having chosen to rely on their own initiative. Note that some from the "non-theist group" who reported use of self-directing coping associated this method with a spiritual dimension. None of the informants from the "theist group" chose Self-Directing Religious Coping with any spiritual connection. The use of self-directing coping among the "theist group" was presented above.

All informants who reported using this method displayed a strong tendency toward self-reliance in overcoming the problems caused by cancer. This diverges from the informants in the "theist group," who believed that God had given them the power to solve the problems themselves. The informants from the "non-theist group":

> did not stress any belief in a power given to them by God, but in a power that they got from a spiritual force or nature or life itself. Whatever gave this power to them, they all aimed to be a part of their treatment and impact their life themselves. They wanted to be active in making a difference in their situation.

In Ahmadi's view, Swedes' strong tendency toward solving their personal problems by relying primarily on themselves – and not on a higher power – is an important factor in informants' insistence on self-reliance in coping with cancer. She sees this tendency as the result of socialization in a society marked by both secularism and individualism.

People using RCOPE-*Spiritual Support* are seeking both comfort and strength in a relationship with God. People using SRCOPE-*Spiritual Support* – who do not believe in God – are not searching for comfort and strength through God, but for love. Two patterns are found here. Ahmadi labels the first pattern "*outworldly*" *spiritual support*, where the patient seeks love from and through a Spiritual Being. She labels the second pattern "*inworldly*" *spiritual support;* here, the patient is looking for love from and in relation to a "spiritual" person, and this search for love is connected to the desire to be loved and understood (Ahmadi 2006: 128).

For some informants, this longing for love when facing difficulties did not involve only the act of seeking love from a spiritual person, but the very act of searching also gave reassurance and comfort. Ahmadi (2006: 130) explains:

> In the framework of a culture like the Swedish, where there exists a kind of spirituality rather than religiosity among people, when a person facing a tragic event does not have faith and does not believe in God, the need for comfort may be directed toward a kind of spiritual support that is not necessarily religious.... One is no longer an isolated creature left alone to suffer without explanation. By ascribing a spiritual meaning to life and regarding oneself as part of an all-embracing life force, one may find comfort and strength. As some informants stressed, this may help the person make a spiritual "connection" with inner forces, in this way consciously transforming her/his reality.

Some informants reported yet another approach, which involved a direct search for love and tenderness that transcended interpersonal love. Ahmadi (2006: 130) writes:

> Unconditional and holistic love may help the person find answers to life's challenges and accept her-/himself and the current situation unconditionally. By searching for love, the person in crisis may develop an awareness of a higher level of consciousness that can help to expand her/his view of reality. This, in turn, paves the way for integrating conflicting issues within her-/

himself and getting comfort. Here, the searching itself may even be a way to achieve relaxation.

Thus far, we have addressed the first question concerning the religious and spiritually oriented coping methods used by cancer patients that can be considered religious coping, as outlined by the Many Religious Coping Methods (RCOPE). Below, we will address the second question by examining new religious and spiritually oriented coping methods that are unrelated to RCOPE.

Existential secular coping methods

The new methods found in the study will be discussed below. By "new" we mean methods that have not been taken up in previous studies. These methods are: Spiritual Sanctification of Nature, Spiritual Connection with Oneself, Positive Solitude, Altruism and Spiritual music. We will call them ECOPE.

Spiritual sanctification of nature

Ahmadi (2006: 133) found that seeking spirituality in nature as a means of coping with cancer was the only method used by all 51 interviewees, regardless of gender, age, or religious beliefs.

The study reveals three different patterns as concerns using nature to cope with cancer: seeing nature as a place for worship – where one goes to find spirituality, seeking the tranquility of nature – as a way to combat stress, and having spiritual contact with nature.

Regarding the first pattern – nature as a place for worship – some informants reported regarding nature as a sacred place, much like a church.

The second pattern – nature as a way to combat stress and find peace – concerns the spiritual sense bestowed by nature.

The third pattern is not a matter of nature being a sacred place (the first pattern) or a spiritual sense that nature bestows (the second pattern), but rather an immediate and unintentional spiritual connection with nature, a sense of oneness with nature – of "the unity of existence."

In their search for meaning, people often sanctify various aspects of life. This search is especially important when people are facing a serious problem. Pargament, who has long explored different groups' views and attitudes concerning sanctification, points out that any object can be seen as sacred. The sacred features include attributions of transcendence (e.g., holy, heavenly), ultimate values and purposes (e.g., blessed, inspiring) as well as timelessness (e.g., everlasting, miraculous) (Pargament 1999: 911).

In the study, several informants reported perceiving a sacred value in nature. For example, a 29-year-old woman from the "atheist group" talked about how, for her, nature had taken on a sacred quality of timelessness; she said:

> So when I have been outdoors, . . . it was peaceful, everything else disappeared. Whatever happens in the world to me or others, nature is still there, it

keeps going. That is a feeling of security when everything else is chaos. The leaves fall off, new ones appear, somewhere there is a pulse that keeps going.
(Ahmadi 2006: 135)

By seeing in nature a circular process that is timeless, the informant, an atheist, portrayed nature as a sacred object that will remain, despite all the chaos and change. By sanctifying nature as a timeless object, she found a spiritual sense that functioned as therapy while she dealt with cancer.

Note that all informants reported having turned to nature during some period of stress or depression. Actually, one of the most important coping strategies found in this study would seem to be the different ways in which informants sanctified nature.

In Ahmadi's (2006: 136) view, one of the explanations for the vital role nature plays in coping may be the crucial role it plays in Swedish culture. Let us look more closely at this point.

In the Christian tradition, God created human beings in His own image. Humankind is, thus, exceptional, in that it derives in part from substance not found in other creatures. In Scandinavia, however, few people share this view of man's basic nature. In an interview survey based with 500 Swedes, 66 percent responded that "humans and animals have the same value," 27 percent that "people have a higher value than animals," and 7 percent were undecided. Among those responding that humans and animals are of equal value, 66 percent felt that animals have a soul and 77 percent that animals have self-consciousness and a sense of morality. Seventy-two percent reported believing that animals' emotional life could be as rich as people's (Uddenberg 1995: 26).

Other studies (e.g., Torbjörnsson et al., 2011; Öhman, 2003) have provides similar pictures of Swedish attitudes toward nature. According to the EVSS from 1990, 44 percent of the 1,000 Swedish informants were of the opinion that it is just as important to save an endangered species as to save a human life (Uddenberg 1995: 27). The EVSS also showed that 55 percent felt people and animals have equal value (Hamberg 1994: 189, footnote 12). While 63 percent agreed that "nature has its own value," only 37 percent agreed that "nature's value is related to its utility for people."

As concerns environmental issues, 66 percent of the Swedish informants reported believing that efforts to protect the environment were of great importance, and 38 percent indicated they would accept tax laws focused on preventing air pollution (Uddenberg, 1995: 27).

The same interest in environmental issues can be seen in the EVSS, Online analysis 2004), where, 71.2 percent of Swedes were willing to pay for environmental protection measures.

According to the Flash Eurobarometer Survey (2011), "the proportion of respondents who said that economic development resulting in damage or destruction of nature protection areas should be prohibited because of the importance of such nature areas" was highest in Sweden, at 67 percent, compared to the other European countries surveyed.

Moreover, the survey shows that, in Sweden, "the proportion of respondents who agreed that it was important to slow down the speed of biodiversity loss as it would make Europe become economically poorer" was 65 percent.

According to the 1994 Study, based on questionnaire responses from 973 Swedes (20 to 69 years of age), only 4 percent felt that "we have no need to be out in nature," whereas 94 percent agreed with the statement "nature makes me feel relaxed and harmonious." Also in the 1994 Study, 51 percent agreed that "human beings would feel much better if they were as natural as animals are."

A number of studies, such as EVSS, the Sifo study (Lindén, 1994), the Uppsala Study of 1986 (Hamberg, 1994), and the 1994 Study (Uddenberg, 1995), have shown that interest in nature and environmental issues is widespread among the Swedish population, particularly young people.

Moreover, both qualitative and quantitative studies have shown that Swedes tend to challenge the traditional Christian notion that human beings are fundamentally different from animals.

What inspires Swedes, in this respect, is the notion that all living creatures – including human beings – are dependent on a single ecosystem that incorporates all living things. Thus, all creatures are interdependent, and the idea that some are more valuable and less useful than others is prejudiced and anthropocentric (Uddenberg 1995: 34).

One indication of the special status nature has in Swedish culture is Allemansrätten (the legal right of access to private land), which means "that everyone has the right to move about freely in the outdoors, even on privately owned land. Certain restrictions apply . . . Allemansrätten is an ancient part of Swedish culture" (Herlitz 1995: 35). The way in which Swedes see nature as sacred and mysterious and their general love of visiting natural environments – where they often experience unity with nature – probably underlie the way in which the informants "turn to nature" to cope with their stressor.

Spiritual connection with oneself

By using this coping method, the patient is not searching for a spiritual relationship with God or any other sacred source, but with her-/himself (Ahmadi 2006: 131). Such a search for inner spirituality can help people cope with their illness. Here, two different patterns can be observed:

- The patient endeavors to increase comfort and decrease stress/ tension by establishing a spiritual contact with her-/himself.
- This search focuses on discovering the spiritual meaning of her/his own existence, which is accomplished by finding oneself.

Analysis of the interviews reveals that searching for one's inner potential and strength can function as a spiritual strategy when dealing with a disease such as cancer. Just like a religious person who is able to find something sacred in all creation, and thus in him-/herself, a non-religious person experiencing a crisis can search for "the sacred" in him-/herself and in this way possibly discover a source of strength greater than self.

Informants who reported using such a coping method seemed to be looking for what Fromm calls self-realization. Here, we focus on the individual's own power (Ahmadi 2006: 132).

In Fromm's view, the purpose of humanistic religion is that each individual achieve the highest degree of strength, not the highest degree of powerlessness; virtue is self-realization, not obedience (Fromm 1950: 37). By finding their own strength, the informants were able to create meaning in their lives and, thus, cope with their disease (Ahmadi 2006: 132).

Humanist religion has a strong foothold in Sweden, which is also characterized by a relatively high degree of individualism. People socialized in the Swedish culture are rather likely to see themselves as an individual and to seek a healing source within themselves.

Positive solitude

This coping method involves achieving a higher level of tranquility and spirituality by being alone, reflecting on one's situation and overcoming the trauma one is experiencing.

One of the strategies the informants reported using to cope with the anxiety and stress associated with cancer involved choosing to be alone and taking time to meditate and reflect on life and existential matters. Actually, several reported having enjoyed being alone during this difficult period. For this reason, Ahmadi chose the term *positive solitude*, which implies appreciation of the state of being alone (Ahmadi 2006: 137).

Both qualitative and quantitative studies (Ahmadi Lewin, 2001; Tornstam, 1997, 2005) have revealed the tendency among Swedes to perceive "loneliness" as something positive. Barinaga (1999: 5) points out how the positive connotations of the word *ensamhet* (solitude) in Sweden astounds immigrants from more collective cultures. According to Barinaga, positive solitude is associated with "inner peace, independence and personal strength. It is a virtue already taught in early years of life" (ibid.). Herlitz (1995) suggests that the Swedish idiom "*att få vara i fred*" (to be left in peace) means not only to be alone and have time for oneself, but also to respect other people's need for peace and positive solitude.

Showing respect for other people's need for solitude is a central feature of Swedish culture, reflecting its strong tendency toward individualism (Barinaga 1999: 5). A Swede is expected to manage life on her/his own and to assume that others are also independent and able to solve their own problems (Ahmadi 2006: 138).

If we consider this tendency toward individualism, it is easier to understand why the Swedish informants made use of positive solitude as a coping method. In an individual-oriented culture where solitude is valued, it is highly likely that people with a serious illness like cancer will not fear being alone with their thoughts and will appreciate undisturbed meditation and reflection.

This does not imply that Swedes want friends and family to leave them alone entirely. Naturally they appreciate, as does everyone else, receiving the care and concern of others in a crisis situation. And certainly having helpful family members, friends and work colleagues makes them feel better. As a coping method, positive solitude provides a means of managing stress and other psychological problems because it allows people to find their inner strength and achieve inner peace. It is in solitude, through thought and meditation, that one finds oneself.

Empathy/Altruism

As Ahmadi writes, the word altruism derives from the Italian *altrui* and was first used by Auguste Comte, one of the founders of sociology, to refer to benevolence. What we today call altruism is complicated, and thus there is no consensus on how to define it. There are, however, several definitions of altruism in which promotion of the welfare of others is the most significant feature. But altruism has also been defined as involving self-destruction for the benefit of others (Costello, 2001).

Ahmadi (2006: 138) suggests that this definition has not been accepted by all scholars because it fails to include the actor's own interests. Few accept the notion that altruism can be completely pure, i.e., without any reward for the altruistic actor. Moreover, definitions that include rewards for altruistic behavior are generally accepted. This only applies, however, when the reward is not a significant motivating factor and when the benefits to the other person are crucial.

However, as Ahmadi (2006: 139) points out, human altruism is not merely an act, but is also interwoven with a sense of empathy. Thus, it is difficult to identify a truly altruistic act in the absence of empathy. Attempts to separate empathy and compassion from altruism, or feelings from actions, have been unsuccessful. In the view of some researchers (e.g., Damasio, 2000), emotions are essential to rational decision-making.

Ahmadi (2006: 139) adheres to Damasio's view that empathy and altruism cannot be separated, defining the pair they form as a voluntary intention/act to assist others at some cost (time, effort or money) to oneself.

Being a good person, fulfilling one's responsibility as a human being and giving the world its due – because one feels one is part of "the whole" – is one of the coping methods used by some informants in Ahmadi's study.

If individualism is a characteristic feature of Swedish culture, then empathy/altruism is the other side of the coin. One of the religious coping methods observed in earlier studies involves receiving help or helping others (empathy/altruism) through religious inspiration. This does not apply, however, to the Swedish cancer patients in the study. The inspiration here was not religious, but a more abstract and transcendent feeling, one of belonging to the great unity, of oneness with all existence – a tendency toward empathy and altruism. In Swedish ways of thinking, the notion that individuals are free, independent and responsible for their own actions does not preclude the existence of social solidarity (ibid.).

As Barinaga (1999: 5) points out and as mentioned by Ahmadi (2006: 140), the idiom "*att göra rätt för sig*" (in English "to carry your own weight") illustrates well the moral dimension of Swedish individualism. According to Barinaga (1999: 5), the idiom refers to the desire to be of service and to help an abstract "other" in addition to one's friends and relations, just as it does in other societies. Actually the idiom is among the pillars of the concept underlying the Swedish welfare system. Everyone should help in creating a secure social system (Herlitz 1995: 14–15).

This abstract solidarity with others and strong feelings for all living creatures reveal the tendency toward empathy and altruism in Swedish culture. This being the case, it may be easy to understand why one coping method used by Swedish cancer patients involves being a good person and assuming responsibility as a good citizen and human being (Ahmadi 2006: 141).

Spiritual music

Some informants also reported using music as an important coping strategy for getting through the stress and anxiety caused by cancer. Music was used as both a spiritual source and a healing method (Ahmadi 2006: 149). This coping method is called *Spiritual Music*.

Some informants reported having used music to cope with their stressful situation. Two patterns were identified here: music as a spiritual source and music as a healing therapy.

According to Pargament and Mahoney (2005), many aspects of life can be considered sacred. Ahmadi (2006: 151) suggests that sanctification of music may be a strategy that can help individuals cope with disease-related anxiety and stress. As the study shows, listening to music cannot only function as a spiritual source, but also promote relaxation and help people deal with the psychological strain brought on by cancer. One reason why spiritual music could be used by the theist, non-theist, and atheist informants alike may be, as previously discussed, the strong tendency toward spirituality observed in Swedish culture and ways of thinking.

Thus far, we have only discussed the new coping methods discovered in the quantitative study of culture and coping among Swedish cancer patients. The analysis reveals the impact Swedish culture has on the individuals' choice of religious and spiritual coping methods. Below, we will discuss the various cultural tendencies that may be crucial in this context. In doing so, we will be addressing the third question: What role has culture played in the choice of religious and spiritually oriented coping methods?

Based on her study, Ahmadi (2006: 180) shows that spirituality is a possible coping resource often overlooked by doctors, psychologists and social care staff in Sweden. Studies have revealed the need to be more sensitive to and to better integrate spirituality when assessing and counseling people afflicted by a serious disease. According to Ahmadi, this requires a range of measures, including more studies on religious and spiritual coping. Addressing this need, she and her colleagues have conducted a questionnaire study among cancer patients in Sweden. The result of this study were published in a book entitled *Coping with Cancer in Sweden – A Search for Meaning* (Ahmadi, 2015). Our discussion below is based on this book.

What do the statistics have to say?

The survey sample includes 2,417 cancer patients (79 percent women and 21 percent men). Almost one-third (29 percent) of the survey respondents were

59 years of age or younger; a greater proportion (38 percent) were between 60 and 69 years. One-third (33 percent) were 70 years or older. Thus, the study consists of three age groups: 18–59 years, 60–69 years, and 70+ years. According to Swedish research ethics regulations, researchers are not (except in special cases) to pose questions about religious affiliation. For this reason, the study lacks data on the informants' religion or faith. It does provide, however, information on informants' belief in a personal God or a higher life-giving force. In response to the question "Do you believe in God?" less than half (49 percent) of informants responded in the affirmative. Those who indicated they did not believe in God were asked to answer the question "Do you think there is a higher power or life-giving force?" Forty-five percent of informants who reported not believing in God indicate their belief in a higher power or life-giving force. One in four respondents (25 percent) reported having no particular faith.

Religious coping methods (RCOPE)

As indicated above, almost half (49 percent) of informants reported believing in God. A large percentage of this group belonged to the oldest age category, 70 years or older. Among women and among those who grew up in towns with 20,000 or fewer inhabitants, the percentage of informants reporting they believed in God was higher than in the younger groups, among men, and individuals raised in larger towns. The European Barometer Study (2010) showed that 2010, just 18 percent of Swedish citizens responded that "they believe there is a god," although a further 45 percent answered that "they believe there is some sort of spirit or life force." In a 2009 Gallup poll, 17 percent answered yes to the question "Is religion an important part of your daily life?" (Crabtree, 2010).

In contrast, the population of cancer patients in the study discussed here showed greater tendencies toward religiosity than that found in the entire Swedish population, perhaps owing to age distribution differences. In the study, only a third (29 percent) of informants were 59 years old or younger. Most (38 percent) were between 60 and 69 years, while one-third (33 percent) were 70 or older.

Study participants were asked to consider whether 24 different factors helped them feel better when they experienced stress, sadness, or depression during or after their illness. There were four alternatives for each factor: the factor in question helped them "not at all," "to a small extent," "to quite a large extent," or "to a very large extent." A numerical scale was used, where 1 was "not at all" and 4 "to a very large extent."

Items covering religious coping focused on the following strategies: praying to God to make things better, thinking that you have done your best and now only God is in control, thinking about God or the life of Jesus or other religious people's lives, thinking that you have ever had a sense of a strong connection with God, going to church, listening to religious music, Seeking spiritual help from a priest or other religious leader. All of the above strategies are RCOPE methods.

As Table 3.2 shows, the factor "Praying to God to make things better" is in thirteenth place (mean =1.7). A fifth of informants (20 percent) reported that this

Table 3.2 Coping methods When you have felt stressed, sad or depressed during or after your illness, to what extent have the following helped you feel better? Percent.

June 2011	Percentage that answers				Mean	Number of answers
	Not at all (1)	Small (2)	Quite large (3)	Very large (4)		
Thinking about God or contemplating the life of Jesus or other religious personages?	63	20	12	6	1.6	2 266
Thinking about a spiritual power?	49	23	18	9	**1.9**	2 264
Going to church?	64	21	10	4	1.5	2 261
Praying?	51	20	17	12	1.9	2 320
Listening to religious music?	65	20	11	3	1.5	2 245
Listening to spiritual music?	56	23	16	5	1.7	2 267
Listening to the "music of Nature" (birds singing/wind rustling)?	13	21	38	28	2.8	2 335
Going for walks or doing other outdoor activities that give you a sense of spirituality?	19	18	34	29	2.7	2 338
Thinking and contemplating the meaning of life and other things, in solitude?	32	36	26	6	2.1	2 307
Helping others to experience spirituality?	50	28	19	3	1.8	2 282
Thinking that you have done your best and the rest is in God's hands?	62	18	13	7	1.6	2 310
Praying to God that He will make things better?	58	21	14	6	1.7	2 302
Trying to control your situation without God's help?	30	20	34	15	2.3	2 283
Trying to stop thinking about your illness by thinking of spiritual matters?	64	25	9	2	1.5	2 327
Seeking spiritual help from a priest or other religious leaders?	86	9	4	2	1.2	2 301
Providing spiritual support to others?	77	16	6	1	1.3	2 290
Having sometime experienced a strong connection to God?	66	16	12	6	1.6	2 324

(*Continued*)

Table 3.2 (Continued)

June 2011	Percentage that answers				Mean	Number of answers
	Not at all (1)	Small (2)	Quite large (3)	Very large (4)		
Having experienced a strong spiritual connection to other people?	57	24	15	4	1.7	2 296
Have you ever believed that your life is part of something greater and higher?	38	27	22	12	2.1	2 323
Having experienced a strong sense of spirituality?	54	23	16	8	1.8	2 314
Believing or feeling that there is a spiritual power within you that helps you cope with your problems?	46	24	20	9	1.9	2 341
Hoping for a spiritual rebirth in this world?	75	17	6	2	1.3	2 285
Preferring to be alone, thinking about your life or contemplating life, to feel better?	43	32	21	4	1.9	2 304
That Nature is an important resource to help you cope with your illness?	11	20	38	30	2.9	2 362

factor had helped them feel better during or after their illness to a large or quite a large extent; one in 20 (6 percent) ranked this method as helping "to a large extent" and one in five (21 percent) as helping only marginally. Nearly three in five (58 percent) chose the option "not at all."

Almost 79 percent of informants chose the alternative "to a small extent" or "not at all" when asked whether they prayed to God to make things better. Praying is clearly not a common coping method among cancer patients in Sweden, despite the fact that most informants were among the elderly group and had, thus, probably received some religious socialization during childhood; they may even have had a religious upbringing. They would have been subject to some degree of Christian indoctrination at school. Given that secularism had not yet fully taken hold during the period of, they may also have experienced other religious influences. We would expect the results for the whole population to be less.

The study results are in line with qualitative findings (Ahmadi 2006: 108) showing that the informants were not comfortable disclosing that they had pleaded to God to make things better. Admitting weakness and that one needs help, even if this someone is God, runs counter to the dominant pattern of socialization in Sweden, where independence and self-reliance are encouraged. Pleading to God for help was likely not part of people's religious behavior in normal situations.

The qualitative study revealed that some informants, particularly those in the "theist group," sought control by praying to God. None of the informants reported having prayed for a miracle.

In sixteenth place (mean = 1.6) was the factor "Thinking that you have done your best and now it's only God who is in control" (Table 3.2). A fifth of informants (20 percent) responded that, when they felt stressed, sad, or depressed during or after their illness, this factor had helped them feel better "a lot or to quite a large extent." Just over one in 20 (7 percent) responded that the factor helped them to a large extent and one in six (18 percent) only marginally. Just over three in five (62 percent) indicated "not at all."

As the study showed, 80 percent of informants reported not having asked for help from God. This is in complete agreement with results on the coping method Self-Directing Religious Coping, where the person seeks control directly through individual initiative rather than help from God. The study indicates that this coping strategy is frequent among cancer patients in Sweden, something we will discuss later. The qualitative study as well showed a strong tendency toward using Self-Directing Religious Coping and a weak tendency toward relying on the method of pleading to God.

The factor "Thinking about God or thinking about the life of Jesus or other religious people's lives" was in seventeenth place (mean = 1.6) (Table 3.2).

One in six informants (18 percent) responded that, during or after their illness, this factor had helped them feel better "quite a lot or to a very large extent." One in 20 (6 percent) responded "to a large extent" and one in five (20 percent) that it had helped only marginally. Just over three in five (63 percent) chose the option "not at all."

In eighteenth place (mean = 1.6), we find the factor "Thinking that you ever had a sense of a strong connection with God" (Table 3,2). One in six informants (18 percent) indicated that this factor had helped them feel better "a lot or to quite a large extent" when they were stressed, sad, or depressed during or after their illness. One in 20 (6 percent) responded that the method had helped "to a large extent," while one in six (16 percent) chose the option "to a small extent." Two in three (66 percent) responded "not at all."

In nineteenth place (mean = 1.5) was the factor "Going to church" (Table 3.2). One in seven informants (14 percent) reported that this factor had helped them to "a larger or very large extent." A few (4 percent) answered "very large extent," and one in five (21 percent) "to a small extent." Nearly two in three (64 percent) chose the option "not at all."

Listening to religious music was ranked in twentieth place (mean = 1.5) (Table 3.2). One in seven informants (14 percent) indicated that, when they had felt stressed, sad, or depressed during or after their illness, this factor had helped "a lot or to a very large extent." A few (3 percent) replied "to a large extent." One in five (20 percent) responded "to a small extent." Nearly two in three (65 percent) indicated "not at all."

In last place (mean = 1.2), we find the factor "Seeking spiritual help from a priest or other religious leader" (Table 3.2). One in 20 informants (6 percent) replied that this factor had helped them feel better "a lot or to quite a large extent." A few (2 percent) responded "to a large extent," one in ten (9 percent) "to a small extent," and six in seven (86 percent) "not at all."

The negative religious coping methods

The informants were asked to rate the above-mentioned eight religious coping methods by indicating the degree to which these methods had helped them feel better during their illness. These coping methods have been considered positive.

In addition to these eight, three other methods were included in the questionnaire; these three were considered negative coping strategies. Negative religious coping has been said to express "a less secure relationship with God, a tenuous and ominous view of the world, and a religious struggle in the search for significance" (Pargament et al. 1998: 712). The following question was posed to address the first negative religious coping method: *Have you wondered whether God has abandoned you or have you been angry that God was not present to assist you?*

As Table 3.2 shows, only 3 percent of informants reported having thought that God had abandoned them or having felt anger toward God and that this had helped them feel better "to quite a large extent" when they felt stressed, sad, or depressed during or after their illness. A few informants (1 percent) responded "to a large extent," one in ten (9 percent) responded that it had helped only marginally and almost nine in ten (88 percent) answered "not at all."

The question addressing the second negative religious coping method was: *Have you ever felt that God has given you your health problems because of your actions or because you have not been sufficiently faithful?* Table 3.2 indicates that only 2 percent of informants chose the option "to quite a large extent." A small number (less than 1 percent) responded "to a large extent." Almost one in ten (8 percent) responded "marginally" and nine out of ten (90 percent) "not at all." No significant differences in responses to this item were found between different groups of informants.

The question addressing the third negative religious coping method was: *Have you ever felt that your illness was caused by an evil power?*

As Table 3.2 indicates, only 1 percent of informants chose "to a large extent" or "to quite a large extent." A small number (less than 1 percent) replied "to a large extent." One in twenty (5 percent) selected "to a small extent," 19 of 20 (94 percent) "not at all." No significant between-group differences were found for this question.

As the results show, very few informants (1 to 3 percent) used any of the three negative coping methods; this is in accordance with the qualitative study.

Drawing specific conclusions based on these findings is difficult, but a hypothesis can be posed: use of these negative coping methods would seem to require a belief in God or Satan: a God who not only created humans, but also controls individuals' actions and destinies, or similarly, a Devil who is able to control and change lives. However, among Protestant Swedes the prevalent view of God is of a Creator God – one who has left humans to determine their own destinies and shape their own history. This is one possible explanation for why these negative coping methods were rare among the informants.

The ranking of religious coping methods presented above shows that the use of such methods is not particularly widespread among cancer patients in Sweden. Besides the two methods (listening to religious music and praying to God to make things better) ranked twelfth and thirteenth – i.e., in the middle – the other methods are ranked in the lowest positions. This reveals how insignificant religious strategies are when it comes to coping with cancer in Sweden.

A brief look at Swedish history shows us that belief in a personal God has decreased in Sweden during recent decades, whereas belief in a transcendent power has increased (Hagevi, 2012; Lövendahl, 2008; Ahmadi, 2006; Hamberg, 1998; Hamberg, 2001; Pettersson & Riis, 1994). Although, until 2001, a large majority of Swedes belonged to the Lutheran Church, only a minority in Scandinavia was committed to the church (Halman & Pettersson, 2002; Pettersson, 2008; Riis, 1992). The difficulty in finding informants who attended church, prayed, or read the Bible for religious comfort in a time of crisis was not unexpected and was in line with findings from other studies (Jänterä-Jareberg, 2010; Pettersson, 2008), including the qualitative study discussed here (Ahmadi, 2006). For instance, a nationwide study among Swedes showed that only 16 percent of respondents prayed weekly and only 9 percent attended church at least once a month (Hamberg 1994: 181). According to statistics from the Church of Sweden, only 2 percent of its members attend worship services on a regular basis (Jänterä-Jareberg 2010: 669). Concerning religious coping, one interpretation of the results of this quantitative study and of the qualitative study (Ahmadi, 2006) is that the few informants who reported having used these coping methods relied not only on God's power, but on their own as well. They felt they were responsible for their own life and saw God as a partner in solving their problems. Thus, God was not seen as a hand that could pull them out of this difficult situation, but a hand to hold to get through it. The informants did not wait passively for God to assist them. Thus, although God was in the picture, helping the individual handle the situation, the individual – not God – was the main actor. The tendency toward independence, control, and self-direction, which is strong among Swedes, was obvious.

As discussed above, the study showed that Self-directed Religious Coping was the most prevalent religious coping method among cancer patients in Sweden. According to Wong-McDonald and Grouch (2000: 150), "People who are less committed tend to be more self-directive or referring, whereas those who are more committed may choose to work collaboratively with God" (Pargament et al., 1998). The qualitative study (Ahmadi, 2006) revealed that the factors of fear and powerlessness cause people to work collaboratively with God in coping. The qualitative study also found a number of informants from the "theist group" and the "non-theist group" who, although less committed Christians or not committed Christians, sought more active collaboration with God or some other higher power in solving their problems. They did this because they felt powerless or were frightened (Ahmadi 2006: 110).

Spiritually oriented coping

As mentioned, informants in the quantitative study were asked to reflect on whether 24 separate factors had helped them feel better when they experienced stress, sadness, or depression during or after their illness. For each factor, four response alternatives were provided: the factor in question helped them "not at all," "to a small extent," "to quite a large extent," or "to a very large extent."

A numerical scale was used, where 1 was "not at all" and 4 "to a very large extent." Factors related to spiritual coping focused on the following methods: thinking about a spiritual force, experiencing a strong spiritual feeling, getting a spiritual feeling by helping others, listening to spiritual music, feeling a strong spiritual connection with other people, trying not to think about your illness by pondering spiritual issues, hoping for a spiritual rebirth in this world, giving spiritual support to others.

As Table 3.2 shows, the factor "Thinking about a spiritual force" is found in ninth place (mean = 1.9). Slightly over a quarter of survey respondents (27 percent) indicated that this factor had helped them feel better "a lot or to quite a great extent" when, during or after their disease, they had felt stressed, sad, or depressed. One in ten (9 percent) responded "to a very large extent," almost one in four (23 percent) "to a small extent" and about half (49 percent) chose the option "not at all."

In eleventh place (mean = 1.8) in the ranking, we find the factor "Experiencing a strong spiritual feeling" (Table 3.2). One in four informants (24 percent) replied that this factor had helped them feel better "a lot or to quite a great extent." Slightly less than one in ten (8 percent) responded "to a large extent," almost one in four (23 percent) "to a small extent" and slightly over half (54 percent) "not at all."

The factor "Getting a spiritual feeling by helping others" (Table 3.2) is found in twelfth place (mean = 1.8). Slightly more than one in five survey respondents (22 percent) indicated that this factor had helped them feel better "a lot or to quite a great extent" when they, during or after their disease, had felt stressed, sad or depressed. A few (3 percent) responded "to a very large extent," slightly more than one in four (28 percent) "to a small extent," and half (50 percent) "not at all."

Listening to spiritual music ranked in fourteenth place (mean = 1.7) (Table 3.2). One in five informants (21 percent) reported that this factor had helped "a lot or to a very large extent" when they felt stressed, sad, or depressed during or after their illness. One in twenty (5 percent) answered "to a very large extent," nearly one in four (23 percent) "to a small extent" and almost three in five (56 percent) chose the option "not at all."

In fifteenth place (mean = 1.7) in the ranking, we find the factor "Feeling a strong spiritual connection with other people" (Table 3.2). About one in five (19 percent) indicated that this factor had helped them feel better "a lot or to quite a great extent," a few (4 percent) chose the option "to a large extent," one in four (24 percent) "to a small extent" and nearly three in five (57 percent) "not at all."

The factor "Trying not to think about your illness by pondering spiritual issues" is found in twenty-first place (mean = 1.5) (Table 2). One in ten survey respondents (11 percent) indicated that this factor had helped them feel better "a lot or to quite a great extent" when they had felt stressed, sad, or depressed during or after their disease. A few (2 percent) answered "to a large extent," one in four (25 percent) "to a small extent" and nearly two in three (64 percent) "not at all."

In twenty-first place (mean = 1.5), we find the factor "Trying not to think about your illness by pondering spiritual issues" (Table 3.2). One in ten survey respondents (11 percent) indicated that this factor had helped them feel better "a lot or to quite a great extent". A few (2 percent) chose the option "to a large extent," one in four (25 percent) "to a small extent" and nearly two in three (64 percent) "not at all."

The factor "Hoping for a spiritual rebirth in this world" is found in twenty-second place (mean = 1.3) (Table 3.2). Slightly less than a tenth of survey respondents (8 percent) answered that this factor had helped them feel better "a lot or to quite a great extent" when they, during or after their disease, had felt stressed, sad or depressed. A few (2 percent) responded "to a large extent," one in six (17 percent) "to a small extent" and three out of four (75 percent) "not at all."

The factor "Giving spiritual support to others" takes next-to-last place (mean = 1.3) in the ranking (Table 3.2). Somewhat more than one in 20 survey respondents (7 percent) indicated that this factor had helped them feel better "a lot or to quite a great extent." A few (1 percent) responded "to a large extent," one in six (16 percent) "to a small extent" and slightly more than three in four (77 percent) "not at all."

Comparing the above findings with the results for RCOPE (religious coping), we see that informants used spiritual coping methods to a higher degree than religious coping methods. As the study shows, almost 24 percent reported that their experience of having a strong sense of spirituality helped them cope with their cancer disease. This does not suggest, however, a strong tendency toward spirituality among the informants. As we saw, the "spiritual" factors were not among the primary methods informants chose to cope with their illness. Actually, the highest rankings are found for what we call "existential secular coping methods" – methods related to "nature." We will discuss these methods later.

Some of the spiritual coping methods, such as "Trying not to think about your illness by pondering spiritual issues," "Hoping for a spiritual rebirth in this world" and "Giving spiritual support to others," do indeed occupy lower positions on the ranking (see Table 3.2).

Note that, in the qualitative study, we categorized the method "Thinking that your life is part of a larger and higher context" as a spiritual coping method, but there is a problem here, which is that about a third of informants (34 percent) reported that this had helped them "a lot or to quite a great extent." It is not clear what informants interpreted as "a larger and higher context" when they chose this option. For instance, they may well have been thinking about *nature*. This hypothesis is supported not only by the qualitative findings, but also by the quantitative results, as we will see later on. It is for this reason, as well as due to our criticism of how the term spirituality was applied in the qualitative study, that we chose to categorize the coping method "Thinking that your life is part of a larger and higher context" as an "Existential secular coping method" in the quantitative study.

In addition to the strategies explained above, informants in the qualitative study revealed several new and effective methods, such as nature, for coping with the emotional and psychological problems associated with their cancer. In the quantitative study, we examined to the prevalence of these methods among cancer patients in Sweden. Thought focused on existential issues, these methods cannot be classified as RCOPE. They have nothing to do with religion or spirituality. These methods are instead characterized by a tendency toward pondering existential questions, thus we call them "existential secular coping methods."

Existential secular coping methods

Factors related to existential secular meaning-making coping focused on the following methods: nature as an important resource, listening to "nature's music," Going for walks or doing other outdoor activities which gives a sense of spirituality, trying to get control of your situation without the help of God (Self-Directing Religious Coping), thinking that your life is part of a larger and higher context, sitting alone and pondering and philosophizing on the meaning of life and other things.

Receiving the highest mean (2.9), thus at the top of the ranking, was the factor "Nature as an important resource" (Table 3.2). Two in three informants (68 percent) indicated that this factor had helped them feel better "a lot or to quite a great extent" when they, during or after their disease, had felt stressed, sad, or depressed. Nearly one in three (30 percent) chose the option "to a large extent," one in five (20 percent) "to a small extent" and one in ten (11 percent) "not at all."

In second place, thus receiving the second highest mean (2.8), was the factor "Listening to the 'music of nature' (birds singing/wind rustling)" (Table 3.2). Two in three informants (66 percent) answered that this factor had helped them feel better "a lot or to quite a great extent." Slightly more than one in four (28 percent) responded "to a large extent," one in five (21 percent) "to a small extent" and just over one in ten (13 percent) "not at all."

In third place, thus receiving the third highest mean (2.7), was the factor "Walking or engaging in any activity in nature that gives you a 'spiritual' sense" (Table 3.2). Three in five informants (63 percent) responded that this factor had helped them feel better "to a very or fairly large extent" when they, during or after their sickness, had felt stressed, sad or depressed. Nearly one in three (29 percent) reported "to a very large extent," one in six (18 percent) "to a small extent" and one in five (19 percent) "not at all."

The factor "Trying to get control of your situation without the help of God" was ranked in fourth place (mean 2.3) (Table 3.2). Half of the informants (49 percent) indicated that this factor had helped them feel better "a lot or to quite a large extent." One in seven (15 percent) responded "to a large extent," one in five (20 percent) that it helped only marginally and nearly one in three (30 percent) "not at all" (Table 3.2).

In fifth place (mean 2.1), we find the factor "Thinking that your life is part of a larger and higher context" (Table 3.2). One in three informants (34 percent) reported that this factor had helped them feel better "a lot or to quite a large extent" when they, during or after their disease, had felt stressed, sad or depressed. Just over one in ten (12 percent) chose the option "to a very large extent," one in four (27 percent) "to a small extent," and nearly two in five (38 percent) "not at all."

In sixth place (mean 2.1), we find the factor "Sitting alone and pondering and philosophizing on the meaning of life and other things" (Table 3.2). One in three informants (32 percent) indicated that this factor had helped them feel better "to quite a large extent." One in 20 (6 percent) reported "to a large extent" slightly more than one in three (36 percent) "marginally" and nearly one in three (32 percent) "not at all."

As we have seen, the highest mean value (2.9) belongs to the factor indicating that, among the Swedish informants, "nature" has been an important resource in dealing with cancer (Table 3.2). The factor with the second highest average (2.8) is "listening to the music of nature (such as birds singing/wind rustling)" (Table 3.2). The factor in third place, with a mean of 2.7, is "going for walks or doing other outdoor activities which gives a sense of spirituality" (Table 3.2). It is clear, then, that the informants in the quantitative study regarded nature and nature-related activities as the most important factors in helping them cope with their illness.

The results suggest that a large number of informants saw a value in nature. Nature is timeless and immense – whatever happens in the world, nature will remain, continuing at its own pace. Nature seems to have had a calming and comforting effect on the severely ill informants; it seems to have provided a feeling of security when everything else was chaotic.

The prominent position of nature in Swedish ways of thinking and culture may explain why experiences of natural environments seem to play such a crucial role in coping. In addition to the EVSS,[3] other relevant studies – for instance the Sifo study (Lindén, 1994), the Uppsala Study of 1986 (Hamberg, 1994), and the 1994 Study (Uddenberg, 1995) – all show that interest in nature and environmental issues is widespread among Swedes, particularly young people. According to the 1994 Study, which was based on a questionnaire survey among 973 Swedes (20 to 69 years of age), only 4 percent reported having "no need to be out in nature," while 94 percent indicated that "nature makes them feel relaxed and harmonious." In the 1994 Study, 51 percent agreed with the statement "human beings would feel much better if they were as natural as animals are."

The finding showing that informants perceived a sacred value in nature can also be explained by previous studies indicating that people living in Sweden are spiritual as opposed to religious. This is because church attendance and other religious activities in the country have declined sharply during recent decades, perhaps even before the mid-20th century (Ahmadi, 2006; Pettersson & Riz, 1994; Sundback, 1994; Gustavsson, 1985). In Sweden, religiosity has shifted toward a subjective, private phenomenon with few public attributes (Sundback 1994: 139). Swedes are more likely to describe their religious lives in spiritual terms. For this reason, it is more appropriate to talk about the existence of a kind of spirituality rather than religiosity among Swedes.

This point was observed in the quantitative study and in the qualitative investigation that preceded it (Ahmadi, 2006).

Two important tendencies observed among people in Sweden have most likely influenced their use of nature as a coping method. These tendencies are seeking closeness with a supreme force and seeking a natural romanticism, both of which render nature an accessible source for coping. One factor that may explain these two tendencies is the influence of culture and ways of thinking on how people deal with their problems. Below, we will discuss the results obtained in the quantitative study by taking a cultural perspective.

The Swedish studies on coping from a cultural perspective

As pointed out by Ahmadi (2006: 82–85), Swedish culture and ways of thinking have played a crucial role in Swedes' modern-day views on religion and spirituality. One aim of the WVS (World Value Study) was to compare basic value systems around the world, starting from each country's culture and ways of thinking.

Pettersson, who has been involved in WVS investigation, discusses the results of a factor analysis on data from 1990/1996; these results are important to understanding the culture underlying the Swedish belief system. Pettersson suggests that two bipolar dimensions play a role here (Pettersson 2000: 14–20):

- Traditional rationality versus secular-rational rationality: traditional rationality is characterized by belief in God and the family is regarded as very important; obedience is of more importance than independence; individuals should have a lot of respect for authority and hierarchy. Secular-rational rationality is characterized by opposite values.
- Survival values versus individual identity and integrity (cultural postmodernization): survival values are characterized by the belief that economic security and safety are much more important than individual identity and integrity; that material working conditions mean more than social and developmental psychology. A strong belief in science and technology and low social confidence are also distinctive features. The other pole, that of individual identity and integrity, is characterized by opposite values (Pettersson 2000: 15).

According to Ahmadi (2006: 82), findings from the WVS show that the value system of the people in the Protestant northern European countries (including Sweden) is marked by a high degree of secular-rational rationality as well as a postmodern view on individual identity and integrity. In the WVS study, Sweden was classified as one of the most secular countries in the world.

Ahmadi (ibid.) claims that the diminishing interest in church attendance and participating in church services as well as the tendency toward disclaiming God as a shepherd, on the one hand, and the growth of secularism, on the other, do not imply that sacred values can no longer be found in Sweden. What we may be witnessing instead is a development toward "post-materialist values," which Luckmann (1990) sees as our times' "sacred values" – a development that goes hand in hand with individualization.

Luckmann (1990: 238) argues further that notions of individual independence and personal autonomy are soon to become part of our times' sacred values. Thus, the decreased significance of traditional faith does not imply disappearance of the sacred. The emphasis on the individual integrity, self-realization, and respect for individual freedom instead becomes a characteristic feature of holiness.

Regarding the position of religion in Sweden, Ahmadi (2006: 84) suggests:

- In Sweden, church practices and other religious activities have declined drastically during the past decades, perhaps even before the mid-20th century, as some researchers (e.g., Gustavsson, 1985) maintain.
- The direction of development of religiousness in Sweden has been toward a subjective, inwardly directed phenomenon with few public attributes (Sundback 1994: 139).
- Swedes are more likely to describe their religious lives in spiritual terms. It seems therefore appropriate to talk of the existence of a kind of spirituality rather than religiosity among Swedes.

Tendency toward natural romanticism

According to Herlitz, "Swedes generally speaking have an almost sacred relationship to nature" (1995: 36). The postmaterialist era has seen an increased tendency toward "private religion" and spirituality among people today, particularly Swedes. As the sacred increasingly becomes private, the role of music, literature, psychoanalysis, and nature in mediating existential and "religious" experiences becomes more prominent. In this respect, nature plays a special role for Swedes. Today, Swedes seem to seek experiences that were previously mediated by Christian culture, but now they do so in other ways. One of these alternate approaches involves experiencing unity with nature. Being in natural environments and feeling unity with nature can provide a spiritual sense of unification with the whole of existence.

As some informants in the qualitative study emphasized, nature becomes the church and unity with the holy becomes unity with nature (Ahmadi, 2006). This view of nature suggests a culture with strong traditions of natural romanticism (Berggren & Trägårdh, 2009). Swedes generally view themselves as a natureloving people (Uddenberg, 1995: 37). For about a century, the Swedish people's national sense has been based on, among other things, a profound love of nature (Sundin, 1981; Johannisson, 1984). Given this, it is easy to understand why many Swedes feel their well-being depends on having contact with nature (Uddenberg

1995: 39) and why such contact is one of the most frequent coping methods reported by cancer patients in the quantitative study.

Considering these results, the possibilities for coping that spending time in and relating to nature offer cancer patients should be taken more seriously by healthcare providers, particularly by therapists trying to address the psychological problems cancer patients face in different phases, such as diagnosis, treatment, and post-treatment. Generally speaking, there should be more focus on developing less conventional therapeutic methods, such as creating opportunities for patients to come into contact with nature. For example, well-designed, health-promoting gardens within clinics would allow patients to engage in gardening, meditation, or just give them an opportunity to feel the earth. In addition to such gardens, seeing plants and hearing birdsong are ways of using nature to meet patients' spiritual needs. The study confirms the notion that meeting such needs is crucial to people dealing with a serious life crisis.

Relying on oneself

As we saw above, the three most frequent coping methods chosen by informants concern nature and nature activities. In fourth place, we find "Trying to get control of your situation without the help of God."

Informants in the quantitative study reported that this factor was the most important coping strategy, following the three existential methods mentioned above. Because Pargament and other researchers in the field consider this strategy a religious coping method, it is interesting to note that, among the RCOPE methods, it is the one most frequently reported.

In the quantitative study, the use of RCOPE methods was examined to some extent, and this self-directing method was categorized as religious coping, just as in Pargament's investigation (Pargament et al. 2000: 522–524). However, other studies (Phillips III et al., 2004; Bickel et al., 1998) have provided conflicting results regarding the correlation between Self-Directing Religious Coping and negative and positive outcomes on different variables, such as depression. One important question raised in these studies is whether a self-directing style is linked to the concept of a deistic God, an abandoning God, or no God at all. However, one of the problems underlying the conflicting outcomes for self-directed coping is that the strategies of people who are trying not to rely on God have been categorized as "religious coping." Some researchers, Pargament among them, have pointed out this problem as one explanation for the mixed results on self-directed coping (Phillips III et al. 2004: 410).

In the qualitative study (Ahmadi 2006: 127), informants belonging to all three groups – the "theist group," the "non-theist group," and the "atheist group" – reported having chosen to rely on their individual initiative rather than on God's help in their efforts to gain control over their difficult situation. Similarly, informants in the quantitative study showed an inclination to trust their own problem-solving abilities more than they trusted other sources of power, such as God or a religious authority. This finding can be seen as partly stemming from the strong role individualism plays in Swedish culture, which values the individual assuming responsibility for his/her own problems. Waiting for a miracle or pleading to God or others for intervention does not coincide with the values and norms of the society these individuals were socialized in, that is, a highly individualistic society embedded in the Protestant ethic – to use Max Weber's term (1964) – where individuals are considered responsible for their own actions.

According to Phillips III et al. (2004: 410), the original assumption in RCOPE concerning Self-Directing Religious Coping is that God has given individuals the ability and freedom to engage in problem-solving. From this perspective, people could assume that God does not intervene, but does support the individual throughout the coping process. People may also believe they have to cope alone because God has abandoned them, or finally, they may adopt self-directed methods because they are not particularly religious and do not involve God in their coping process. It is interesting that, in this connection Phillips III et al. (2004: 410) discussed the possibility of someone being "not very religious," but not being a non-theist or atheist. This may be because the research on which the coping methods are based was conducted in the United States where, according to the WVS (http://www.wvsevsdb.com/ wvs/WVSAnalize.jsp), religion plays an important role in the lives of 55.1 percent of the population.[4] Replicating this research on coping methods in cultural contexts other than the American one may give different results. In cultural settings like Sweden, where only 10.1 percent of the population regard religion as very important in their lives,[5] the last explanation for the self-directing coping method – the participant is not particularly religious and does not involve God in the coping process – can be expected to be more pertinent than the others.

Concerning the role of culture in coping, the tendencies described below were observed (Ahmadi 2006: 177–179):

Tendency toward spirituality: it is the individual's own spiritual ideas about a higher power that are in focus rather than his/her participation in religious or social activities. As mentioned, during the past three centuries, Swedish society has moved toward increased individualism and secularism, and religion has become less organized and more privatized. This and other characteristics of Swedish culture, such as nature romanticism, likely underlie Swedes' tendency to choose spirituality over religiosity.

Tendency toward control and self-direction: Sweden is one of the world's most secular countries, and its people are highly individualistic (Pettersson & Riis, 1994). Having been socialized in a secular and individual-oriented society has doubtless reinforced Swedes' tendency toward solving personal problems primarily through self-reliance rather than looking to a higher power. If we take into consideration the combination of strong individualism, secularism, and privatization of religion found in Sweden, the informants' strong tendency toward using self-directed coping methods is completely understandable.

Tendency toward privacy: another tendency revealed in the study is that informants appreciated seclusion and avoided involving others. To understand this, we must consider that Swedes are individualistic and seek positive solitude. This does not mean that no one suffers from loneliness. Certainly many elderly people do. But, as we can read in a guide for newcomers to Sweden, Swedes like being alone. This guide, which is written in English, states that as long as solitude is not permanent or forced, most Swedes not only accept but even enjoy being by themselves. Swedes take for granted that others share the same preference for privacy and try to respect this.

Tendency toward nature romanticism: all informants in the study, regardless of religious belief or philosophical view, reported "using" nature to deal with the problems caused by their disease.

We have discussed the results showing an increased tendency toward privatized religiosity and spirituality among Swedes. As the sacred becomes more private, the role that music, literature, psychoanalysis and nature play in mediating existential, spiritual and religious experiences becomes more important. This partly explains the special position nature holds among Swedes. It would seem that Swedes today are seeking experiences in other ways than through traditional religion. One of these experiences involves the sense of being one with nature (Ahmadi 2008: 178).

Swedes, on the whole, have been said to have an almost sacred relationship with nature (Herlitz 1995: 36). Being in natural environments and feeling a part of them promotes spiritual feelings of the unity of existence. Some informants pointed out that, for them, nature is like a church and unity with nature is like unity with the sacred. Spending time in nature can result in a sense of spirituality and total connectedness.

Tendency toward rationalism and pragmatism: the informants' rejection of choice of some coping methods such as praying to God for a miracle, is regarded as a sign of their socialization into the rationalism and pragmatism that predominates in Swedish culture. Rationalism and pragmatism are considered two of the most important features of Swedish ways of thinking (Pettersson & Riis, 1994).

The Swedes are renowned for their practical approach. According to Runblom (1998), the Swedish tradition is marked by a high degree of pragmatism in solving social problems. For instance, the internationally acclaimed Swedish model of corporatist policy has also been referred to as "principled pragmatism" (Helco & Madsen, 1987).

In Ahmadi's view (2006: 179), having been socialized into a highly rational and pragmatic culture may result in individual preferences for some coping methods over others. Methods that are not rational or that are harmful and require belief in fatalism are less likely to be used by Swedes.

Notes

1 In this chapter, we have used some results, which are already published. Copyright permissions have been obtained.
2 The large number of people who are members of trade unions should not been seen as an indication that Swedes are collectivists and that the Swedish culture is group oriented. The strong position of trade unions in Sweden is actually related to Swedes' strong inclination toward organization and a result of the cooperative arrangement of society, which is completely different from collectivism.

3 The European Values Study is a large-scale, cross-national, and longitudinal survey research program on basic human values, initiated by the European Values Study Group (EVSSG) in the late 1970s, which at that time was an informal grouping of academics. Now, it is carried on in the setting of a foundation, using the (abbreviated) name of the group: European Values Study (EVS).
4 The American Religious Identification Survey (ARIS 2008: 9) showed that, when asked about the existence of God, less than 70 percent of Americans reported believing in the traditional theological concept of a personal God. According to other sources, 76 to 80 percent self-identify as Christians (Putnam & Campbell, 2010), while about 3.9 to 5.5 percent of the adult population belong to non-Christian religions (Kosmin & Keysar, 2009).
5 According to several sources (Kallenberg et al., 1996; Hamberg, 1994), the proportion of people in Sweden who self-identify as religious varies between 18 and 23 percent. A sociological survey indicated that 46 to 85 percent of the Swedish population can be categorized as atheists, agnostics, or non-believers (in God) (Zuckerman, 2007).

References

Ahmadi, F. (2006). *Culture, religion and spirituality in coping: The example of cancer patients in Sweden.* Acta Universitatis Upsaliensis. Studia sociologica Upsaliensia 53. Uppsala: Uppsala University.

Ahmadi, F. (2008). *Kultur och Hälsa (Culture and Health).* Lund: Studentlitteratur.

Ahmadi, F. (Ed.). (2015). *Coping with cancer in Sweden: A search for meaning.* Acta Universitatis Upsaliensis. Studia sociologica Upsaliensia 63. Uppsala: Uppsala University.

Ahmadi Lewin, F. (2001). Gerotranscendence and different cultural settings. *Ageing and Society,* 21(4): 395–415. Barinaga, E. (1999). *Swedishness through Lagom. Can words tell us anything about a culture?* Research paper series 6: Centre for Advanced Studies in Leadership.

Berggren, H. & Trägårdh. L. (2009/2006). *Är svensken människa? (Is a Swede human?)* Stockholm: Norstedts.

Bickel, C. O., Ciarrocchi, J. W., Sheers, J. J., Estadt, B. K., Powell, D. A., & Pargament, K. L. (1998). Perceived stress, religious coping styles and depressive affect. *Journal of Psychology and Christianity,* 17(1): 33–42.

Costello, B. (2001). Altruism: Selfless or selfish. Article online. *Serendip.* Second Web Report. Biology 202. Retrieved from: http://serendip.brynmawr.edu/ b/neuro/neuro01/web2/Costello.html.

Crabtree, S. (2010). Religiosity highest in world's poorest nations. *Gallup Global Reports.* Retrieved from http://www.gallup.com/poll/142727/religiosity-highest-world-poorest-nations.aspx.

Damasio, A. (2000). *The feeling of things: Body and emotion in the making of consciousness.* New York: Harvest.

Fromm, E. (1950). *Psychoanalysis and religion.* New Haven, CT: Yale University Press.

Gustavsson, A. (Ed.). (1985). *Religiösa Väckelserörelser i Norden Under 1800- och 1900-Talen. (Religious revivalist movement in Nordic countries during the nineteenth and twentieth centuries.* Lund: Centrum för religionsetnologisk forskning.

Hagevi, M. (2012). Beyond church and state: Private religiosity and post-materialist political opinion among individuals in Sweden. Journal of Church and State, 54(4): 499–525.

Halman, L. & Pettersson, T. (2002). Moral pluralism. Journal of *Yearbook for the Scientific Study of Religion,* 13:173–204.

Hamberg, E. (1994). Secularization and value change in Sweden. In T. Pettersson & O. Riis (Eds.), *Scandinavian values: Religion and morality in the Nordic countries* (pp. 179–195). Uppsala: Acta Universitatis Uppsaliensis.

Hamberg, E. (1998). *Kristen på Mitt Eget Sätt: En Analys av Materialet Från Projektet Livsåskådning i Sverige.* Stockholm: Religionssociologiska Institutet.

Hamberg, E. (2001). Kristen Tro Och Praxis i Dagens Sverige. In C. R. Bråkenhielm, *Världsbild och Mening: En Emperisk Stidie av Livsåskådningar i Dagens Sverige.* Nya Doxa: Nora.

Helco, H. & Madsen, H. (1987). *Policy and politics in Sweden.* Philadelphia: Temple University Press.

Herlitz, G. (1995). *Swedes: What we are like and why we are as we are.* Uppsala: Uppsala Publishing House AB.

Jänterä-Jareberg, M. (2010). *Religion and the secular state in Sweden. National report on Sweden.* Research Programme: The Impact of Religion: Challenges for Society, Law and Democracy. Uppsala: Uppsala University, Sweden. Retrieved from http://www.crs.uu.se/digitalAssets/55/55502_Religion_in_the_Secular_State.pdf.

Johannisson, K. (1984). Det sköna i det vilda. (*The beauty in the wild nature*). In T. Frängsmyr, (Ed.), *Paradiset och Vildmarken (The paradise and the wild region).* Stockholm: LiberFörlag.

Kallenberg, K., Bråkenhielm, C. R., & Larsson, G. (1996). *Tro och värderingar i 90-talets Sverige. Om samspelet livsåskådning, moral och hälsa.(* Faith and values in the 90's Sweden. About the interaction of life, moral and health.) Örebro: Libris.

Kosmin, K. B. & Keysar, A. (2009). *American religious identification survey (ARIS) 2008.* Hartford, CT: Trinity College.

Lindén, A. L. (1994). *Människa och Miljö (Human being and Environment).* Stockholm: Carlsson.

Lövendahl, Lena. (2008). Privatreligiositet. In I. Svenberg & D. Westerlund, (Eds.), *Religion i Sverige (Religion in Sweden)* (pp. 29–32). Stockholm: Dialogos Förlag.

Luckmann, T. (1990). Shrinking transcendence, expanding religion? *Sociological Analysis,* 50(2):1 27–138.

Öhman, J. (2003). Miljöfostran i naturen (Nature experiences and environmental commitments). In L. Östman. (Ed.). *Nationell och internationell miljödidaktisk forskning: En forskningsöversikt (National and international research in environmental education: A review)* (pp. 65–89). Educational Research in Uppsala 148. Uppsala: Department of Education, Uppsala University.

Pargament, K. I. (1997). *The psychology of religion and coping.* New York: Guilford Press.

Pargament, K. I. (1999). The psychology of religion and spirituality. Yes and no? *The International Journal for the Psychology of Religion,* 9(1): 3–16.

Pargament, K. I., Koenig, H. G., & Perez, L. M. (2000). The many methods of religious coping: Development and initial variation of the RCOPE. *Journal of Clinical Psychology,* 56: 519–543.

Pargament, K. I. & Mahoney, A. (2005). Sacred matters: Sanctification as a vital topic for the psychology of religion. *The International Journal for the Psychology of Religion,* 15(3): 179–198.

Pargamnent, K. I., Zinnbauer, B. J., Scott, A. B., Butter, E. M., Zerowin, J., & Stanik, P. (1998). Red flags and religious coping: Identifying some religious warning signs among people in crisis. *Journal of Clinical Psychology,* 54: 77–89.

Pettersson, T. (2000). Svenskan och religionen. In L. Lewin (Ed.), Svenskt Kynne. Uppsala: Acta Universitatis Upsaliensis.

Pettersson, T. (2008). Sekularisering. In I. Svenberg & D. Westerlund (Eds.), *Religion I Sverige* (pp. 34–38). Stockholm: Dialogos Förlag.

Pettersson, T. & Riis, O. (Eds). (1994). *Scandinavian values. Religion and morality in the Nordic countries.* Uppsala: Acta Universitatis Uppsaliensis.

Phillips III, R. E., Pargament, K. I., Lynn, Q. K., & Crossley, C. D. (2004). Self-directing religious coping: A deistic God, abandoning God, or no God at all? *Journal for the Scientific Study of Religion*, 43(3): 409–418.
Riis, O. (1992). *Secularization in Scandinavia*. Paper for the Nordic Conference for the Sociology of Religion. Skálholt, Iceland.
Riis, O. (1994). Patterns of secularization in scandinavvia. In T. Pettersson & O. Riis (Eds.), *Scandinavian values. Religion and morality in the Nordic countries* (pp. 99–128). Uppsala: Acta Universitatis Uppsaliensis.
Runblom, H. (1998). Sweden as a multicultural society. *Current Sweden Series 418*. Swedish Institute online publishing.
Sundback, S. (1994). Nation and gender reflected in Scandinavian religiousness. In T. Pettersson & O. Riis. (Eds.), *Scandinavian Values. Religion and morality in the Nordic countries* (pp. 129–150). Uppsala: Acta Universitatis Upsaliensis.
Sundin, B. (1981). Från riksparken till bygdemuseum. Om djurskydds-, naturskydds- och hembygsrörelserna i sekelskiftets Sverige (From national park to rural community museum. On prevention of cruelty to animals – environment protection – and rural community movements in Sweden at the turn of the century). *Naturligtvis*, 14. Uppsatser om natur och samhälle tillägnade Gunnar Eriksson. Umeå : Inst. för idéhistoria, Umeå Univ.
Torbjörnsson, T., Molin, L., & Karlberg, M. (2011). Measuring attitudes towards three values that underlie sustainable development. *Utbildning och Demokrati, Örebro: Örebro University*, 20(1): 97–121.
Tornstam, L. (1997). Gerotranscendence in a broad cross sectional perspective. *Journal of Aging and Identity*, 2(1): 17–36.
Tornstam, L. (2005). *Gerotranscendence: A developmental theory of positive aging*. New York: Springer Publishing Company.
Uddenberg, N. (1995). *Det Stora Sammanhanget. Moderna Svenskars Syn på Människans Plats i Naturen.* (*The great whole: The modern Swede's view of the human beings' place in nature*). Lund: Nya Doxa.
Weber, M. (1964). *The sociology of religion*. Boston: Beacon Press.
Wong-McDonald, A. & Grouch, R. L. (2000). Surrender to God: An additional coping style? *Journal of Psychology and Theology*, 28(2): 149–161.
Zuckerman, P. (2007). Atheism: Contemporary rates and pattern, In M. Martin (Ed.), *The Cambridge companion to atheism*. Cambridge: University of Cambridge Press.

Internet sources

European Values Study. (1990). Retrieved from http://www.gesis.org/en/services/data-analysis/survey-data/european-values-study/2nd-wave-1990/.
European Values Study, Online Analysis. (2004). Retrieved fromhttp://www.worldvaluessurvey.org/WVSOnline.jsp.
The American Religious Identification Survey (ARIS). (2008). Retrieved from http://commons.trincoll.edu/aris/.
The European Barometer Study. (2010). Retrieved from http://ec.europa.eu/commfrontoffice/publicopinion/archives/ebs/ebs_341_en.pdf.
The Flash Eurobarometer Survey. (2011). Retrieved from http://ec.europa.eu/public_opinion/flash/fl_316_en.pdf.
WVS. Retrieved fromhttp://www.wvsevsdb.com/wvs/WVSAnalizeQuestion.jsp

4[1] The study in East Asia

The study in South Korea

In the framework of the international project on meaning-making coping, a qualitative interview study was conducted in South Korea to explore the use of meaning-making coping (existential secular, spiritual and religious coping) among cancer patients in Korea and to investigate the impact of culture on choice of coping methods. Interview questions for the study in Korea were mainly constructed based on the results from the Swedish study (Ahmadi, 2006; Ahmadi, 2015). Some questions were modified to adapt them to the Korean culture.

A convenience sample was chosen. In total, 33 participants were recruited in Seoul and surrounding suburban areas. The patients who participated in the study had either survived cancer or were still undergoing chemotherapy. Both men and women participated (age 20 years and older). They self-identified as either non-religious, spiritual, or religious (Protestants, Catholics, and Buddhists are three largest religious groups in Korea). More detailed information can be found in Table 4.1.

Table 4.1 Demographic characteristics of the participants, South Korea

Characteristics		N
Gender	Male	17
	Female	16
Age	20~39	3
	40~59	15
	60+	15
Education	High school graduate or less	17
	College graduate or higher	16
Children	Yes	29
	No	4
Monthly Household income*	Mid-low or less	14
	Mid-high or higher	19
Employment status	Housewife	7

(*Continued*)

Characteristics		N
Religion	Student	1
	Working	15
	Retired/On leave	10
	Buddhist	5
	Catholic	6
	Protestant	11
	No religion	11

N=33

*Low=less than 2,000; Mid-low=2,000~less than 4,000;

Mid-high=4,000~less than 6,000;

In this chapter, we focus on some selected results. Detailed reports of the results of the study in South Korea have already been published (Ahmadi et al., 2016, 2017).

Religious coping methods

The findings indicate that the use of religious coping methods was not prevalent among the interviewees in South Korea.

Some researchers have claimed that religiosity or spirituality has a positive effect on subjective well-being among cancer patients (Koenig, 1995; Pargament, 1997; Schreiber & Edward, 2015), while others have questioned the importance and effectiveness of such an impact (Poole & Higgo, 2010; Powell et al., 2003; Sloan, 2006; Sloan, Bagiella, & Powell, 2001). Looking at cancer patients in Sweden, Ahmadi (2015) revealed that existential secular meaning-making coping methods, especially nature and having a sense of self-control, were the most meaningful coping strategies. South Korea is not a particularly religious country. According to Gallup Korea (2015), about 50 per cent of South Koreans adhere to some religion (Buddhism 22 percent, Protestant 21 percent, and Catholic 7 percent); many, however, are spiritual and incorporate features of Shamanism into their daily life. For instance, some people make frequent visits to fortune tellers or shamans when they must make a critical decision (e.g., concerning a wedding, job); they may also attach wish ribbons to old trees, make piles of wishing stones in the mountains, and some believe that the ghost of the deceased is present during a memorial service. Whether or not Koreans are aware of it, their behaviors reveal a high degree of spirituality. It is, thus, not surprising to find that, in Korea, people with cancer report relying greatly on a transcendent power, irrespective of their level of religiosity.

The results of the South Korean study revealed the following coping methods, which can hardly be categorized as religious. We categorize them as existential secular coping methods. They are: (a) belief in the healing power of nature; (b) mind-body connection; (c) relying on a transcendent power; and (d) finding oneself in relationships with others.

Existential secular coping methods

Belief in the healing power of nature

When asked what their most effective coping resource was, some participants mentioned nature. Just as in the Swedish study (Ahmadi, 2006, 2015), the Korean participants also reported finding relief in the healing power of nature. They believed being close to nature would heal and comfort their mind and body during their struggle with cancer. Their belief in the healing power of nature can be characterized using two themes: *mountains as a healer* and *the healing power of natural foods*.

The greater Seoul area contains numerous mountains. Koreans are fond of spending time in nature and enjoy going to the mountains (Ministry of Culture, Sports, and Tourism, 2013). Popular Korean books and television programs have described people curing disease by living in the mountains or eating healthy, natural foods. Participants reported having experienced or heard about the benefits of mountains and specific natural foods in curing cancer. They followed the advice of physicians, but also had faith in the healing power of nature. Some stated that human life came from nature and must return to nature when the body and mind malfunction.

Following their cancer diagnosis, they tried to stay near a mountain, believing it contained a healing energy capable of revitalizing all living things. The participants not only believed that a mountain could cure cancer, but they also found comfort by simply being on it.

While discussing how the healing power of nature served as an effective coping resource, almost all of the participants mentioned natural foods. They believed natural foods could function as anti-cancer medicine. Among the foods mentioned, the fast-fermented yellow bean paste (called Chung-Gook-Chang in Korean) was the most common.

The reason the Korean participants believed in the healing power of mountains and natural foods is probably linked to their understanding of the mechanisms of nature, which are thought to be based on the theory of Yin-Yang and Five Elements. Koreans share in the broader oriental philosophy according to which human beings are part of nature and will return to nature – the root of all living beings (Jean, 1998). The natural foods the participants believed would help cure their cancer were produced from the earth. They reported experiencing comfort and vitality when they spent time on the mountains or when eating healthy foods, and they trusted that their mind and body would be healed in the arms of nature.

Mind-body connection

When we asked whether they had ever thought about why they got cancer, participants pointed to the stress of a busy lifestyle and having an uneasy mental state. They believed that experiencing a negative and complex mental state could harm the body and cause dysfunction. This can be interpreted as showing their belief in a body-mind connection. Several participants used the Korean term "Ah-dung-bah-dung," which means they had done their utmost to endure and achieve material success. They reported regretting their "Ah-dung-bah-dung" lifestyle following the cancer diagnosis, realizing that a peaceful mental state was helpful in overcoming a life crisis. While struggling with cancer, participants tried to achieve and maintain a balance between mind and body as well as a positive state of mind. We found two patterns of coping related to the mind-body connection: *peaceful mental attitude* and *positive life perspective.*

The participants' suspicion that the cancer might have been caused by stress and a negative mental state had made them pay attention to their mental attitudes. They often reported having tried to empty their mind or push away all obsessive thoughts, whether these thoughts concerned their work or their relationships. Enduring the psychological problems associated with cancer and thinking about the possibility of death made concerns about other life issues and relationships meaningless. They felt that too much thinking about ethical and moral codes had led to stress and their cancer. They started being less concerned with such issues. They reported that, after being stricken with cancer, the most important task was to attempt to achieve peace of mind.

Some participants expressed their appreciation for having had or currently having cancer. According to them, their painful journey with cancer had made them feel more grateful at present, bringing about "a turning point" in life and new attitudes. While struggling with cancer, participants reported having used the positive-life-perspective coping method. This was accomplished either by interpreting the situation from a positive perspective or by strengthening their sense of self-responsibility.

Participants revealed a high level of resilience in how they faced their cancer. They tended to believe that survival depended on how they approached coping with cancer. Instead of blaming external factors, they tried to discover solutions by taking responsibility for their own actions.

Koreans have a saying that originated from the History of Three States in China: "Do your best, then God will do the rest." Among the participants, having a self-responsible attitude toward cancer means reflecting this idea in one's actions: One should first do one's best and then let God (or the universe) do the rest to cure the cancer. Through their stories, the Korean participants showed their high levels of self-responsibility, which had helped them take an active approach to coping with cancer. A high level of self-responsibility is also found in Confucianism, a philosophy that has affected South Koreans' ways of thinking. Confucianism stresses assuming responsibility for one's own life.

Relying on a transcendent power

All participants – the religious as well as non-religious – reported having prayed to God prior to surgery. Regardless of how they defined a supreme power – the Lord, Buddha, their deceased parents, or the universe – they felt the need for an omnipotent being to rely on. Cancer operations are not necessarily fatal, but participants reported fearing death and worrying about the family members they would leave behind. Religious people use coping methods in accordance with their religiosity, and the non-religious were also comforted by coping methods, such as spiritual meditation.

Finding oneself in relationships with others

When participants were asked to name the most helpful resource in coping with cancer, several mentioned "the people around me." Loneliness is not an uncommon feeling among people struggling with cancer. The participants explained that, when dealing with cancer, they gradually realized they were not alone. They were surrounded by family, friends, neighbors, or other patients in the hospital, all of whom offered support. It was comforting to know that people cared and were praying for them.

Prior to the cancer diagnosis, participants reported having guarded themselves against other people as a way of avoiding being hurt by them. However, after experiencing cancer, participants understood that the people around them loved them and that there was no need to be wary of human relationships. They felt grateful for the unconditional care they had received, and this caused them to reflect on their life and relationships. Being aware of relationships with others helped the participants cope with cancer. The Korean participants talked about one positive aspect of having cancer: realizing people would help them cope with their illness and thinking about what they could do to help others. The participants in the study in Sweden expressed gratitude for those who helped them cope with cancer, but perhaps equally helpful for them was the coping method "positive solitude." Positive solitude helped the Swedish participants find themselves and the strength to deal with the psychological effects of cancer; it allowed them to be by themselves and to think about life, particularly existential matters (Ahmadi, 2006, 2015).

In contrast, the Korean participants became self-aware in their relationships with others and preferred the company of others while struggling with cancer. Social support or social relationships have been shown to have a positive effect on quality of life among Koreans, especially among those struggling with cancer (Han & Lee, 2011; Kim, Kwon, Kim, Lee, & Lee, 2008; Lee, Yoo, & Hwang, 2014). The population of Seoul and its surrounding suburban Gyonggi area is more than 22 million. About 20 percent of the Korean population lives in Seoul, causing overcrowding in the city. Moreover, South Korea is considered to have the highest-speed Internet in the world. Thus, advanced technology would seem to make Korean society highly interconnected. However, Koreans may experience ambivalence in their crowded, interconnected society. They may have a sense of "solitude in the crowd," as American sociologist David Riesman called it in his book *Lonely Crowd* (Riesman, Glazer, & Denney, 2001). Korean people may also feel even lonelier when fighting cancer, because people with no experience of cancer may find it hard to understand the situation and feelings of others who are on a "day-to-day cancer journey" (Wilkes, O'Baugh, Luke, & George 2003: 414). Therefore, people with cancer may appreciate others coming, unexpectedly, to take care of them and offering unconditional support.

In sum, the aim of the Korean study was twofold: to explore the coping resources the Korean participants found most helpful and to examine the impact of culture on choice of coping methods.

We observed four coping resources among the Korean participants: 1) belief in the healing power of nature, 2) mind-body connection, 3) relying on a transcendent power and 4) finding oneself in relationships with others. Although experiences of cancer varied across participants, one shared meaning derived from these experiences could be characterized as "a turning point in life." Fighting cancer has been a great ordeal for all of them, but the outcome of their struggles included positive aspects. Experiences of struggling with cancer gave the Korean participants a chance to appreciate the small things in life, to stop worrying about what others think, to realize the futility of petty arguments, and to find themselves in relationships with family and friends they love.

The study in China

China is one of the East Asian countries included in our international project on meaning-making coping. The study aim was to examine the use of meaning-making coping (existential secular, spiritual, and religious coping) among cancer patients in China as well as the impact of culture on choice of coping methods.

China has the world's largest non-religious population (The Washington Post, 2015). Despite limiting certain forms of religious expression and assembly, China's constitution protects religious freedom; the Chinese government does not promote any religion. According to a 2015 Gallup poll, the proportion of convinced atheists in China is 61 percent, with a further 29 percent saying that they are not religious and only 7 percent reporting that they are religious (ibid.). In the study in China, 74 cancer patients (30 female and 44 male) were interviewed. The informants were 18+.

The study was conducted at the Provincial Tumor Hospital of Guizhou, which is located in southwestern China. We interviewed 33 cancer patients (16 female and 17 male). All interviewees were more than 60 years old. Twenty-five patients had urban Hukou,[2] and 49 had rural Hukou. Interviewees' education level varied from primary school, to junior high school and above. The predominant pre-retirement occupations were working in agriculture or freelancing; many of interviewees still owned a small business. Owing to their low pensions, most of interviewees were being financially supported by their child or other relatives. All of the interviewees had been diagnosed with cancer fewer than five years before being interviewed. Fourteen patients were in a severe stage and were disabled.

Five informants informed us that they were religious (four Buddhists, one Christian). Interestingly, only one of these five had religious beliefs prior to being diagnosed with cancer. The other four reported that they began visiting a temple/church in order to pray after the diagnosis.

Religious coping methods

The study indicates that use of religious coping methods was not prevalent among our Chinese informants. As stated above, however, a few reported having adopted a positive attitude toward religion after receiving their cancer diagnosis.

Despite serious gaps in our knowledge about the impact of health on changes in religiosity and spirituality, it has been suggested that traumatic events or serious illness, such as cancer, can result in increased religiosity, although the findings are inconsistent. Several factors may influence such a change. One factor that affects changes in religiosity associated with a cancer diagnosis is culture. Religiosity and health are closely linked in some cultures, but not in others. Culture, which is a system of norms and values shared by members of a society, is vital to the construction of individuals' identities as well as to their ethical/moral world, which in turn functions as an orienting system. The orienting system serves as a frame of reference (which is material, biological, psychological, social, and spiritual in nature) for thinking about and dealing with life situations, and it guides and grounds individuals faced with a crisis. As Ahmadi emphasizes (2006: 26), an orienting system "actually represents the way in which culture imposes its impact on the individual's life and therefore the way she/he copes with stress when facing intrusive circumstances." In societies where the orienting system does not promote a relation between religiosity and health, people's possibilities for turning to religion when facing a crisis are not great (Ahmadi, 2006, 2017). Having been socialized in a non-religious society – where the dominant norms and values are not based on religious teachings and axioms – the majority of our Chinese informants did not use religious coping methods or turn to religion after being diagnosed with cancer.

Existential secular coping methods

Family relationships

As our study shows, the sanctification of family has been a crucial meaning-making coping method among informants.

Pargament and Mahoney define sanctification as "as a process through which aspects of life are perceived as having divine character and significance" (Pargament & Mahoney 2005: 183). They regard sanctification as a "psychospiritual" construct, because it focuses on perceptions of what is sacred, and also as spiritual, because of its point of reference, which is the sacred (Pargament and Mahoney 2001). According to them, many classes of objects can be viewed or experienced as sacred, including family relationships.

Although Pargament and Mahoney (2005: 187–188) define "sanctification as a process of potential relevance not only to theists but to nontheists as well," their understanding of sanctification remains within the framework of religiosity (Ahmadi 2006: 67–69), and therefore can hardly be applied when studying coping among people who were socialized in non-religious societies (ibid.). Despite this criticism of Pargament's definition of spirituality and sanctification, Ahmadi (2006: 133–137) has found the concept of "sanctification" useful and has applied it without necessarily relating it to a religious context. Actually, when looking at coping among non-religious populations in our project, we have observed existential secular "sanctification."

As Ahmadi (2006: 32) mentions:

> When facing a difficult situation, people invest different available resources in order to cope. Sanctification may play an important role (negative or positive) in this respect. Through sanctification of different objects such as one's job, children, marriage, etc., people reorient their focus of attention in times of crisis.

A change in focus from the problem to the "sacred object" may give individuals a sense of security, even if they are non-theists and do not regard the "sacred object" as a manifestation of any divine entity.

In our study among cancer patients in China, we found *family* to be the most important coping method among informants. Almost all of them explained that they would adhere to treatment and never give up because of their family. What we saw was a "sanctification of family relationships," especially of one's children.

Regarding children (often only one child per family) and grandchildren as a source of happiness and the reason for their daily attempt to survive, the interviewees found meaning in life and a reason to fight their illness and survive. One of the reasons for having such a view on family relationships can be found in Chinese culture and social structure.

As a key component of Chinese society, the family has been one of the most important issues in every Chinese person's personal and social life for thousands of years. Different aspects of Chinese life are related to honoring one's parents or ancestors. Most of the "five relationships" advocated by Confucius are centered on the notion of family. This explains the survival of the extended family structure in Chinese society up until modern times. According to Shi (2015: 51), the Chinese people have traditionally preferred extended families, especially having three generations under one roof – something that is thought to represent happiness. One greeting common during the festivals can be translated as: "may your whole family enjoy happiness." In addition to liking extended families, many Chinese people also prefer to stem[3] family, especially men and their parents. They consider this to be the highest state of filial piety, and one that fully expresses the Chinese idea of "family centeredness."

A Chinese person's quality of life is determined by the condition of his or her family. For Chinese people, the family is where one primarily takes shelter and receives nurturing. Historically, Chinese people have regarded duty to family as an important way of achieving a career, which in turn is viewed as a measure of success. Shi (2015) goes on to explain that, in China, people find it difficult to accept the idea of sending the elderly to a nursing home, let alone to do so in practice. As long as the sons and daughters are living, this should preferably not occur. In China, the father-son relationship is considered one of the most important of the various family ties. This relationship entails that the father should be kind and the son should be filial. Being kind means to love, while filial piety is the core of the traditional Chinese ethic. This ethic, in turn, serves as the foundation of morality.

The one-child policy[4] makes the extremely close relationship between parents and the child even more complicated. Parents are afraid of losing their only child or her/his support, on the one hand, and become highly emotionally attached to their child and see him/her as the only support they have, on the other. To this we should also add the problem of the Little Emperor Syndrome (or Little Emperor Effect)[5] as an aspect of China's one-child policy. The little emperors, being the only child, receive excessive amounts of attention from their parents and grandparents. Although the effects of these children, as adults, on Chinese social and economic life have not been as drastic as once believed (Hvistendahl, 2013), there is no doubt about parents' great attachment even to their adult child.

The 1,000-year-old traditional culture of Chinese intra-familial relationships, filial piety, and extended family support has not been stable and has been impacted by the emergence of modernity, industrialization, and urbanization, but as studies (e.g., Oxfeld, 2010) have shown, "the ethical obligations continue to serve as a primary source of identity construction and moral standing especially out of mega cities" (Jankowiak & Moore, 2016).

The significant role of family in the social life of Chinese people and the family's impact on different aspects of their personal life make quite clear why "sanctification" of the family is, as it seems, an important existential secular meaning-making coping method for our Chinese informants.

Inner peace

Of the meaning-making coping methods, inner peace was found to be an important coping strategy among the interviewees. In Chinese culture, inner peace refers to a deliberate state of psychological (or "spiritual") calm despite the potential presence of stressors. Inner peace is considered a state of consciousness or knowing oneself, which can be reached in different ways, for example through meditation, tai chi, or yoga. Harmony is the keyword (Xuezhi, 2007). Harmony and equilibrium are the cornerstones of traditional Chinese culture. The following statement, the Doctrine of the Mean, shows this clearly:

> This equilibrium is the great root from which grow all the human actions in the world, and this harmony is the universal path which they all should pursue. Let the states of equilibrium and harmony exist in perfection, and a happy order will prevail throughout heaven and earth, and all things will be nourished and flourish.

In addition, in the Book of Changes, we read, "The harmony is beneficial to all things." Here, the balance of Yin and Yang, which is essential to all things, and the long-term stability of the state, in a word *the unified relation of body and mind,* are in focus. In traditional Chinese philosophy, we find several modalities of the body-mind relationship. As Xuezhi (2007: 379) mentions:

> Ancient Chinese philosophers were inclined to preserve the doctrine of a unified body and mind rather than to engage in a discussion on the separation of

the two. In addition, most traditional Chinese philosophers stressing in particular the function of mind. Based on the tradition of believing in the concept of qi, they traced the cause of their spiritual activities to the natural effect of the qi. The modalities display a phenomenological characteristic that looks at mental activities lightly, and examines language and action as a natural revelation of material force, qi.

The ability of the mind to promote "healing" has deep roots in Chinese medicine. Perceiving body, mind and spirit as inseparable, Chinese medicine has, for thousands of years, treated ailing persons using different healing modalities.

Such being the case, it is not surprising that our informants – having been socialized within a cultural framework where inner peace is considered a strong way of reaching a balance in life and the key to a healthy body and mind – have used inner peace as a meaning-making method of coping with their illness. The impact of culture on their choice of coping methods is undeniable.

Listening to music to ease the pain

Our study revealed that some interviewees reported using traditional Chinese music as a form of meaning-making coping.

A number of publications have described the specific benefits of music for cancer patients. Interactive music interventions – such as instrumental improvisation, drumming and singing – have shown promise in improving the mood of cancer patients (Burns et al., 2005; Cassileth et al., 2003, Krout, 2001; Magill 2009). Some studies have examined the effects of receptive interventions – such as music listening, music and imagery, or of a combination of music therapy interventions – on outcomes such as decreased pain and nausea, improved mood, increased family communication and improved quality of life among cancer patients. Examples of such studies are Burns et al. (2001), Sahler et al. (2003), Cassileth and Gubili (2009), Nainis et al. (2006), Hart (2009), and Kaliyaperumal and Gowri Subash (2010). The integration of music therapy into the healthcare system in various countries is related to, among other things, the dominant culture of the society. China is one of the countries in which music has historically played an important role in patients' healing process.

According to Changzhen (2014), physicians in ancient China developed a complex system to incorporate musical notes into the healing process. In China's first medical text, *The Yellow Emperor's Classic of Medicine*, written 2,300 years ago, we find the use of music as therapy. Music therapy is an aspect of five-element theory, which is actually the basis of traditional Chinese medicine. Considering all things in nature to be composed of the elements of earth, water, fire, metal and wood, classical Chinese music was composed on the basis of five notes or sounds: jiao, zhi, gong, shang, and yu. To achieve different healing methods, Chinese medicine has used the relationship between internal organs and their five-element correspondences, such as musical notes. In modern China, Five Phases Music Therapy (FPMT) is still used by physicians. FPMT "employs the theory of five phases and five music scales or tones (Gong (do), Shang (ri), Jue (mi), Zhi (so) and Yu (la)) to analyze and treat mind-body illness" (Zhang 2017).

Studies (Ahmadi 2009, 2010, 2013, 2016; Pavlicevic, 2005; Stige, 2016; Barbara Wheeler, 2002) have shown that the role of music in coping with cancer is not only personal in nature, but also cultural. Thus, the role of culture in applying music as a coping method is important for grasping how and why individual cancer patients use music as a way to cope with their illness.

Briefly, the Chinese may not be inclined toward religion, but may be more interested in philosophy. Moreover, their sense of spirituality seems to be an integrated part of their strong preference for philosophy. It is perhaps for this reason we did not find religious coping methods to be prevalent among our interviewees. Instead, we observed meaning-making coping methods such as *sanctification of family* and *inner peace,* which are based on the traditional Chinese philosophical doctrine of the body-mind-spirit relation. The ancient philosophers' discussions on Yin and Yang, Auspiciousness and Ominousness, harmony and sameness, which are based on the doctrine of body-mind-sprit, still have a strong impact on the Chinese family culture, business culture and healing culture. For instance, according to Dong (2013):

> modern medicine includes consensus on several theories and concepts of traditional Chinese medicine, and usage of several treatments and prescriptions of traditional Chinese medicine including commonly used Chinese herbs.

The strong position of the body-mind-spirit doctrine in the Chinese culture and ways of thinking is, as our study also shows, an important factor in the choice of meaning-making coping methods when facing a crisis like a cancer diagnosis.

Summing up, in this study, we did not find the use of any religious coping methods besides visiting church and praying. Regarding "spiritual" coping methods, none of the conventional spiritual meaning-making coping methods could be found among our Chinese informants, despite the fact that some reported believing to some extent in a mysterious spiritual power, without being able to explain this belief clearly. The existential secular meaning-making coping methods were, as it seems, prevalent among the informants; these methods are *family*, *inner peace* and *listening to music to ease the pain*. In the following, we discuss the results from a cultural perspective.

Culture and meaning-making coping in East Asia

In this section, we discuss the results of our studies in two East Asian countries: South Korea and China. As the results show, in both countries, the relation between body and soul has an impact on the use of meaning-making coping strategies among cancer patients.

Development of the idea of body-mind-spirit in the ways of thinking of people in East Asia is primarily influenced by a holistic system of thought advocated by Eastern philosophers, particularly the Chinese. Chinese civilization has greatly influenced other civilizations in East Asia, including Japan and Korea as well as Southern Asia. At the core of both the Chinese and Korean idea of body-mind-spirit is a holistic perspective: "The holistic perspective that only the whole exists and the parts are linked relationally, like 'the ropes in a net,' is related to the Chinese orientation toward practicality as a method of knowing" (Lee et al. 2009: xxxv)

Use of various body-mind-spirit techniques to ease pain or to cope with illnesses is an old traditional cultural habit among people in East Asia. We find among both Chinese and Korean informants the use of meaning-making coping methods related to the doctrine of a body-mind-spirit relation: *inner peace* among the Chinese and *peaceful mental attitude* among South Koreans. Certainly their body-mind-spirit techniques varied, but not the nature of coping.

We do find, however, a considerable difference between these two groups concerning the role of the family in coping.

While the participants in both groups were afraid of death and worried about family members who would be left behind, the Korean participants had a more critical attitude toward their relation to family.

Ahmadi et al. explain this as follows:

> The suspicion that cancer might have been caused by stress and a negative mental state caused participants to pay attention to their mental attitudes. Participants often stated that they tried to empty their mind of or push away everything they were obsessed with, whether these obsessions concerned their work or their relationships. Going through the psychological problems caused by cancer and thinking about the possibility of death made concerns about life issues and relationships meaningless for them. They believed that too much thinking about ethical and moral codes had made them stressed and caused their cancer. They began to be less concerned about these issues. The most important task after being struck by cancer was, as they explained, to try to attain peace of mind.

The Korean informants reported that the constant pressure of duties and family obligations for many years had caused mental stress, which had affected their body and caused cancer, or at least made them more vulnerable to being hit by cancer. They tried, therefore, to think less about family relationships and to live in peace. Some interviewees even have chosen positive solitude as a coping method.

A similar critical attitude was not found among our Chinese participants. This may be because that high level of performing traditional family duties, which still we find among South Korean people, is not as prevalent in China. This could be due to the fact that the Chinese informants had been socialized in a socialist society, where some aspects of children's traditional responsibilities for parents, and vice versa, are supposed to be assumed by the state. For this reason, perhaps Chinese individuals do not find themselves in as stressful a situation regarding family duties as Korean individuals do. Moreover, as discussed before, the Chinese traditionally have extremely positive attitudes toward family relationships and sanctify such relationships. Another important difference, which may cause South Koreans to feel more stressed regarding their family duties, is the issue of worshiping ancestors and the traditional ceremonies associated with this. This is not the case among the Chinese people. Presiding over ancestor worship in Korea is, according to Lee (2008: 15), inherited along the line of agnatic primogeniture, "viewed as a more important privilege than inheriting family headship or property." This is, he maintains (ibid.), a sign of the rigid application of the patrilineal principle in how the Korean traditional family is run.

Actually, because the patrilineal principle still underlies the basic structure of authority in Korea, the substantial duties in relation to the elderly and ancestors have a strong presence in the Korean family.

As Lee (2008: 6) explains:

> At first glance, the Korean traditional family looks so similar to the Chinese one that many observers have sometimes seen it as a minor variant of the Chinese model. But a careful examination reveals that the Korean family differs in many respects. The basic difference lies with the Korean emphasis on patrilineal, consanguine continuity, and on ancestor worship. In contrast to China, economic considerations played no role in the evolution of Korean family institutions. To a large extent, the patrilineal principle underlies the basic structure of authority in Korea. As a result, not much room is left for horizontal exchange relations within the traditional family.

As Lee emphasizes, the Chinese approach to family shows "a more individualistic orientation than that of the other two Asian countries" (Lee 2008:1 2), and the Chinese have maintained a flexible family structure (p.10), while "Instead of adjusting its family structures to the task of modernization, Korea has managed to project the basic values associated with its notion of family onto modern organizations, decisively influencing the actual operations of contemporary institutions." According to Lee (2008: 13), when comparing China, Korea, and Japan, "Korea appears to be most patriarchal."

Although China and South Korea have a common cultural tradition of broadly defined Confucianism, their societies differ considerably when it comes to family structure, the roles of family members, and adaptation to modern norms and values. As it seems, being more patriarchal and more traditional concerning the duties and responsibilities of family members to each other and to ancestors means that Koreans have to endure difficult family-related obligations. This, as mentioned, results in a stressful life situation, which according to our Korean informants, who have internalized the doctrine of body-mind-spirit, leads to serious health problems like cancer.

Thus, for our Korean informants, trying to break free from the bounds of family relationships is an important aspect of meaning-making coping. On the contrary, for our Chinese informants – who do not feel the same kind of stress related to family duties and who have a cultural tradition of regarding the family as an important resource for a healthy life – sanctification of the family becomes an essential coping method. In both countries, however, we see traces of the body-mind-spirit relationship.

Notes

1 In this chapter, we have used some results, which are already published. Copyright permissions have been obtained.
2 A hukou is a record in the system of household registration required by law in both mainland China and Taiwan (but not Hong Kong and Macau). The system itself is more properly called "huji," and has its origins in ancient China. For more information see https://en.wikipedia.org/wiki/Hukou_system.
3 A family system in which a couple's firstborn child lives with them in the family home, and that child's spouse moves into the home of said in-laws, so that the younger couple's children are raised in the home of their grandparents. Usually, the younger offspring move out upon marriage. The inheritance, depending on the culture, may or may not be the most favorable to the firstborn. (https://en.wiktionary.org/wiki/stem_family).
4 The one-child policy, a part of the family planning policy, was a population planning policy of China. It was introduced in 1979 and began to be formally phased out in 2015. The policy allowed many exceptions and ethnic minorities were exempt. Provincial governments imposed fines for violations, and the local and national governments created commissions to raise awareness and carry out registration and inspection work. Coming into effect in January 2016, China,s new universal two-child policy was the culmination of years of loosening its family planning laws, which, since 2014, permitted ethnic minorities, rural couples with a first-born girl, as well as any couple in which at least one of the parents is an only child (2013, to have two children.
5 Although Little Emperors have been primarily an urban phenomenon, they are increasing more and more even in rural areas, due the continued development of these areas. Still, the one-child policy was generally only applied in urban communities.

References

Ahmadi, F. (2006). *Culture, religion and spirituality in coping: The example of cancer patients in Sweden*. Uppsala: Uppsala University, Acta Universitatis Upsaliensis, Studie Sociologica Upsaliensia 53.
Ahmadi, F. (2009). Hard and heavy music: Can it make a difference in the young Cancer patients' life? Voices: A world rorum for music therapy, 9(2). (A refereed online journal). Retrieved July 2, 2009, from http://www.voices.no/mainissues/mi40009000302.php
Ahmadi, F. (2010). Song lyrics and the alteration of self-image. *Nordic Journal of Music Therapy*, 20(3): 225–241.
Ahmadi, F. (2013). Music as a method of coping with cancer: A qualitative study among cancer patients in Sweden. *Art and health*, 5(2): 152–165.
Ahmadi, F. (Ed.). (2015). *Coping with cancer in Sweden: A search for meaning*. Uppsala: Uppsala University, Acta Universitatis Upsaliensis, Studie Sociologica Upsaliensia 63.
Ahmadi, F. (2016). Coping with cancer through music: Three studies among cancer patients in Sweden. In M. Hashefi (Ed.), *Music therapy in the management of medical conditions*. New York: Nova Science Publishers.
Ahmadi, F. & Ahmadi, N. (2013). Nature as the most important coping strategy among cancer patients: A Swedish survey. *Journal of Religion and Health,* 52(4): 1177–1190.
Ahmadi, F., Park, J., Kim, M. K., & Ahmadi, N. (2016) Exploring existential coping resources: The perspective of Koreans with cancer. *Journal of Religion and Health*. DOI 10.1007/s10943-016-0219-6; http://rdcu.be/ksP2
Ahmadi, F., Park, J., Kim, K. M., & Ahmadi, N. (2017). Meaning-making coping among cancer patients in Sweden and South Korea: A comparative perspective. *Journal of Religion and Health*. Retrieved from http://link.springer.com/article/10.1007/s10943-017-0383-3.

Burns, D. S., Sledge, R. B., Fuller, L. A. A., Daggy, J. K., & Monahan, P. O. (2005). Cancer patients' interest and preferences for music therapy. *Journal of Music Therapy,* 42(3): 185–199.

Burns, S., Harbuz, M., Hucklebridge, F., & Bunt L. (2001). A pilot study into the therapeutic effects of music therapy at a cancer help center. *Alternative Therapies in Health & Medicine,* 7(1): 48–56

Cassileth, B. & Gubili, J. (2009). Integrative oncology: Complementary therapies in cancer care. In D. S. Ettinger (Ed.), *Supportive care in cancer therapy* (pp. 1–9). Totowa, NJ: Humana Press.

Cassileth, B. R., Vickers, A. J., & Magill, L. A. (2003). Music therapy for mood disturbance during hospitalization for autologous stem cell transplantation: A randomized controlled trial. *Cancer,* 98(i12): 2723–2729.

Changzhen, Gong. (2014). Musical therapy in Chinese medicine. *The Edge.* Retrieved from http://www.edgemagazine.net/2014/08/musical-therapy-in-chinese-medicine/.

Dong, J. (2013). The relationship between traditional Chinese medicine and modern medicine. *Evidence-Based Complementary and Alternative Medicine.* http://dx.doi.org/10.1155/2013/153148.

Gallup, Korea. (2015). *The religion of Koreans 1984–2014.* Seoul: Gallup Korea Research Institute.

Han, I. & Lee, I. (2011). Study on the factors that affect the posttraumatic growth of cancer patients. *Social Welfare Research,* 42(2): 419–441.

Hart, J. (2009). Music therapy for children and adults with cancer. *Alternative and Complementary Therapies,* 15(5): 221–225.

Jankowiak, W. R. & Moore R. L. (2016). *Family life in China.* Cambridge: Polity Press.

Jean, G. H. (1998). *Environmental ethics: Natural preservation and respect to life in the East and the West.* Seoul: Minum Publisher.

Kaliyaperumal, R. & Gowri Subash, J. (2010). Effect of music therapy for patients with cancer pain. *International Journal of Biological and Medical Research,* 1(3): 79–81.

Kim, H., Kwon, J., Kim, J., Lee, L., & Lee, K. (2008). Exploring the factors of posttraumatic growth among breast cancer survivors. *The Korean Journal of Health Psychology,* 13(3): 781–799.

Koenig, H. G. (1995). *Research on religion and aging.* New York: Greenwood Press.

Krout, R. E. (2001). The effects of single-session music therapy interventions on the observed and self-reported levels of pain control, physical comfort, and relaxation of hospice patients. *American Journal of Hospice Palliative Care,* 18(6): 383–390.

Lee, H. Y. (2008). A comparative study of Korean, Chinese, and Japanese traditional family and contemporary business organizations. EAI Working Paper Series 14.. *Frontiers of Philosophy in China* 2 (3): 379–401.

Lee, M. Y., Chan, C., Ng, S-M., & Leung, P. (2009). *Integrative body-mind-spirit social work: An empirically based approach to assessment and treatment.* New York: Oxford University Press.

Lee, M. Y., Yoo, Y., & Hwang, E. (2014). Experiences of self-help group activities among breast cancer patients. *Korean Journal of Adult Nursing,* 26(4): 466–478.

Magill, L. (2009). The meaning of music: The role of music in palliative care music therapy as perceived by bereaved caregivers of advanced cancer patients. *American Journal of Hospice and Palliative Medicine,* 26(1): 33–39.

Ministry of Culture, Sports, and Tourism (2013). *A white paper on leisure.* Seoul: Krihongbo.

Nainis, N., Paice, J. A., Ratner, J., Wirth, J. H., Lai, J., & Shott, S. (2006). Relieving symptoms in cancer: Innovative use of art therapy. *Journal of Pain and Symptom Management,* 31(2): 162–169.

Oxfeld, E. (2010). *Drink water, but remember the source: Moral discourse in a Chinese village.* Stanford, CA: Stanford University Press.

Pargament, K. I. (1997). *The psychology of religion and coping.* New York: Guilford Press.

Pargament, K. I., & Mahoney, A. (2001). Spirituality: Discovering and conserving the sacred. In C. R. Snyder (Ed.), *Handbook of positive psychology.* Oxford: Oxford University Press.

Pargament, K. I. & Mahoney, A. (2005). Sacred matters: Sanctification as a vital topic for the psychology of religion. *The International Journal for the Psychology of Religion,* 15(3): 179–198.

Pavlicevic, M. (2005). *Music therapy in context: music, and meaning and relations.* London: Jessica Kingsley Publishers.

Poole, R. & Higgo, R. (2010). Psychiatry, religion and spirituality: A way forward. *The Psychiatrist,* 34, 452–453.

Powell, L. H., Shahabi, L., & Thoresen, C. E. (2003). Religion and Spirituality: Linkages to physical health. *American Psychologist,* 58 (1): 36–52.

Riesman, D., Glazer, N., & Denney, R. (2001). *The lonely crowd: A study of the changing American character.* New Haven, CT: Yale University Press.

Sahler, O. J., Hunter, B. C., & Liesveld, J. L. (2003). The effect of using music therapy with relaxation imagery in the management of patients undergoing bone marrow transplantation: A pilot feasibility study. *Alternative Therapies in Health & Medicine,* 9(6): 70–74.

Schreiber, J. A. & Edward, J. (2015). Image of God, religion, spirituality, and life changes in breast cancer survivors: A qualitative approach. *Journal of Religion and Health,* 54, 612–622.

Shi, L. Z. (2015). Differences between Chinese and American family values in pushing hands. *Cross-Cultural Communication,* 11(5): 50–53. Retrieved from http//www.cscanada.net/index.php/ccc/article/view/7000. DOI: http://dx.doi.org/10.3968/7000.

Sloan, R. P. (2006). *Blind faith: The unholy alliance of religion and medicine.* New York: St Martin's Press.

Sloan, R. P., Bagiella, E., & Powell, T. (2001). Without a prayer: Methodological problems, ethical challenges, and misrepresentations in the study of religion, spirituality, and medicine. In T. G. Plante & A. C. Sherman (Eds.), *Faith and health: Psychological perspectives* (pp. 339–354). New York: Guilford Press.

Stige, B. (2016). Culture-centered music therapy. In J. Edwards (Ed.), *The Oxford handbook of music therapy.* Retrieved from http://www.oxfordhandbooks.com/view/10.1093/oxfordhb/9780199639755.001.0001/oxfordhb-9780199639755-e-1.

Wheeler, B. (2002). Cultural aspects of music therapy. *Voices.* Retrieved from https://voices.no/community/?q=fortnightly-columns/2002-cultural-aspects-music-therapy.

Wilkes, L. M., O'Baugh, J., Luke, S., & George, A. (2003). Positive attitude in cancer: Patients' perspectives. *Oncology Nursing Forum,* 30(3): 412–416.

Xuezhi, Z. (2017) Severalmodalities of the body-mind relationship in traditional Chinese philosophy. *Frontiers of Philosophy in China,* 2 (3): 379–401.

Zhang, H. (2017). Five phases music therapy (FPMT). *In Chinese Medicine: Fundamentals and Application. Preprints.* Retrieved from https://www.preprints.org/manuscript/201704.0145/v1.

Other sources

Map: These are the world's least religious countries. The Washington Post. Retrieved 24 December 2015 from https://www.washingtonpost.com/news/worldviews/wp/2015/04/14/map-these-are-the-worlds-least-religious-countries/?utm_term=.ce51ef520afa.

"End of year survey 2014: Regional and country results." WIN-Gallup International. Retrieved 16 November 2015.

Hvistendahl, M. (2013). Making a selfish generation by Fiat. Science, 339(6116): 131. DOI: 10.1126/science.339.6116.131.

5[1] The study in Muslim countries

The study in Turkey

The results from the Swedish study (Ahmadi, 2015) were used to formulate the interview questions for the study conducted in Turkey. The two psychologists participating in our data collection translated the original interview guide from English to Turkish. In this relation, some terms were modified to better suit Turkish culture, for instance, the word church was replaced by "mosque" and the notion of God replaced by "Tanrı." Nevertheless, among older generations and in religious environments, the word "Allah" is more commonly used than the term "Tanrı," but for the new generations, the word "Allah" has a strong religious connotation, therefore, in the interviews the word "Tanrı" was used systematically. For the qualitative study, we chose a convenience sample. A total of 25 participants were recruited in one oncology center and one psychiatric clinic in Istanbul. These patients had survived cancer or were still undergoing chemotherapy and radiotherapy. Upon receiving the patients' consent to participate in the study, the psychologists participating in the study conducted the interviews. For more details about informants, see Table 5.1.

Table 5.1 Demographic characteristics of the participants, Turkey

Characteristics		N
Gender	Male	7
	Female	18
Age	20~39	5
	40~59	14
	60+	6
Education	High school graduate or less	10
	College graduate or higher	15
Employment status	Housewife	1
	Not working	11
	Working	10
	Retired/On leave	3
Religion	Muslim	21
	Believe in God	2
	No religion	2

N=25

Religious coping methods (RCOPE)

In order to categorize these methods, we used the Five Key Religious Functions that constitute the basis of RCOPE; Religious Methods of Coping to Find Meaning, Religious Methods of Coping to Gain Control, Religious Methods of Coping to Achieve Comfort and Closeness to God, Religious Methods of Coping to Achieve Intimacy with Others and Closeness to God, Religious Methods of Coping to Achieve a Life Transformation.

Benevolent Religious Reappraisal, which involves using religion to redefine the stressor as benevolent and potentially beneficial, is one of the religious methods of coping to find meaning. We observed the use of a coping method by some informants that can be categorized as Benevolent Religious Reappraisal. Using the coping method Benevolent Religious Reappraisal, the individual tries to find a lesson from God in the event or to see how the situation could be spiritually beneficial.

Here we have found two patterns. In the first one, we can see the act of talking with God, prayer itself, as a way of dealing with the stressor and achieving a feeling of relaxation. In the second pattern, praying seems to have helped the informants re-examine their past life and find a lesson there.

Punishing God Reappraisal, another method in the category of religious methods of coping to find meaning, involves redefining the stressor as a punishment from God (sins I have committed in my life). As Ahmadi explains, applying Punishing God Reappraisal as a coping method "presumably requires a belief in a God who can determine the course of individuals' lives: a God who not only created man, but also continually controls man's deeds and his destiny" (Ahmadi 2006: 106). The prevalent notion of God among many Muslims tends toward this view.

Passive Religious Deferral concerns passively waiting for God to control the situation. This method belongs to the category "Gain Control." We found that, for some interviewees, their way to achieve comfort and to cope with the stressor that cancer had brought about was Passive Religious Deferral.

Regarding illness as a test imposed by God is an old idea. Illness may be seen as the result of God's will and therefore accepted or, as in the story of Job, seen as educational theodicy (Dein, 1997). Perhaps religion functions by removing the responsibility from the sick person, lessening self-blame and consequently leading to a better psychological outcome (Gotay, 1985; Linn et al., 1982). The notions of testing (Ekhtebar) and being patient (*Sabr*) are quite strong among Muslims.

Active Religious Surrounding also belongs to the coping category "Gain Control." It refers to actively giving up control to God (I did my best and now I am relying totally on God).

Some interviewees reported having used this coping method. They admitted that they had handed over control to God after having done their best. When they could no longer fight, they left the battle to God.

Here we are dealing with the notion of *Kader,* which means "fate" or "predestination." In Islamic thought, *Kader* is the concept of divine destiny. According to some Muslims, God wrote down all that has happened and all that will happen in the *Preserved Table* ("al-Lauḥ al-Maḥfūẓ"). This means that God has ordained everything that occurs in the world (cosmos) and has done so based on his prior knowledge and states of wisdom.

Pleading for Direct Intercession refers to seeking control indirectly by pleading to God (praying). This coping method belongs to the category "Gain Control."

The study reveals that some informants tried to gain comfort by pleading to God for a positive outcome. In some cases, we detect a trace of desperation, as it seems pleading did not help them totally overcome their psychological problems. Here, there is a risk that pleading to God will have negative effects, such as depression, or that the patient will become disappointed in God, believing that God is not listening or has abandoned her/him (Boscaglia et al., 2005). In other cases, the pleading method has yet another positive effect. Here, it is not only pleading that plays a positive role in gaining comfort, but also the patient's strong faith. Here, the risk of becoming depressed or thinking God has abandoned you is smaller; if the worst comes to the worst, it can turn into a case of educational theodicy (Job's story), i.e., believing that the illness is a matter of God testing you.

Collaborative Religious Coping, which belongs to the category "Gain Control," refers to the coping methods of individuals who seek control through a partnership with God (God and therapy).

Our understanding is that, when using this method, the interviewees were not passively relying on God to help them, but also relying on their own power. As the study shows, the interviewees using this method did not plead for miracles, but they hoped their treatments would be effective. Here we see a collaboration between the patient, the physicians, and God. It may be that these interviewees saw God as a partner, as a hand not for pulling them out of the difficult situation they were facing, but a hand to hold to get through it. In other cases, the interviewees seemed to have relied even more on themselves, only hoping that God would see their efforts and be at their side in fighting their illness.

Religious Purification is a coping method that involves searching for spiritual cleansing through religious actions (visiting the mosque, reading religious texts).

Our study reveals that some interviewees used this coping method. Praying or having any kind of exchange with a transcendent power, reading religious or spiritual texts – regardless of whether one believes in any God or transcendent power – are not passive approaches to facing a crisis; they are active attempts to understand one's situation and place it within a comprehensive context. By establishing a relationship with an "entity" other than her-/himself, the patient tries to achieve a feeling of comfort and control. Moreover, because many people have been socialized in a cultural setting in which prayer is an integrated part of life, when they face a crisis, these religious actions help them control their emotions and overcome their fear and anxiety. Praying, reading religious texts, and especially visiting religious places are integrated into the everyday life of people in Muslim countries, including Turkey. Thus, it is quite reasonable that these interviewees would use *Religious Purification* as a coping method, and that they would try to cope with their psychological problems by searching for spiritual cleansing through religious actions.

Spiritual Discontent – a coping method belonging to the category "Gain Comfort and closeness to God" – signifies expressing confusion and dissatisfaction with God's relationship to the individual in the stressful situation (God has abandoned me).

By questioning the existence of God, some show their discontent with religion and faith. Some interviewees were angry because they had been stricken with cancer. They called into question God's existence. What these informants were facing is called the Theodicy Problem. They wonder why God, who is supposed to love his children, has inflicted such a terrible illness on them. Perhaps there is no God. This method of religious coping can be harmful, but according to some researchers, expressions of religious anger can be understood as "positive disintegration" (cf. Dabrowski, 1964), which is a painful step in the process of constructive change (Pargament 1997: 291).

Seeking Support from Clergy or Congregation Members involves searching for comfort and reassurance through the love and care of congregation members and clergy (an imam). This is one of the coping methods in the category "Gain Intimacy with Others." Here, searching for comfort takes place with the help of other people, i.e., congregation members, clergy, imams, or other spiritual or religious authorities. Some interviewees reported having used this method.

Existential secular coping methods

Finding power inside oneself

Some interviewees reported using existential secular coping methods, which involves finding power inside oneself, as a way to deal with the stressors brought about by cancer. As shown in a similar study conducted in Sweden (Ahmadi, 2006), finding oneself, searching for inner possibilities and realizing one's inner force may be a spiritual outcome. According to Ahmadi (2006: 112), a spiritually oriented person facing a difficult situation may search for the "sacred" in her-/himself and in doing so find a force greater than the self – a source of strength. Ahmadi (ibid.) emphasizes that "Here, we are neither witnessing "the incorporation of the sacred into the self" (Pargament 1997: 253), as is the case in religious conversion, nor "'dying unto oneself' or 'loss of self' through unification with a greater existence, as in the case of self-inhibition" (Ahmadi & Ahmadi, 1998). What we may be witnessing is what Fromm (1950) calls *self-realization* in his discussion of "humanistic religion." Through realization of the self in the stressful situation caused by cancer, some of our informants found a way to give meaning to their life and, thereby, cope with their illness.

Altruism (being a good person)

Altruism, which the informants called "being a good person," was found to be one of the existential secular coping methods used by some informants.

Ahmadi (2006: 139) explains:

> "Human altruism is not only an act, but is interwoven with an emotion: empathy. Altruism is then as a prosocial behaviour a voluntary intention/act to help others at some cost to oneself (time, effort or money)"
>
> (ibid.).

In the study among Swedes, a similar coping method was found (Ahmadi 2006: 139–141).

Although Swedish and Turkish ideas about what constitutes prosocial behavior seem to be similar, there are differences between individualistic and collectivistic ways of thinking. While for Swedes altruism takes the form of improvement of *la Condition Humaine* (Ahmadi 2006: 140), in the Turkish case, it involves helping people in one's community and is primarily construed as a religious duty.

Below, Hinde and Groebel (1991: 90) explain the reason for differences in prosocial behavior between individualistic and collectivistic ways of thinking. Note, however, that they are referring primarily to China and Japan, and that most Asian countries are not individualistic but instead collectivistic.

> Asian considerations of what constitutes prosocial behavior are very similar to those of the west: altruism, kindness, considerateness, sympathy, aiding ... However, Asian considerations differ from those in the west because of their conception of the role of the individual in relation to family and society. We in the west place great emphasis on the importance of the individual and on the development of an independent, self-directed child.

In Eastern societies, however, the emphasis is on the interrelation between the child and members of the family and society (ibid.).

Another factor to consider here is religion. In societies where religion plays a significant role in people's relations, any sense of altruism may be related to religious belief and duties. In Islam, altruism is manifested through hospitality and generosity, which are foundational virtues. Several duties, such as *fasting*,[2] *zakat*,[3] and *sadageh* (donation) are intended to help develop a sense of empathy and altruism among Muslims (Homerin, 2005). In our interviews in Turkey, this factor – i.e., the role of religion – was quite evident in relation to this coping method.

Family relationships

In a collectivistic society such as Turkey, the importance of family results in another coping method: "Family relationships."

As Mahoney et al. (2003: 222) maintain:

> For many people, family relationships involve more than biological, psychological, and social processes; people often believe these bonds tap directly into the spiritual realm ... in short, people often view family relationships as sacred.

These authors suggest that people may sanctify the entire family system (ibid.).

Confirming this idea, our study among cancer patients in Turkey shows that sanctification of the family may serve as a coping strategy. Actively trying to recover and not allowing one's health problems to disturb family relations or make family members unhappy can be a powerful method of dealing with the psychological problems caused by cancer. In this connection, religion may play a critical role. According to Zimmerman (1974: 6), "the most sacred or divine aspect of society is considered to be the family system and being religious is tantamount to being a good husband, a good wife, or a good parent, child or kinsman."

Given that our Turkish interviewees were socialized in a group-oriented society, it is understandable that "family relationship" seems to have played a role in the meaning-making methods they reported using to cope with cancer. We will return to this issue in the next chapter.

Searching for meaning by contemplating philosophical issues

For some of our interviewees, searching for existential meaning – by thinking about the meaning of life and death – seemed to have functioned as an existential secular meaning-making method of coping with their cancer.

In contrast to informants in the Swedish study, the Turkish interviewees were religious and were contemplating existential issues through their religiosity.

Positive life perspective (finding new meaning in life by changing priorities)

We found that enduring the painful process of having cancer caused some interviewees to appreciate their present life and everyday life experiences. This led to "a turning point" that caused them to change their priorities in life. This new attitude helped them cope with their illness, and has been called the "positive life perspective coping method" (Ahmadi et al., 2016a).

The study indicated that culture plays an essential role in the choice of coping methods.

What do the statistics say?

Following the qualitative interview study among cancer patients in Turkey (Ahmadi et al., 2016b), a quantitative survey study was conducted (Ahmadi et al., 2017). The survey aimed to deepen the knowledge obtained through the qualitative study and to identify the main meaning-making coping methods used by informants. A cultural perspective was employed when analyzing the results. Due to the nature of the population and the possibilities at hand, we did not attempt to secure a quota or use random sampling. Instead, using convenience sampling, the questionnaire was distributed to former/current cancer patients as an electronic survey through the media website of the *Cancer Survivors Association*.

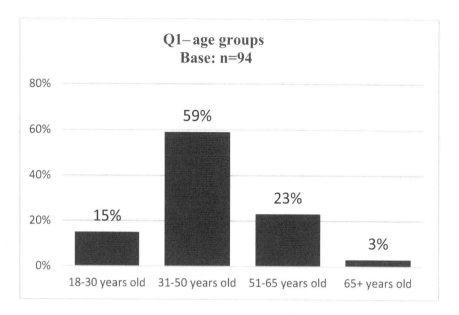

Figure 5.1 Description of the sample – age – Turkey

More than 8 out of 10 are between 31 and 65 years old. The largest age group is the lower-middle aged group between 31 and 50 years old – 59 percent.

The target group for the quantitative study was people 18+ who had been struck by cancer. The final sample size was 95 male and female respondents (for more detailed information see Figure 5.1).

Religious coping

One of the RCOPE methods focused on in the quantitative study is *Spiritual Connection,* which refers to having a sense of a stronger connection with God. The majority of informants (56 percent) reported feeling a strong connection to God. Only 14 percent reported never having felt this.

Another RCOPE method tested is *Active Religious Surrender.* This involves realizing one has done one's best and actively giving up control and turning the situation over to God. A majority (68 percent) reported thinking they have mainly done their best and now there is only God. Moreover, 31 percent reported always having done so.

The third method in focus in the quantitative study is *Passive Religious Deferral.* Here, the person is waiting passively for God to take over and control the situation. Thirty-five percent of informants reported constantly asking God to make things better. An additional 24 percent reported doing so often, while 15 percent responded "never." A Chi-square test showed a significant association between gender and the variable asking God to make things better ($\chi^2(3, n = 95) = 17.14$, $p = .001$), where females (41 percent) were more likely than males (14 percent) to respond that they always do so.

One RCOPE method tested in the study is *Spiritual Discontent,* which involves expressing confusion and dissatisfaction with God's relationship to the individual in the stressful situation. Here individuals may wonder whether God has abandoned them or feel angry that God was not there for them. The vast majority reported not blaming God. Sixty-five percent reported never having wondered whether God had abandoned them or becoming angry because God had not helped them. Only 8 percent did so "always," 8 percent "often" and 18 percent "sometimes."

Pleading for Direct Intercession, which refers to seeking control indirectly by pleading to God (praying), is another RCOPE method considered in the quantitative study. The most common response was praying (65 percent); only 6 percent responded that they had never prayed. A Chi-square test indicated a significant association between gender and the variable praying ($\chi^2(3, n = 95) = 7.64, p = .05$), where females (43 percent) were more likely than males (27 percent) to report that they had prayed often.

Another RCOPE method in focus is *Seeking Support from Clergy or Congregation Members.* This method involves searching for comfort and reassurance through the love and care of congregation members and clergy. Surprisingly, the majority of informants reported not having asked for help from a religious leader (73 percent responded "never"). One possible reason is the fact that the majority of informants in the quantitative study are women and, as it seems, Turkish women do not tend to contact imams. A Chi-square test indicated a significant association between gender and the variable seeking spiritual help from a religious leader ($\chi^2(3, n = 95) = 9.19, p = .03$), where females (78 percent) were more likely than males (55 per cent) to respond that they had never done so.

In Turkish society, there is a significant gender difference concerning the place of Muslims in Islamic space. According to the World Values Survey (Wave 6, 2010–2014),[4] only 11.8 percent of females reported visiting a mosque once a week or more than once a week, while the corresponding figure for males is much higher: 54 percent. Although in recent years Turkey has made several developments aimed at greater inclusion and gender equality in its religious spaces, Zein (2015) points out that disregard for women is still pervasive. Many women are deliberately excluded from entering mosques, and women seldom have contact with imams.

Another reason may be age group. A Chi-square test indicated a significant association between age group and the variable seeking spiritual help from a religious leader ($\chi^2(3, n = 95) = 8.30, p = .04$), where the older group (83 percent) was more likely than the younger group (65 percent) to respond that they had never done so.

Yet another reason may be the fact that, in Turkey, religious leaders, like imams, mainly provide everyday advice (lead Islamic worship services, serve as community leaders, and provide religious guidance), not spiritual support. According to

Sunni scholars, the imam (or caliph, as they prefer to say) can be either elected, nominated by the preceding caliph, or selected by a committee. Consequently, there is no great expectation that an imam will go beyond giving mundane advice and help people with spiritual issues. This does not apply to Islamic mystics, however, who regard their religious leaders as highly spiritual. Note that this does not negate the fact that in a number of Islamic countries, like Egypt, Morocco, Jordan, and Pakistan, many Sunni imams and scholars do offer spiritual advice to the seriously ill. Turkey is a special case because Ataturk first abolished the class of *'ulama* and then created a government-run school to train a new class of *imams* – who are government employees to a certain extent. Even in Turkey, however, there are certainly some imams who are not merely government employees and who do offer spiritual advice to the destitute, especially imams who are devoted to Sufism (Islamic mysticism) and members of a Sufi order.

Besides this coping method, two religious coping methods that, according to the quantitative survey study, were not particularly prevalent among informants are *Punishing God Reappraisal* and *Demonic Reappraisal. Punishing God Reappraisal*, one of the RCOPE methods included in the study, is considered a negative coping method. It involves redefining the stressor as a punishment from God for the individual's sins.

The individual wonders whether God was punishing her/him for lacking in faith or sinning. A majority (75 percent) reported never having had such thoughts. Only 4 percent thought in this way "always" and 5 percent "often." A Chi-square test showed an almost significant association between gender and the variable God has caused the cancer because they have not believed enough ($\chi^2(3, n = 95) = 8.74$, $p = .068$), where females (81 percent) were more likely than males (55 percent) to report never having thought this.

These findings show that the idea of illness being a punishment inflicted by God or being caused by an evil power was not strong among the informants in the quantitative study, despite the primacy of the notion of the "Evil Eye" in Turkish culture. One possible explanation may be rooted in the views on suffering and the position of evil in Islam. Applying *Punishing God Reappraisal* as a coping method requires seeing punishment as being grounded in the idea of free will. Note that the problems of predestination and free will have been conceived of in various ways among Muslim thinkers, but the problem of theodicy, as it appears in Christianity, is neither as dominant nor as important among Muslims as it is among Christians. One of the central theological controversies in Christianity is the problem of theodicy, i.e., the contradiction between the existence of human suffering and the notion of God's goodness – something that, as Turner mentions, gives rise to the idea of reconstructing the world. The main contradiction in Islam, however, concerns "God's omnipotence and human free will." In this connection, in a discussion of the lack of a comprehensive confessional apparatus in Islam, Gilsenan (1973: 70) writes:

> Certainly, the sense of sin, of the fall from grace, of spiritual guilt and the whole theodicy of suffering are virtually absent from Islam by comparison with most of the Christian churches.

Demonic Reappraisal – which involves redefining the stressor as an act of the "Devil"/an evil power – is another coping method in this group. The quantitative findings indicate that the majority (70 percent) of informants reported never having had such thoughts. Only 7 percent reported "always" or "often" having thought that the illness was caused by an evil power.

Applying *Demonic Reappraisal* as a coping method would seem to require belief in a Devil who can control the course of individuals' lives – who has the power to change mankind's "destiny." Discussing this necessitates a detailed examination of the anthropology of evil and theodicy in Islam. To help readers understand the results on the *Demonic Reappraisal* coping method, we try below to briefly explain the prevailing view of the position of evil/Satan in Islam and how this differs from the dominant view in Christianity[5]. According to Taylor (1968: 35), in the Christian evolution of the idea of Satan, matters take a different turn (from Judaism). Christianity took over the apocalyptic worldview, which was basically dualistic. Thus, Satan came to mean all that was opposed to God. He was Prince of this world, and all the kingdoms of the world were under his control.

The opposition between Satan and God, which later transformed into the conflict between Satan and Christ, went through different phases, but never disappeared from the Christian tradition.[6] In Islam, however, Satan (Eblis/Shaytan) is considered a creation of God and never "evil as such"; he remains a necessary instrument in God's hands, because, in Islam, there is hardly a conclusive dualism between good and evil or God and Satan. The Quran does not depict Satan as an enemy of God, because God is greatest and supreme over all creation and, thus, Satan is merely one of his creations. Satan's only enemy is humankind. Thus, a Muslim who believes in an omnipotent God and does not believe that Satan has the power to change the course of events against God's will can hardly redefine her/his stressor as having been caused by an evil power; everything is in God's hands, not Satan's. In Turkish culture, however, we do find, as mentioned, the idea of the Evil Eye. but this is more a product of superstition than of a theological belief in the power of Evil, like we see in Christianity. Thus, for some Muslim cancer patients, the Evil Eye may explain the cause of their illness, but they can hardly use this belief as a way to deal with their stressor. Accepting defeat at the hands of an evil power means accepting that God has no power to help them, and that they should regard their illness as the act of an enemy of God. Such acceptance is in complete conflict with belief in a supreme, omnipotent God among people (here Muslims) who do not believe in the power of the Devil, like we see in parts of Christianity.

Another factor that has most likely impacted the results on both the *Punishing God Reappraisal* and *Demonic Reappraisal* is the informants' education level. Though a chi-square test did not show a significant association, as mentioned above, the majority of informants were well educated (60 percent of respondents had at least a university degree). Concerning the impact of education on having superstitious ideas, researchers' opinions differ drastically. In a future survey study among cancer patients in Turkey, we plan to include informants belonging to lower educational and socioeconomic strata. It will be interesting to see what the results of this study reveal about the prevalence of the coping methods *Punishing God Reappraisal* and *Demonic Reappraisal*.

Summing up the findings on the RCOPE methods *Spiritual Connect, Active Religious Surrender, Passive Religious Deferral, Spiritual Discontent,* and *Pleading for Direct Intercession,* we see clearly that these coping strategies have been of great importance to the informants. The quantitative results strongly support the conclusion of the qualitative study, which stressed the importance of religious coping in Turkey (see Ahmadi et al., 2016b). What these findings bear witness to is the great influence of the idea of subordination to and acceptance of the will of God, and the fact that illness may be considered the result of God's will. As suggested by some researchers (Gotay, 1985; Linn et al., 1982), religious belief may serve to lift the responsibility from the ailing person and lessen self-blame, which in turn may result in a better psychological outcome. This is due to the notions of testing (*Ekhtebar*) and being tolerant/patient (*Sabr*), which are quite strong among Muslims, including those living in Turkey. We will return to these concepts later on.

Existential secular meaning-making coping methods

Our project shows that some informants, especially those in Sweden, South Korea, and Japan, saw health as "sacred" and assigned it special meaning (Ahmadi, 2006, 2015; Ahmadi et al., 2016a). For this reason, some informants in these countries employed coping methods connected to holistic therapy. Meditation and visualization, approaches that are tied to *Holistic Health,* are among such strategies. In *Holistic Health*, each person is thought to be a unified whole and both mind and spirit are assumed to play vital roles in healing the body. Holistic or "wholistic" health claims to deal with all parts of the individual, not just the physical body where illnesses are often most apparent. The methods considered in our study were *Meditation and Visualization.*

It was against this background that we chose to look at these methods in our study in Turkey as well, which shows that the non-religious meaning-making coping methods were not particularly frequent among informants.

As regards *Holistic Health,* the results from our informants in Turkey show that use of any form of holistic health was not particularly common. Only 12 percent reported having used it "always" or "often." A majority (55 percent) reported never having used this method.

Concerning *Meditation*, 62 percent reported never having regularly meditated as a way to cope with their illness. Another 31 percent reported having done this only "sometimes." A Chi-square test revealed an almost significant association between education and the variable regular mediation ($\chi^2(3, n = 95) = 7.34$, $p = .06$), where respondents who had been through higher education (10.6 percent) were more likely than those with a lower standard of education (2.6 percent) to respond that they "often" or "always" meditate.

Looking at *Visualization*, 58 percent reported not having used it to cope with their illness. Another 28 percent reported having used this method "sometimes."

A Chi-square test showed a significant association between area of residence while growing up and the variable using visualization (χ^2 (3, n = 95) = 9.59, p = .02), where respondents growing up in a big city (44 percent) were more likely than those living in a smaller town (13 percent) to respond that they "sometimes" or "often" use visualization, while the opposite was true of the extreme response alternatives "never" and "always."

Besides the above-mentioned non-religious coping strategies, there is a method that Pargament assigns to the RCOPE methods, but that we have not classified as RCOPE here. In the RCOPE measurement instrument, this method is called *Self-Directing Religious Coping*. The self-directed religious style refers to seeking control directly using one's own individual initiative rather than seeking God's help. Although self-directing has been regarded (Pargament 1997: 181–182) as a religious strategy, we see no reason to see it this way. If a person chooses not to rely on God, but instead gains control through her/his own initiative, it is difficult to accept categorizing this approach as religious (for more discussion, please see Ahmadi 2006: 34–38).

As many as 54 percent of the Turkish informants reported "never" having tried to control the situation directly without seeking God's help. Another 34 percent reported having done so "sometimes." As the results show, this kind of will to cope without relying on God is not particularly prevalent among the informants; they preferred to lean to God instead. Only 6 percent responded "always" and 6 percent "often."

Here, once again, we see the strong impact of religion on coping with cancer among our Turkish informants. Given that the majority of our informants had achieved a high education qualification (60 percent with at least a university degree; only 7 percent with a secondary and 4 percent a primary school diploma) and that the majority lived in big cities (77 percent), we find it reasonable to maintain that the strong impact of religion on coping seen in the results can be generalized to the entire population. This is because, in non-developed countries, people who have a low level of education or live in villages are usually more religious than people who have a high level of education or who live in big cities.

Summing up, the findings from the study in Turkey reveal that several religious coping methods that have been found to be prevalent in other countries – such as *Spiritual Discontent, Seeking Support from Clergy or Members, Punishing God Reappraisal,* and *Demonic Reappraisal* or *Self-Directing Religious Coping* – were not applied by the Turkish informants. Nor were the non-religious coping methods highly prevalent among these informants. The most important coping methods used by cancer patients in Turkey were the RCOPE methods, especially *Spiritual Connection, Active Religious Surrender, Passive Religious Deferral,* and *Pleading for Direct Intercession.*

Both the qualitative and quantitative studies in Turkey illustrate the impact the religious culture has on choice of coping methods. Although Turkey is at the junction of strong religiosity and secularism, the country whose population is 96.4 percent Muslim (KONDA Research and Consultancy, 2007), is characterized by cultural homogeneity, traditional values, and religious commitment, all of which influence the way people deal with everyday life, including life crises.

To investigate how religion and culture affect choice of meaning-making coping strategies in a Muslim society that is not religiously homogenous, we have chosen the example of Malaysia.

The study in Malaysia

Malaysia is a multiracial, multi-religious country in South-East Asia. The Malaysian population includes the Malay (68.6 percent), Chinese (23.4 percent), Indians (7 percent) and other (1 percent) ethnic groups (Department of Statistics Malaysia, 2016). Islam, the official religion of Malaysia, is the most widely professed religion, followed by Buddhism (19.8 percent) and Hinduism (6.3 percent). The Federal Constitution of Malaysia (Thomas 2006: 18–19) states that all religions "are free to be practiced in peace and harmony." However, Malaysia does not allow any denominations of Islam other than Sunni Islam. Any teaching departing from the official Sunni code is illegal; thus, all other forms of Islam are forbidden (Global Security, 2011). Islam has a great influence on many aspects of the lives of the Malay people (Oka, Hussin, & Hagström, 2017).

Among the three major ethnic groups in Malaysia – the Malay, Chinese, and Indian – the incidence of cancer is the highest among Malay females. Statistics have shown that Malay people run a high risk of being diagnosed with certain cancer types, such as lymphoma (Esoof, 2013), ovarian cancer (Isaman, 2015), and nose and throat cancer (Online journal, Berita Harian, 2015). Nonetheless, we know very little about how Malay people cope with cancer. Thus, the aim of the Malaysian study was to deepen our understanding of how Malay cancer patients use elements of both religiosity and spirituality in coping with their illness. The study also aimed to investigate the role of culture in the choice of various meaning-making coping methods. We have only conducted a qualitative interview study in Malaysia.

Twenty-nine participants were recruited to the Malaysian study by posting a recruitment advertisement in a closed Facebook group, where interested cancer patients/survivors could post a comment indicating their intention to participate. Only Muslim informants were chosen. Although Facebook users in this closed group had been checked by several administrators, the researchers also applied a strict verification process prior to the interview. Potential participants were asked to prove their status by sharing documents related to their medical and treatment histories. The documents were then verified by an oncologist. The data were obtained from 29 Malay cancer patients, women and men between 29 and 60 years of age (for more details, see Table 5.2).

Religious coping methods

To categorize these methods, we used the Five Key Religious Functions that constitute the basis of RCOPE. Above, when discussing the use of Religious Coping (RCOPE) in Turkey, we explained these methods. Here we only mention them briefly.

Table 5.2 Demographic characteristics of the participants, Malaysia

	Category	Amount
Gender	Female	21
	Male	8
Age	25–30	2
	31–40	15
	41–50	9
	51–60	3
Education	High School	7
	Undergraduates	17
	Post graduates	5
Employment status	Housewife	6
	Businessman	3
	Private sector	5
	Government sector	5
	Retirees	2
	Educators	8

N=29

Benevolent Religious Reappraisal: We observed a coping method, used by some informants, that can be categorized as Benevolent Religious Reappraisal. We found two patterns. The first pattern refers to cancer as a lesson from God. In the second pattern, as in the story of Job, suffering is seen as educational theodicy (Dein, 1997).

In the first pattern, the individual tries to find a lesson from God in the event or to see how the situation could be spiritually beneficial. As the study shows, some interviewees regarded the illness as a turning point. They saw cancer as a gift from God – a gift that helped them see their life in a new light, which led them to God and their family; in this way, they could deal better with the stressor and feel some relaxation. In other words, being struck by cancer caused them to re-examine their past life and find a lesson there.

The second pattern is "educational theodicy." Regarding illness as a test that God imposes on us is an old idea. Illness may be seen as the result of God's will and therefore accepted or, as in the story of Job, seen as educational theodicy (Dein, 1997). As the study shows, some interviewees reported believing that God had allowed them to suffer in order to test them and then help them achieve a better life – as in the story of Job. Thus, suffering helps the person appreciate the good things in life, and therefore to grow.

Punishing God Reappraisal: We found this coping method among some interviewees. Ahmadi (2006: 106) suggested that applying Punishing God Reappraisal as a coping method "presumably requires a belief in a God who can determine the course of individuals' lives: a God who not only created man, but also continually controls man's deeds and his destiny." Among many Muslims, the prevalent notion of God tends toward this view. In this connection, as mentioned in the previous chapter, Aflakseir and Coleman (2011: 46) explain that Islamic teachings encourage people to be patient in times of need.

Demonic Reappraisal – Several informants reported believing in *black magic* and therefore used the coping method of Demonic Reappraisal. Black magic or dark magic has traditionally meant the use of supernatural powers or magic for evil and selfish purposes. The idea of black magic and Shamanism in Southeast Asia can be traced back to the region's prehistoric tribal people. However, Muslim scholars regard the practice of shamanism as shirk (idolatry, deification of figures other than Allah). What we see here is the impact of the culture on health beliefs, which are stronger than fundamental religious axioms. We will return to this point in the discussion section.

Passive Religious Deferral: Some interviewees sought comfort and coped with the stressor using this coping method. A passive approach to facing one's illness and totally relying on God was observed among interviewees. Analysis of the interviews reveals that we are dealing with the idea of *Kader,* which, as already mentioned, means "fate" or "predestination." We discussed that the ideas of testing (*Ekhtebar*) and being patient (*Sabr*) are quite strong among Muslims. It would seem that the notion that the problems of this world are put there to test people and to encourage them to have patience is strong among people in Muslim countries, including Malaysia.

Active Religious Surrounding: The interviewees revealed how they had handed over control to God after having done their best and undergone various treatments. Here, although we see an Active Religious Surrounding method, there is also a trace of belief in fate, or *Kader* as it is called in Islam.

Pleading for Direct Intercession: Here, the informants tried to gain comfort by pleading to God to make things turn out positively.

Collaborative Religious Coping: When using this method, the informants are not being passive and only relying on God to help them, but they are also relying on their own power. The interviewees did not only plead for miracles; they also relied on themselves and physicians. What we see here is a collaboration between the patient, physicians, and God.

Religious Purification: We found interviewees who used this method by reading Quranic verses, especially, sura Al-Inshirah. The Al-Inshirah is a famous *sura* (passage) in the Quran. It informs Mohammad (the Prophet) that he will soon be freed from his burden and difficulties, which he must endure because of his prophetic mission. In fact, the passage says that with each difficulty there is ease. The informants were drawn to the passage, and probably many other Muslims facing serious problems are as well. People read it and are comforted by the idea that God will lift their burden, as He once promised he would do for Mohammad. Muslims consider the Quran to be miracle of Islam and the direct words of God; for some Muslims, reading the Al-Inshirah is an integrated part of daily life. Thus, it is logical that the interviewees would have used *Religious Purification* as a coping method and tried to cope with their illness by searching for spiritual cleansing through reading Quran. Reading religious texts is not a passive approach to dealing with a crisis. It is, instead, an active attempt to understand what one is experiencing and to place these experiences in a broader context. In cultural settings where prayer is an integrated part of everyday life, people facing a crisis readily turn to religious texts. Reading is a way to control one's emotions and overcome fear and anxiety.

Seeking Support from Clergy or Congregation Members: In the Malaysian study, we did not find informants who had searched for comfort by seeking out the love and care of an imam or any other religious leader. We did, however, identify informants who had received treatment from practitioners of shamanism or alternative medicine. Just as in the case of religious coping through *Demonic Reappraisal*, here we are also dealing more with the influence of culture than with that of religion. As it seems, the impact of shamanism, and of the shamanic view of health, on people's ways of thinking is strong and causes them to seek alternative treatment rather than the spiritual guidance provided by imams.

Existential secular meaning-making coping methods

Finding power inside oneself

In the study among cancer patients in Malaysia, we identified some informants who used the coping method "finding power inside oneself." Just as similar studies conducted within the framework of the international project . . . also confirmed, finding oneself and searching for inner possibilities as well as actualizing one's inner force may constitute a spiritual outcome. As explained above, here we are looking at what Fromm (1950) calls *self-realization.*

Family relationships

Several informants in our study in Malaysia reported that family had been a tremendously important factor in coping with their illness. As we explained above, in collectivistic societies such as Malaysia and Turkey, sanctification of the family is not unusual. In the case of Malaysia, the impact of religion (Islam) and East Asian culture (Chinese and Indian) makes this sanctification even stronger. When discussing the case of Turkey, we pointed out the role of religion in how Muslims view the family; the role of group-oriented culture in how the family becomes an integrated and crucial factor in the life of individuals has also been revealed in the case of China in Chapter 4. So we will not repeat these discussions here.

Nature

We found several interviewees who described the importance of nature in coping with their illness. Malaysians' perspectives on nature are associated with their religious background. Malay people are, for example, greatly influenced by the spirit of nature. According to Ani, Mohamed, and Rahman (2012), Malay people practice ritual or "adat" as a part of their Malay identity. Nature is a part of this ritual event. From childbirth to death, the elements of nature play important roles in their rituals. Skeat (1900) described the folk religion of the Malays as being distinct from orthodox Islam – as a "natural religion" in which most natural things were thought to possess a soul and some distinctive natural landmarks, such as oddly-shaped rocks or huge trees, were thought to have a spirit, namely Keramat.

Keramat also refers to a sacred shrine, typically where a holy person has been buried. This belief is a symbolic reflection that is represented in Malay Muslim, Indian, and Chinese traditions in Malaysia (Davary, 2012). People worship Keramat to achieve their personal goals, such as getting protection or acquiring wealth.

The act of worshiping Keramat is described as *shirk* in Islam, as it involves human beings having faith in sources other than Allah. The Malaysian government plays an important role in highlighting and forbidding this activity. As a result, Malay people who follow Islamic teachings holistically describe nature as reflecting God's power. As written in the Quran, nature is a sign of Devine creativity and existence, and Muslims should worship nothing else but Allah (AlIsra', https://quran.com/17/44).[7]

In sum, the Malaysian study indicates that informants used several RCOPE methods, both passive and active. It also shows that shamanism – although it is in opposition to the religion of our informants (all of whom were Muslims) – plays a role in how they have coped with cancer. The study highlights the important role of culture in the choice of coping methods. However, for some interviewees, the role of culture in coping may be even stronger than that of fundamental religious axioms. Phenomena such as applying the coping method *Demonic Reappraisal*, believing in black magic and getting help from shamans/bomohs for alternative treatment reveal the strong role of cultural beliefs, even when such beliefs are in opposition to religious axioms.

Culture and meaning-making coping in Turkey and Malaysia

As the studies in Turkey and Malaysia indicate, some of the RCOPE methods seem to be highly relevant for the interviewees. Just as for our interviewees in Turkey (Ahmadi et al., 2016b), for those in Malaysia, religion is a "larger part of [their] orientation system" (Ahmadi 2006: 28). Religion is, indeed, constantly available in people's sociocultural context. Given this, it is understandable that, when facing a life-threatening illness like cancer, people turn to religion rather than to other resources. An orienting system is based on culture and impacts the individual's life. When religion is a highly accessible factor that is constantly available in the individual's sociocultural context, it is likely that she/he will turn to religion rather than to other resources in times of crisis. Naturally, in most societies, religion is not the only resource available in an individual's orienting system. There are other dimensions of life – e.g., biological, psychological, social, and environmental – to which individuals also can turn. In societies with great non-religious resources and where religion does not play a major role in individuals' everyday life, religion's role in the coping process will be less extensive. In our project, Sweden, China, and South Korea provide some examples of this. Choosing to "turn to religion in coping" is primarily a question of religion's position in the culture the individual was socialized in. When religion does not play a prominent role in individuals' orientation systems, and is therefore less relevant to their life experiences, it will also play a minor role in coping (Ahmadi, 2006; Ellison, 1991; Ferraro, & Koch, 1994; Kesselring et al., 1986; Neighbors et al.,

1983; Wicks, 1990). If a larger number of non-religious resources had been part of the everyday life of our Turkish and Malaysian interviewees, the role of religion in coping that we observed might not have been equally strong. Nevertheless, when religion does play a dominant role as a coping resource, it is often because there are few or limited alternatives available in the individual's immediate sociocultural context.

Religion appears to be an immediate means of coping among individuals in Turkey and Malaysia, whose orienting system is greatly influenced by religion.[8] It is convenient to maintain that the reason people in Turkey and Malaysia turn to religion in times of crisis is that religion has a prominent position in people's ways of thinking. Yet there are certain differences between these two countries.

Although Turkey is constitutionally a secular country, Islam plays an enormously important role in the everyday life of most Turkish people (World Values Survey, Wave 6, 2010–2014).

The role of religion in daily life and in society can be looked at from different perspectives, among them a sociological perspective, which is used by Inglehart (1997) to compare cultures. Inglehart has developed a two-dimensional model for positioning societies based on their scores on various value data, gathered through the World Values Survey. The first dimension, with traditional values at one end and secular-rational values at the other, includes measures of, e.g., the importance of religion, obedience, respect for authority, and national pride (Esmer, 2007). The second dimension – the survival and self-expression values – emphasizes, e.g., economic/physical security or quality of life, individual happiness, degree of acceptance of homosexuality, and interpersonal trust (ibid.). As shown by the World Values Survey (Wave 6, 2010–2014), for many Turks religion is an important aspect of life (92.7 percent responded that religion is *very* or *rather important in life*), as is prayer (80.1 percent reported praying *several times a week/once a day/several times a day*). The data from Turkey indicate that the meaning of religion is to make sense of life after death (74 percent) and life in this world (22.1 percent). However, attending religious services is not necessarily as common (11.8 percent of females responded *once a week* or *more than once a week*, while the corresponding figure for males was much higher: 54 percent). Note that attending religious services is much lower among females owing to cultural and gender factors, and that low attendance does not reflect lack of religiosity, because within Islam attendance does not play the crucial role it does within, for instance, Christianity. Turkish culture is greatly influenced by religion, especially Islam. For Turkish people, praying, reading religious texts, and especially visiting religious places are integrated parts of everyday life. Mosques are common features of the urban landscape, and people take time to say prayers during the day. However, as also seen in the World Values Survey results, religious attitudes and values are stronger than religious practices.

In the case of Malaysia, despite the elevated position of Islam as the official religion, spiritual beliefs among Malay people are greatly influenced by animism, Hinduism, and Buddhism, all of which preceded the Islamization of Malaysia (Osman, 1988). Concerning the Malay people's indigenous knowledge about illness, some believe in witchcraft, black magic, or *santau*, which originated from ancient mystic rituals. These ancient mystic rituals are believed to involve *jinn* and demons. They are used to destroy friendly relations among family members, to end spousal relationships, to bring about insanity and illness, and at the very worst, to cause the death of their victims (Mahyuddin, 2014). Santau, which is a popular term among Malay people, is described as a poison that is sent using black magic or physically by the sender (Daud, 2010). The impetus for sending santau is usually feelings of hatred or jealousy. It is believed that illnesses caused by santau and black magic cannot be cured using conventional medical treatments (Sahad & Abdullah, 2013); what is needed is religious treatment. *Ruqyah*, which refers to prayer therapy, is a common treatment among Malay people.

Some Malay people believe that all illness is caused by unexpressed *angin* (wind) that has got stuck in the body and induced pathology (Haque, 2005; Ng et al., 2003). *Angin* is believed to be a whirl of wind that becomes trapped in some parts of the body, causing discomfort. Some also believe in supernatural causes, such as being possessed by *jinn* (genie) or affected by santau (black magic), typically sent by enemies (Haque, 2005). Such beliefs open up other treatment possibilities. People may choose either a conventional medical doctor or a traditional healer, called a *pawang* or *bomoh*, to rid themselves of any spiritual possession that may be causing their physical and psychological illnesses.

In the Malay world, shamans include pawings (a specific kind of black or white magician) or dukuns and bomohs (spiritual counselors, traditional healers, or medicine men). The bomoh's original role was that of healer. Prior to European colonization, bomohs – as well as Buddhist monks and Hindu holy men – were frequently exempt from paying taxes because they typically had few material belongings. The bomohs' craft remained largely the same even after Islam prevailed, and up until the Islamic revival in the 1970s and 1980s. Bomohs were then seen as deviating from the Muslim faith because they invoked spirits, and they were accused of practicing harmful black magic. This period saw a sharp decline in traditional herbalism and many dishonest practitioners moved in to fill the void. As a result, bomohs are currently regarded with suspicion, although some Muslims still consult them.

In Malaysia, shamanism and cosmology are made up of various elements of belief and religion, such as animism, Hinduism, and Buddhism. Some shamans have attempted to adapt their practice to modern Islam, for example by reciting verses from the Quran or invoking the name of Allah, but conservative shamans find this practice superficial. Similar objections were also made by Muslim leaders. As mentioned above, Muslim scholars regard the practice of bombo as shirk (idolatry, deification of figures other than Allah), which is a great sin in Islam.

It is thought that the Malay originally believed in animism. This belief still exists in modern times among certain ethnic groups, such as the Senoi, Semang, Negrito, Kenak, Dayak, and others. As Daud (2010: 183) maintains:

> Their mystical views are replete with a variety of spirits connected with the forest, mountains, the sea, large trees, and hillocks and such things like. These

spirits are an integral aspect of their lives and form a channel to realize their existence and their lives. Before the arrival of Islam approximately in the fourteenth century, peninsula Malays are said to have adhered to Hindu-Sivaism and subsequently to Hinayana Buddhism. . . . Slowly but surely, Hinduism and animism were set aside and were replaced by a belief system based on Islam. However, because animistic and Hindu elements were so firmly implanted in the Malay souls, Islam did not succeed in obliterating them completely.

(Mohamed Ghouse Nasuruddin 2006: 10)

The interesting point here is the impact of the culture on health beliefs, which may be even stronger than central religious axioms. According to Ahmadi (2015), culture is a basic element in the construction of a belief system. The myths, symbols, and rituals connected to a religion can be seen as offering ways to understand the world. Cultural belief systems regarding heath explain what causes illness, how to cure or treat it, and who should be involved in the process. For instance, applying *Demonic Reappraisal* as a coping method would seem to necessitate belief in a Devil who can control the course of people's lives – who has the power to change human "destiny." Indeed, in Islam, the Devil is thought to be God's creation and is never depicted as "evil as such"; he always remains a necessary instrument in God's hands; there is no real clear dualism between good and evil or God and Satan. In the Quran, Satan is not portrayed as an enemy of God. God is greatest and supreme over all creation. Satan is merely one of his creations, and Satan's only enemy is humankind.

Thus, a Muslim who believes in an omnipotent God and does not believe Satan possesses the power to change the course of events is unlikely to redefine her/his stressor as an act of an evil power. Shamanism was often condemned as *shirk* (idolatry) by religious Muslim leaders referring to Quran, which denounces magicians and shamanists[9]:

. . . and the magician will never be successful, no matter what amount (of skill) he may attain. (Taa Haa, 20: 69)[10]

Despite this opposition to shamanism, the notion of black power seems to be quite strong in Malay culture (and generally among East Asian people), but it is better characterized as a superstition than as a theological belief in the power of Evil. Thus, what we seem to be witnessing here is the strength of old pre-Islamic cultural beliefs, which survived long after Islam became the predominant religion.

The studies in Turkey and Malaysia also indicate that, in both countries, the notion of being tolerant (*sabr*) was important among the informants when they were coping with the psychological problems caused by cancer. In this regard, Aflakseir and Coleman (2011: 46) emphasize "Islamic teachings encourage people to be patient, to perform prayer, and trusting and turning to God in times of need and for guidance." They (Aflakseir and Coleman, 2011) also explain that, according to the Quran and tradition, one way of achieving a state well-being and of coping with problems is to "remember the Name of your Lord and devote yourself with a complete devotion" (Quran verses 73: 8).[11] For this reason, the notion that the problems of this world are meant to test people and encourage them to have patience is highly influential among people in Muslim countries, including Turkey and Malaysia.

Notes

1 In this chapter, we have used some results, which have already been published Copyright permissions have been obtained.
2 Fasting is an act of empathy. The fast is intended to remind Muslims of the suffering of those less fortunate than themselves. Muslims often donate to charities during the month of fasting and feed the hungry.
3 Zakat, the giving of alms to the poor, is one of the five pillars of Islam.
4 World Values Survey (2010?2014), corresponded to the fifth wave of the World Values Survey. This study has been carried out by 57 countries all over the world.
5 This is because the RCOPE methods are based mainly on studies conducted among Christians.
6 It is clear that different Christian traditions, particularly Catholicism and Protestantism, have adopted different approaches to the issue of the necessity of evil and the doctrine of Original Sin and, accordingly, to the notion of Satan. Delving into these approaches is beyond the scope of the present work, so we restrict ourselves to the general claim that the notion of there being a conflict between Satan and Christ - despite many varying interpretations of it - is still strong among Christians.
7 On the other hand, people other than Muslims, like Chinese people in Malaysia, are also heavily influenced by nature. The ancient Book of Rites describes in detail religious ceremonies. For example, sacrifices were offered to Heaven, the Earth, the Sun, the Moon, the seasons, the mountains and forests, and all natural phenomena were regarded as living spirits. Feng shui is an example of a practice that influences Chinese people in their lives. Feng shui refers to the art of living in harmony with the nature (Thongtaab, 2001). Feng shui is used to channel nature's positive forces and correct negative ones. This process is used to promote better health, wealth, and relationships (Moran, 2002). Chinese people usually rely heavily on feng shui to determine the location of their houses and the arrangement of decorations in their houses, the goal being to promote goodness in their life. This is similar to the belief among Indian people in Malaysia that nature is God's body. Humans and their societies are embedded in nature and dependent upon cosmic forces (Coward, 2003). This reflects how Indian people appreciate nature and define it as something important in their lives.
8 An orientation system refers to the way in which culture influences an individual's life (Ahmadi 2006: 45).
9 Some Muslim groups, like some Sufi sects, have practiced shamanism, but Sufis have always been condemned and insulted by religious leaders and fundamentalists in many Islamic countries; some have even been executed. Sufi ways of thinking can then hardly be considered predominant among Muslims. The influence of shamanism among some Muslim sects in the Middle East can be traced back to the thirteenth century, when the Mongols conquered the Middle East. Shamanism was predominant among Mongols, dating as far back as the eighth century.
10 http://corpus.quran.com/translation.jsp?chapter=20&verse=69.
11 http://corpus.quran.com/translation.jsp?chapter=73&verse=8.

References

Aflakseir, A. & Coleman, P. G. (2011). Initial development of the Iranian religious coping scale. *Journal of Muslim Mental Health,* 6 (1): 44–61.

Ahmadi F. (2006). *Culture, religion and spirituality in coping: The example of cancer patients in Sweden.* Uppsala: Acta Universitatis Upsaliensis.

Ahmadi, F. (Ed.). (2015). *Coping with cancer in Sweden: A search for meaning*. Uppsala: Uppsala. University, Acta Universitatis Upsaliensis, Studie Sociologica Upsaliensia 63.

Ahmadi, F., Certez Ö., Erbil, P., Ahmadi, N., & Ortak, A. (2017) A survey study among cancer patients in Turkey: Meaning-making coping. *Illness, Crisis and Loss*. Retrieved from http://journals.sagepub.com/doi/pdf/10.1177/1054137317720751.

Ahmadi, F., Park, J., Kim, M. K., & Ahmadi, N. (2016a). Exploring existential coping resources: the perspective of Koreans with cancer. *Journal of Religion and Health*. DOI 10.1007/s10943-016-0219-6; http://rdcu.be/ksP2.

Ahmadi, N. & Ahmadi, F. (1998). *Iranian Islam: The concept of the individual*. London: Macmillan.

Ahmadi, N., Ahmadi, F., Erbil, P., Certez, Ö. A. (2016b), Religious meaning making coping in Turkey: A study among cancer patients. *Illness, Crisis and Loss*. DOI: https://doi.org/10.1177/1054137316672042. Retrieved from http://journals.sagepub.com/doi/full/10.1177/1054137316672042.

Ani, A., Mohamed, N.m & Rahman, N. A. (2012) Socio-cultural influences in the composition of traditional Malay house compounds in rural Melaka. *International Journal of Sustainable Tropical Design Research and Practice*, 5 (1): 63–78.

Boscaglia, N., Clarke D. M., Jobling, T. W., Quinn, M. A. (2005). The contribution of spirituality and spiritual coping to anxiety and depression in women with a recent diagnosis of gynecological cancer. *International Journal of Gynecological Cancer* 16(5): 755–761.

Coward, H. (2003). Ethics and genetic engineering in Indian philosophy, and some comparisons with modern western. *Journal of Hindu-Christian Studies*,16(9): 1–10.

Dabrowski, K. (1964). *Positive disintegration*. Boston: Little Brown & Co.

Daud, H. (2010) Oral traditions in Malaysia, *Wacana*, 12(1): 181–200.

Davary, B. (2012). Islam and ecology: Southeast Asia, Adat, and the essence of Keramat. Asian Network Exchange, 20(1). ˑετριεϭεδ φροµ https://www.asianetworkexchange.org/articles/abstract/10.16995/ane.44/.

Dein, S. (1997). Does being religious help or hinder coping with chronic illness? A critical literature review. *Palliative Medicine*, 11: 291–298.

Ellison, C. G. (1991). Religious involvement and subjective well-being. *Journal of Health and Social Behavior*, 32(1): 80–99.

Esmer, Y. (2007). Globalization, "McDonaldization" and values: Quo vadis? In Y. Esmer and T. Pattersson (Eds.), *Measuring and mapping cultures: 25 years of comparative value surveys* (pp. 79–98). Leiden: Brill:.

Esoof, N. D, (2013). Orang melayu paling ramai hidapi barah limfoma (Malays are most likely to be affected by lymphoma cancer). Retrieved from https://www.ttsh.com.sg/uploadedFiles/TTSH/About_Us/Newsroom/News/210313%20BH%20Pg%203.pdf.

Ferraro, K. F. & Koch, J. R. (1994). Religion and health among black and white adults: Examining social support and consolation. *Journal for the Scientific Study of Religion*, 33(4): 362–375.

Fromm, E. (1950). *Psychoanalysis and religion*. New Haven, CT: Yale University Press.

Gilsenan, M. (1973). *Saint and sufi in modern Egypt; An essay in the sociology of religion*. Oxford Monographs on Social Anthropology, 248. Oxford: Clarendon Press.

Gotay, C. C. (1985). Why me? Attributions and adjustment by cancer patients. *Social Science and Medicine*, 20: 825–831.

Haque, A. (2005). Mental health in Malaysia: An overview. In Z. A. Ansari, N. M. Noor, & A, Haque, *Contemporary issues in Malaysian psychology*. Singapore: Thomson Learning.

Hinde, R. A. & Groebel, J. (1991). *Cooperation and prosocial behaviour* (1st ed.) New York: Cambridge University Press.
Homerin, E. (2005). Altruism in Islam, In J. Neusner & B. Chilton (Eds.), *Altruism in world religions*. Washington, DC: Georgetown University Press.
Inglehart, R. (1997). *Modernization and postmodernization: Cultural, economic, and political change in 43 societies*. Princeton, NJ: Princeton University Press.
Isaman N. I. (2015). *Lebih ramai wanita hidap barah ovari, wanita Melayu berisiko lebih tinggi (More women are affected by ovarian cancer; Malay females have a higher risk)*. Retrieved from http://berita.mediacorp.sg/mobilem/singapore/lebih-ramai-wanita-hidap/1916396.html.
Kesselring, A., Dodd, M. J., Lindsey, A. M., & Strauss, A. L. (1986). Attitude of patients living in Switzerland about cancer and its treatment. *Cancer Nursing*, 9(2): 77–85.
Linn, M. W., Linn, B. S., & Stein S. R. (1982). Beliefs about causes of cancer in cancer patients. *Social Science & Medicine*, 16: 835–839.
Mahoney, A., Pargament, K. I., Murray-Swank, A., & Murray-Swank, N. (2003). Religion and the sanctification of familyrRelationships. *Review of Religious Research*, 44: 220–236.
Mahyuddin I. (2014). Bewitchment as a defence in divorce cases according to Islamic law. *The Islamic Quarterly*, 58(4): 283–292.
Mohamed, G. N. (2006). Unsur mistik dalam teater tradisional. *Dewan Budaya*, 28(4): 9–13.
Moran, A. (2002). *The complete idiot's guide to feng shui*. Upper Saddle River, NJ: Pearson.
Neighbors, H. W., Jackson J. S., Bowman P. J., & Gurin G. (1983). Stress: coping, and black mental health: Preliminary findings from a national study. *Prevention in Human Services*, 2(3): 5.
Ng, L. O., Teoh, H., & Haque, A. (2003). Clinical psychology in Malaysia: A brief overview. *ASEAN Journal of Psychiatry*, 6: 11–16.
Oka. T., Hussin, N. A. M., & Hagström, A. S. (2017). The diversity of indigenous wisdom on grief: Exploring social Work approaches to bereavement. *The IAFOR International Conference on the Social Sciences*, Hawaii 2017. Retrieved from http://25qt511nswfi49iayd31ch80-wpengine.netdna-ssl.com/wp-content/uploads/papers/iicsshawaii2017/IIC-SSHawaii2017_33556.pdf
Osman, M. T. (1988). The concept of national culture: The Malaysian case. *Bunga Rampai: Aspects of Malay culture* (p. 276). Kuala Lumpur: Dewan Bahasa dan Pustaka.
Pargament, K. I. (1997). *The psychology of religion and coping*. New York: Guilford Press.
Sahad M. N. & Abdullah S. (2013). Santau and Malay society: An analysis from the perspective of Islamic Aqidah. Retrieved from http://jurnalmelayu.dbp.my/wordpress/wp-content/uploads/2014/09/223-242-Santau.pdf.
Siemienska, R. & Zuasnabar, I. (2010). *Changing human beliefs and values, 1981–2007: A cross-cultural sourcebook based on the world values surveys and European values studies*. México, D.F.: Siglo Veintiuno Editores.
Skeat, W.W. (1900). *Malay magic: An introduction to the folklore and popular religion of Malay Peninsula*. New York: Benjamin Bloom.
Taylor, E. B. (1968). The science of culture. In M. H. Fried (Ed.), *Readings in Anthropology: Cultural and Anthropology* (Vol. 2, pp. 1–18). New York: Thomas Y. Crowell.
Thomas, T. (2006). Is Malaysia an Islamic state? *Malayan Law Journal Article* (*MLJA*), XV, 15–17.
Thongtaab, S. (2001). *The philosophy of feng shui*. Bangkok: Sangdoa.
Wicks, J. W. (1990). *Greater Toledo area survey*. Bowling Green, OH: Population and Society Research Center.

Zein, Z. (2015). The place of Muslim women in Islamic space. *Solutions*, 6(5): 37–39.

Zimmerman, C. C. (1974). Family influence upon religion. *Journal of Comparative Family Studies*, 5 (2): 1–16.

Other references

Department of Statistic Malaysia (2016). Siaran akhbar anggaran penduduk semasa, Malaysia 2014–2018. Retrieved from https://www.dosm.gov.my/v1/index.php?r=column/pdfPrev&id=SzVuRjlvV3JsUXUyOStZcTQyNEVGQT09.

Global Security (2011). Malaysia Religion. Retrieved from http://www.globalsecurity.org/military/world/malaysia/religion.htm.

KONDA Research and Consultancy (2007, 9 September). Religion, Secularism and the Veil in daily life. Milliyet. Archived from the original on 25 March 2009.

Online journal Berita Harian (2015). Barah hidung, tekak turut jejas ramai Melayu (Nasal cancer, throat affect many Malays). Retrieved from http://www.beritaharian.sg/gah/barah-hidung-tekak- turut-jejas-ramai-melayu.

World Values Survey, Wave 6, (2010–2014). Retrieved from http://www.worldvaluessurvey.org/WVSDocumentationWV6.jsp.

6 The relationship between culture and health

In this chapter, we will discuss the importance of taking cultural differences into consideration when studying the meaning-making coping methods used by people who are facing a serious crisis.

Cancer patients use a multitude of meaning-making coping methods, be they spiritual, religious or existential. The strategies people employ when they are stricken by disease, accidents, misfortune, etc., are cultural and historic constructions. Culture can affect the coping process in four ways: First, the cultural context shapes the type of stress individuals are likely to experience. Second, culture may affect assessment of the stressfulness of a given event. Third, culture affects selection of the strategies an individual uses in a given situation. Fourth, and finally, culture provides the institutional mechanisms individuals may use when trying to cope with stressful situations.

The findings of our studies verify the third way, i.e. "culture affects selection of the strategies an individual uses in any given situation." In the following, proceeding from our studies on meaning-making coping with cancer in different cultural settings, we will first discuss the relation between culture and health and then the relation between religion and health. In the final section, we will focus on the role of sanctification in coping from a cultural perspective.

Health

Although our studies show clearly the impact of culture on coping, they also demonstrate that being stricken with a serious crisis such as cancer can, itself, affect one's view of health and sickness, regardless of culture of socialization.

In this regard, one of the interesting finding of our studies was that going through the psychological problems caused by cancer and thinking about the possibility of death caused concerns about life issues, one's own life, possibilities and limitations. For quite a few informants, this concern has brought about a new picture of what it means to be healthy and sick. The meaning of health has changed for them, in that health is no longer considered a state one experiences introspectively. Health is rather a kind of presence, an active and fruitful commitment to what is important in life. Thus, well-being is a state that can make us receptive to new things,

ready to deal with new problems without forgetting ourselves and the demands and strains we face.

In such a view, health is not a matter of never getting sick, but being able to both become ill and recover. For a cancer patient, the illness often entails falling out of one's everyday context. Thus, health means being able to fall and rise again. Health does not mean constant harmony, because you cannot invite anything new into your life without the balance being disturbed. Therefore, health does not need to rule out worry or even moderate anxiety. There is a kind of anxiety that should be understood as an existential road to rising again after a fall; it shows that one is on the way back to "life."

Health and culture

Studies showing a link between health and culture have made different assumptions about the impact of culture on health. Already in 1987, Angel and Thoits (1987) argued that subjective experiences of illness are culture-bound. The cognitive and linguistic characteristics that characterize an illness in each culture limit the interpretation and action framework the patient needs to respond to the problems caused by the disease. This assumption is based on what Rundström (1997: 38) calls the macro-sociological perspective. We will use and adapt Rundström's thesis on the macro-sociological in our discussion on culture and health.[1]

A macro-sociological perspective

From a macro-sociological perspective, each culture is a unique entity with its own special health system. Public health systems differ from one another. As Rundström (1997: 38) explains, from a macro-sociological perspective, everyone is considered to belong to a demarcated group characterized by common values, behaviors, customs, and practice, which is termed "a culture." The cultures are considered to be more or less unique to each group. People are born and raised into their parents' culture, which shapes their values and behaviors for the rest of their lives.

The culture-based view of morbidity is basically based on how, in a given cultural setting, people view the body and its structure and function. Here we are dealing with what are called "layman's theories."

As Helman (2000: 91) explains, layman's theories are based on a certain belief in the body's structure and function and about what makes the body malfunction. Although these theories, or rather models, are based on scientifically incorrect premises, according to Helman (ibid.), they often have an internal logic and consistency that helps the disease victim get an answer to the question of what happened to him/her and why. In most cultures, these models are part of a complicated, inherited folklore. In industrialized countries, this folklore is often influenced by concepts borrowed from the media. Generally, layman theories locate the cause of ill health in any of the following:

- The individual
- The natural world
- The immediate environment
- The supernatural world

According to Helman, we can perhaps say that while social and supernatural etiologies[2] tend to be a feature of societies in the non-industrialized world (especially in rural areas), natural and patient-centered explanations of diseases are more common in the Western industrialized world. However, this explanation is obviously generalized and one-sided.

The view as to where the cause of illness is located is directly related to the view of the body and is mainly culturally constructed. It also impacts the way people cope with their illness. In the following, proceeding from the results of our studies, we try to shed light, from a cultural perspective, on an explanation of where the cause of morbidity is located in relation to the above-mentioned four causes.

The individual: The layman's theories, which locate the cause of morbidity in the individual, see sickness as a functional problem in the individual's body, sometimes related to a change in diet or behavior. Here the responsibility lies mainly (but not entirely) with the sick person him-/herself.

This view is especially common in individual-oriented (primarily Western) societies. In these societies, the responsibility is often imposed on the victim. She is accused of not taking care of her body, her diet, her hygiene, her lifestyle, her relationships, her sexual behavior, or that she has smoked and consumed alcohol, not exercised, or taken care of her physical problems in time.

In our interviews among cancer patients in Sweden, we have observed this view. Several interviewees cited their lifestyle or stress as the reason they were afflicted by cancer. Here we can see traces of the cultural doctrine of individual responsibility for health. Owing to the strong individualism, on the one hand, and the well-established welfare system in Sweden, on the other, individuals are increasingly expected to live healthy lifestyles and avoid dangerous habits.

As our studies indicate, such a view can result in more individual-oriented coping methods.

The natural world: In some layman theories, different aspects of the natural environment, both living and non-living, are considered to be the cause of ill health. Common in such theories is, for example, emphasizing climate-related circumstances such as cold, heat, wind, rain, snow or moisture. Other natural causes of morbidity include damage caused by different animals and, at least in the West, infections caused by microorganisms. Here, for instance, cancer is regarded as an invasion of the foreign body by a living entity – something that then grows and "consumes" the body from within. In our studies, we found examples of this view of cancer. Some said they used visualization[3] as their coping method to remove the "cancer bugs."

In the same vein, nature can be attributed a healing power and viewed as an effective coping resource. In our studies, natural foods were sometimes regarded as anti-cancer medicine, or living near a mountain could be seen as a way to protect oneself from cancer.

Such understandings of the cause of morbidity can perhaps be found in cultural settings where people strongly believe in a direct body-mind relationship. Here the meaning-making coping methods – either religious, spiritual, or existential – tend to relate in different ways to nature and natural phenomena.

Social environment: Accusing others of causing one's own illness is a common feature in cultural settings where a group-oriented ideology is predominant. In such cultures, we have observed interpersonal relationships that are characterized by strong duty toward members of the group and, on the contrary, by ongoing conflicts.

Concerning this sense of duty, some of our informants from group-oriented societies were suspicious that their illness – cancer – might have been caused by stress arising from having too many family-oriented duties and thinking about ethical and moral codes. In coping with cancer, they have then used meaning-making in an attempt to achieve peace of mind.

Regarding the ongoing conflicts resulting from the intensive interrelation found in the group-oriented societies, common forms of accusation concerning morbidity are sorcery, black magic and the evil eye. In all three cases, morbidity is seen as the result of another person's hostility or wretchedness, consciousness or unconsciousness. It should be mentioned that such beliefs often occur among groups whose lives are characterized by poverty, insecurity, danger, feelings of inadequacy and powerlessness.

The idea of "the evil eye" as a cause of morbidity and illness can be found throughout Europe, the Middle East and North Africa. The main features of the "evil eye" are connected with the fear of envy in the eyes of the observer, and that its influence can be avoided or counteracted by objects that distract attention, and through the practice of magic. Jealousy, when channeled through the eyes, can kill. It can also cause several types of disease. The one who has "the evil eye" usually causes injury unintentionally. As noted above, people in some group-oriented communities believe that other people can cause morbidity through magic powers, such as magic, black art, or the "evil eye."

In our studies, informants in some cultural settings reported believing in black magic, having applied the coping methods Demonic Reappraisal and have received help from shamans for alternative treatment. In some cases, the strong role of such cultural beliefs is in clear opposition to the people's religious axioms, just as in the case of the Malaysian informants discussed in Chapter 5.

The supernatural world: As Helman (2000: 94) points out, some people attributed morbidity to the direct actions of supernatural entities, such as gods, spirits, or ancestral shadows.

Studies have shown that some Americans described morbidity as a "reminder" sent by God for their wrongdoing or oversights, such as failing to visit church regularly, not reading nightly prayers or not thanking God daily for one's blessing. Sickness was perceived as a divine punishment for sinful behavior. Here, as Snow (1978) emphasizes, "cures and regrets, not penicillin" culminate in the sin committed. In some societies, morbidity was attributed to whimsical, evil spirits. Such a view of obsession with a spirit – *jiin* – is common in the Islamic world. Jiins are beings with their own free will, created by smoke-free fire from God. Jiines have a great deal in common with people. They eat, marry, sleep, die, and so on. They are invisible to humans, but they can see humans. Sometimes they are unintentionally exposed to humans. They can be both good and evil. They can turn into animals or humans. They can also possess people. They have more power than humans and live longer. Some people can control them using magic powers.

The notion of black power seems to be quite strong among East Asian people, but it is better characterized as a superstition than as a theological belief in the power of evil. As we discussed in Chapter 5, some Malay people believe in witchcraft, black magic, or *santau*, which derives from the ancient mystical rituals. Santau is a method of poisoning one's enemies. It can be executed either by physical means or by the wind. The reason for sending santau is usually feelings of hatred and jealousy. It is believed that the illnesses caused by santau and black magic cannot be treated using conventional medical treatment (Sahad & Abdullah, 2013), but require religious treatment.

Supernatural explanations of morbidity are divine punishment or demise, but these are less common in secular individual-oriented societies. However, there are counterparts to such explanations, such as beliefs in luck, fate, the stars, or "acts of God." However, in many religious groups, the blame for morbidity lies in the ailing person having acted immorally, or having not thought or acted in a sufficiently spiritual manner. The various "layman's theories" mentioned above do not go beyond a single reason in their explanations for the causes of morbidity. They assume that several causes may be working together. This means that explanations locating the cause of disease to the individual, nature, the immediate environment, or supernatural powers are not mutually exclusive, but linked to each other.

Globalization, health, and culture

When discussing the issue of health and culture, we should remember that we are not talking only about different cultural settings that are separated from each other geographically. These settings are not islands. In a world that is becoming more and more linked to international trade, immigration and electronic communication, health issues are increasingly affected by both global and local forces and cultures are becoming more and more connected. The populations of many societies consist of people with different cultural and ethnic backgrounds. Therefore medical and healthcare professionals should know the distinct cultural characteristics of the population they are serving, because these characteristics form the common link that connects all humanity.

There is a wealth of literature on health and culture that can help students in medicine and healthcare create a moral, political, and scientific bridge between culture-specific and more universal approaches, and better understand the tension that exists between the two. One example is Airhihenbuwa's book *Health and Culture: Beyond the Western Paradigm* (1995). Freudenberg (2000: 508) points out, in his interesting review of this book, that the author believes culture should play a central role in health promotion. Airhihenbuwa proposes a model to help healthcare students address climate-related factors under different circumstances. The proposal is based on his experiences from different parts of the world. Although Airhihenbuwa acknowledges the role of socioeconomic factors in health, he believes that emphasizing these factors at the expense of the cultural reduces the impact of health promotion interventions.

Airhihenbuwa's *Health and Culture* criticizes Eurocentric approaches to culture, health, and health promotion. The author believes that the European and North American world image underestimates the role of culture in health issues, emphasizes an authoritarian education model that creates a dichotomy between education and learning, defines development in ridged economic terms, and prefers medical-oriented explanations and solutions to public-health-oriented ones. These problems reflect, according to Airhihenbuwa, a colonial or postcolonial worldview in which Western hegemony is believed to be a norm.

The universal and culture-specific approaches are not mutually exclusive in theory. The goal should therefore be to maximize both of these values. In practice, however, these two strategies may conflict with each other. The following example provides an illustration (Freudenberg 2000: 508–509).

Many suburbs in a large number of cities around the world accommodate persons belonging to different ethnic minorities or subcultures. Living in some districts of metropolitan areas, such as London, Paris, New York and Stockholm, are people who speak different languages, eat different foods, practice different religions, and experience different health systems. According to Airhihenbuwa, this diversity helps create positive energy and a nice atmosphere, but at the same time creates problems for the professionals planning public healthcare. How can they plan a healthcare system that will be accepted by different groups, when each culture has its own view of health and care? What should be done if part of the population dislikes basic socially dominant values, such as sexuality? Are public health educators content to emphasize the values that are common to all groups in an attempt to not violate anyone, and do they never omit such fundamental values, which may create conflict? Or does each group require a separate intervention? According to Airhihenbuwa, who has rich experience in such measures, assuming a separate agenda is not a good solution. If that is done, culture-specific interventions and groups will be polarized, making dialogue between them even more difficult and giving rise to strong segregation (Freudenberg 2000: 509).

Global changes require that the importance of culture and, consequently, its effect on care be reviewed. The blend of cultures resulting from relocation and immigration has always been a factor in world history, but now it is occurring faster than ever. The emergence of a cultural world dominated by multinationals that are striving to make huge profits by spreading consumerism across the globe affects the desires and values of all people. We can appreciate or dislike these trends, but we can hardly deny their existence.

In reality, we all belong to many cultures; our parents, partners, friends and neighbors, our colleagues, our mass media, and the culture of the social class we are part of. These many cultures can overlap. Global trends, however, suggest that they have become more heterogeneous, no more equal. On the other hand, one of our cultural identities may appear stronger than the others or affect our relationship to health and care more directly.

Airhihenbuwa's book offers definitions of culture-specific and universal approaches to health promotion efforts. The book helps identify the issues that we should address if we wish to successfully integrate these two approaches, but it does not offer any specific solution – because there is no simple solution.

When studying meaning-making coping among people with different cultural backgrounds, we had to integrate these two approaches when analyzing the results. Although we have emphasized, in our book, the role of culture in the various coping methods, we must remember that the patient should not be seen merely as a member of an ethnic or cultural group, but also as an individual.

The relationship between religion and health

Over the past two decades, a growing number of publications in important journals in medicine, public health, psychology and other social sciences have been devoted to the relationship between religion and health.

The increase in studies on the role of religion in health is partly related to the world's current social and political circumstances. These circumstances have paved the way for the "comeback" of religion. For instance, the idea that religiosity, in general, and belief in a creator, in particular, are healthy for a society has gained more popularity. It is in this context that some researchers have decided to test this idea empirically.

According to Gregory and Baltimore (2005), however, these studies have a limited perspective and are often conducted among religious populations.

We agree with Gregory and Baltimore. After studying a large number of the studies on religious coping conducted in the United States for many years, we can observe that these studies almost exclusively concern religious people (Ahmadi 2015). Perhaps this is partly due to the fact that the majority of the US population is religious, thus making it difficult to find a representative sample of victims of crisis who both use coping strategies and are not religious.

To test the hypothesis that belief in a creator is healthy for a society, Gregory and Baltimore (2005) compared different democratic Western countries with regard to degree of religiosity, crime, and health. They point out that the notion that religiosity is socially useful and healthy is based on the assumption that a high rate of faith in a creator, as well as prayer and other religious activities, should have a positive correlation with a low degree of fatal violence, suicide, non-monogamous sexual acts, abortion and improved physical health. In other words, the hypothesis implies that religiosity leads to a healthy and moral life, which in turn prevents people from committing crimes or living unhealthily. According to Gregory and Baltimore (2005), such a religiously virtuous way of life should be achievable if people believe God created them for a particular purpose, thus encouraging them to follow the strict moral dictates imposed on them by religion. In the United States, people's belief in the cultural and moral superiority of religion is so strong that doubt about God's existence is ranked as a major societal fear factor.

If the data had shown, Gregory and Baltimore (2005) suggest, that the level of social health is higher in the United States than in more secular democratic countries, one could find support for the above hypothesis, but statistics show the opposite. Gregory and Baltimore (2005) point out that, for the first time in history, only more secular pro-evolution democracies have come close to achieving practical "cultures of life" that exhibit a low level of fatal crime, teenage/adult mortality, gender-related dysfunction as well as abortion. The least theistic and most secular developed democracies, such as those found in Japan, France, and Scandinavia, have been most successful in this regard. Therefore, believing in God and practicing a religion are no guarantee for a healthy society. At the same time, this does not mean that individuals in a non-religious society like Sweden have no existential needs, do not care about non-material aspects of life, or do not think about spiritual aspects of existence.

The conflicting discussions and different opinions about the influence of religion on health make it difficult to argue that religion is a necessary factor for maintaining a healthy society or for the well-being of the individual, but this does not rule out that religion – and especially spirituality – may, in some circumstances, be a factor that positively or negatively affects the health of individuals. The influence of religiosity and spirituality has to do with many other factors, including the cultural context in which religion is exercised.

Modern times have largely been characterized by a rational and science-based mindset, which has led to strong antipathy toward the involvement of religion in medicine. This antipathy has dominated the area of physical health. In terms of mental health, however, discussions concerning the influence of religion have been more open.

Viewed from a historical perspective, the Western authors in medicine have had different views on the relationship between religion, spirituality and health. For example, Plato described madness from a medical perspective, but regarded it as a state of divine enthusiasm. Thielman (1998: 3) emphasizes that ancient Jews have described madness in both natural and supernatural terms during different periods. Many Christian thinkers have not seen a natural contradiction between a medical perception of madness and a Christian view that acknowledges the existence of supernatural powers that work in the world. Islam has a long tradition of compassion for the mentally ill, and a very complicated view of the spiritual implications of madness.

It seems that philosophers and doctors in the pre-modern era had some acceptance for the notion that religion and spirituality might affect mental health both positively and negatively

However, during the modern era, the influence of religion was neglected. In our postmodern times, especially during the past decade, some researchers, especially in the United States and a few other religious countries, have tried to demonstrate the positive impact of religion on mental health. However, any negative effect of religion has not been noted. Recent discussions about religion and health appear to have turned into a duel between those who totally deny the role of religion in health and those who want to show that religion is a positive element of the health of individuals and communities. However, no matter what doctors and philosophers claim about the influence of religion on health, especially mental health, there is a reality beyond this discussion. Individuals have their own perceptions of mental health and morbidity. These perceptions, which are partly influenced by the cultural and religious views they have regarding their body and mind, affect their behavior in response to disease and their coping strategies. Therefore, to help patients effectively, it is important that healthcare professionals understand the different perceptions patients have of their illness. These perceptions are culturally constructed, and one of the most important stones in such a construction is religious belief. Here, we are referring to the impact of the religion on culture, regardless of whether the society is secular or religious. For instance, Sweden is a Protestant country, which means that the dominant religion is Protestantism. This does not mean that the majority of Swedes are "practicing Protestants," but one cannot deny that Swedish culture and mentality have been influenced by Protestantism and its ethics. A good example is the attitude toward work found in Swedish society.

In the next part, we will describe religion and mental health from a macro-perspective and try to understand how religious tradition may affect a person's understanding of his/her own health. However, we should remember that generalizations about the characteristic features of a religion are too coarse to apply to an individual. So we will only discuss possible trends in some actions associated with health-related problems. A religious tradition is a complex phenomenon composed of doctrine, community, identity, structure, stories and rituals. When we consider religion and health from different religious perspectives, it is important to remember that individuals, even within a particular religious community, differ in their ideological views despite their resemblance to other members. Thus, regardless of belonging to a religious community, it is the individual and not the group that should be the focus of a healthcare encounter, because it is the individual who has internalized the religious mindset and, therefore, the individual's characteristic features that should be taken into account. Just as an individual's mental life has been formed, schooled and, in some cases, "deformed" by his/her family as well as his/her mental status and life experiences, the person has also been formed, educated, and perhaps "deformed" by his/her experience of religious education, which has taken place in a broader context.

The influence of Protestantism

We can divide the Protestants into different groups. The first group we will look at includes the fundamentalist Protestant churches, for which the Bible is the primary source of authority and for which the criterion for determining whether someone is religious or not is obedience to biblical norms and laws (Malony, 1998).

According to *Fundamentalist Protestants*, people who are spiritually healthy obey God's precepts from the Bible and prepare to enter the Kingdom of Heaven when they die. The only other kind of health that is conceivable for this group is physical health, which has nothing to do with spiritual health. There is no such thing as mental health, which is not synonymous with spiritual health (ibid.). People who are depressed or disturbed have not responded to the calling of God.

Coping as a way to achieve good mental health in times of crisis is therefore only accomplished through spiritual health, i.e., by answering the calling of God. Any psychological problems caused by cancer are, for instance, often regarded as punishment. A cancer patient with a fundamental Protestant view is more likely to face a religious struggle.

According to Malony (1998), the second group is the Traditional Protestant churches. For traditionalists, historical tradition is the prime source of authority. Active involvement in a particular religious group is the criterion for judging who is and who is not religious.

The other group is *Liberal Protestant Churches,* for which rational thinking is the primary source of authority and for which the criterion for judging whether or not someone is religious is the person's ethical conduct.

Liberal Protestants understand health/mental health in the same way as the fundamentalists do, but from a completely different perspective. They also claim that the best mental health can be defined by the term "obedience." However, obedience is less a matter of personal ethics and true faith than one of obeying the biblical appeal to love thy neighbor and work for justice.

Liberal Protestants do not deny that physical health is completely separate from spiritual health, but they definitely assert that mental health is surrounded by spiritual health, which is defined as obedience to biblical teachings about creation, justice, and peace (ibid.).

The third group is *Evangelical Protestant Churches*, for which experience is the primary source of authority. Their criterion for judging whether or not someone is religious is that an event has resulted in an emotional assurance of salvation.

Evangelical Protestants and traditionalists do not associate spiritual health and mental health, which fundamentalists and liberals do. Evangelical and traditional Protestants claim that both spiritual and mental health are real, but separate. For example, evangelists distinguish between the expressions "joy" and "happiness" – both are desirable feelings, but they refer to different areas. Joy is the goal that spiritually healthy people aspire to, while happiness is the goal of those who wish to achieve mental health. Joy refers to the promise that one will be "born again" and that God will provide companionship in everyday life. Happiness is the experience of being well-integrated and productive in a social environment (ibid.).

Because Evangelical Protestants' religious traditions are usually accepted by society, they easily adapt to the differences between sacred and secular. They find themselves comfortable in their role as churchgoers and, at the same time, as public citizens; they have no problem considering the state and the church to be two separate entities. Both are of cultural importance. They are not in competition with each other; they refer to different areas. In this kind of Protestantism, there is hardly any reflection on how spiritual and mental health may differ.

An important issue taken into consideration by Malony (1998: 207) is what effects differences between fundamentalist, liberal, and evangelistic Protestants might have on coping and treatment. Maloney suggests that the differences should be as follows (note that the treatment implications described below regarded hypothetically those who practice their religion and take it seriously and heartily).

Fundamentalists who turn to a psychologist or counselor may feel guilty about being there and may be suspicious of any kind of counseling outside their church. Therefore, they may only trust the advice offered by a Christian counselor in their church, who would encourage them to test their devotion to biblical norms.

Evangelists may accept the advice they receive, but wish they could check that the psychologist or counselor is a "born again" Christian. In addition, they may expect counseling to begin with prayer and biblical and religious resources to be recommended in the treatment.

Traditionalists would probably not question the religious background of the psychologist or counselor, but would like to know whether the person is well-educated and proficient. They would be surprised if the psychologist or counselor were to mix religious and psychological views. They may, in the particular situation that has caused them to turn to a psychologist or mentor, become more bound to their own religious practices. However, they would not expect the psychologist or counselor to recommend such practices.

Liberals cannot help using the regular religious resources or religious practices offered by their church; they are also open to other opportunities for high-level psychological treatment and meditative exercises that help them achieve a harmonious relationship to their bodies and universe.

The influence of Catholicism

In discussing the view on health in Catholicism, we draw on the ideas of the well-known health and medicine researcher Nancy Clare Kehoe, from Harvard Medical School. As Kehoe (1998: 212) points out, there are specific Catholic teachings and educational programs, although there cannot be "a Catholic perspective." The Roman Catholic Church is universal. Its structure and its protagonist, the Pope, are highly visible. Papal statements are typically public and sometimes dedicated to the citizens of the world. Thus, familiarity with Catholicism is, in this respect, greater than with other religions across the world, and there may be more negative transference due to the authoritarian structures and public nature of certain official statements. However, the Catholic collectivization or subculture is not the same as the Catholic Church as an institution. There are several factors that may be important to the Catholic psychology and that may affect coping among Catholic patients.

One of them, according to Kehoe (1998: 219–222), is the dominance of authorities and the reduction of individual responsibility. In their investigation of the implications of psychotherapy with a Catholic patient, Hailparn and Hailparn (1994: 277) state the therapist has a unique role. In contrast to regular analysis focusing on propulsive transmission (Projected Transference), a targeted attack on the superego is vital. The old superego must be minimized and a new and accepting ego put in place. The authors further claim that therapists then exorcise the punishing superego and replace it with a loving and accepting self.

Another area with implications for treatment of and coping among persons with a Catholic education is, as Kehoe (ibid.) mentions, *imagination*. The "Confiteor," a prayer usually read at the beginning of collections, contains the following formulation: "I have sinned especially in thought, expression, and deed." This is a problematic expression, because it concerns both the person's inner world and his/her actions, expressions and deeds. Although it is true that many who repeat these words do not mean what they are saying, the words can have damaging effects on some conscientious people. In order to prepare young children for their first confession, they must consider whether they have sinned in thought, expression, or deed. The problem is that there is no difference between spontaneous thoughts, lusts, or fantasies and selfish thoughts, lusts or fantasies, sustained by the accompanying desire to act them out. When the therapist asks a patient about his/her fantasies, the patient may understand this as meaning "tell me what you have done wrong" or "tell me about your sins." Sexual fantasies, anguish, emotions of jealousy, etc., may be considered equivalent to sins. The patient's reaction may be resistance based on feelings of shame and guilt, but this reaction may be misunderstood if the therapist is ignorant of the patient's Catholic upbringing. Illnesses such as cancer may also be regarded as resulting from sinful behavior or thoughts, and this probably influences the patient's choice of coping method.

The third factor is religious messages and language. In Catholicism, certain religious messages are taught in schools, within families, or preached from the altar (Kehoe 1998). Catholic teachings include the concepts of hell and the Devil as well as heaven and angels. How a person relates to these convictions and how the person sees her-/himself in relation to them affect the coping methods he/she chooses.

According to Pargament (1997: 285–286), some religious coping methods, such as God's punishment and pleading for divine intercession, are related to negative outcomes. These methods are directly or indirectly associated with the guilty feelings. An example of this is the religious coping method *Punishing God Reappraisal*, which involves redefining the stressor as a punishment from God/a Spiritual Being for the individual's sins. Here, the patient may be wondering whether God/a Spiritual Being was punishing me for my lack of faith or my sins. Another example is the religious coping method *Demonic Reappraisal*, which redefines the stressor as an act of the "Devil"/an evil power. Here, the Devil's decision to make horrible things (such as deadly illness) happen is regarded as the result of a person being sinful.

Naturally, what is written above does not apply to all societies and all Catholics. There are many different approaches to Christian messages. One of the better-known approaches to Christianity and health is *Christian Science*. This is a religious teaching regarding the effectiveness of spiritual healing based on Mary Baker Eddy's interpretation of the Bible, as presented in her book entitled *Science and Health with Key to the Scriptures* (published in 1875). Students in Christian Science are usually, but not necessarily, members of the Church of Christ, Scientist. *Science and Health* is based on an entirely metaphysical view of Christianity, where sin, sickness, and death do not come from God and are, therefore, not real. According to this doctrine, these "false convictions" can be removed from our experience by striving for spiritual understanding of the world as the perfect creation of God (Kehoe, 1998)

Such a view can pave the way for understanding a life-threatening illness like cancer as a lesson from God and for trying to see how the situation could be spiritually beneficial. Here, the religious coping method *Benevolent Religious Reappraisal* may be an option.

Without a doubt, there are different ways of viewing disease and health in Christianity. For instance, there is the authoritarian view, which reduces the individual's responsibility and reinforces the role of doctors and other authorities that renounce disease and pain. One thing common to the various Christian treatment methods is the emphasis on the role of some religious practices, such as prayer, church visits, and the like, in healing. This has given rise to the emergence of the different religious coping methods we discussed earlier when explaining RCOPE.

The influence of Islam

In an interesting article, El-Kadi studies Islamic medicine. According to El-Kadi (2007), Islamic medicine can include all modalities of modern medicine, but it nonetheless differs from modern medicine by meeting the following criteria:

It is a medicine of faith and priesthood; it guides and orientates. Furthermore, it is extensive and attentive to both the body and the soul, the individual and society; it is universal and uses all available resources, offering its services to all people, not just Muslims. Finally, it is scientific. El-Kadi claims that modern medicine fails to fulfill these criteria, i.e., to offer guidance and to be ethically oriented, comprehensive, universal, and scientific.

Without necessary accepting El-Kadi's views on Islamic medicine or modern medicine, his discussion of the criteria of Islamic medicine can be important in understanding coping among Muslims.

One of the most important of these criteria is that Islam is a religion that presents an overall picture of the relationship between body and mind. This becomes particularly important with regard to the Islamic perspective on how to cope with life-threatening illness.

Syed Arshad Husain (1998: 279–290) describes this perspective. According to him, the Islamic strategy for promoting mental health and well-being is based on acknowledgment of congenital human defects and therefore calls for systematic and constructive action to overcome these deficiencies. The Quran focuses on some specific mental processes and behaviors, one of which is suicide. There are clear, exact, and definite regulations about suicide in the Quran. One verse in the Quran clearly states: "Do not take away your life, because God is merciful to you." This verse plays a major role in prevention of suicide in the Muslim community. In Islam, elimination of guilty feelings involves an exercise of religious conviction and a practical learning process through action, which is a systematic, step-by-step implementation of spiritual but also worldly acts. First, the person should face her/his sins, and then she/he should meet and understand her/his mistakes. After this, the person should sincerely promise not to repeat these wrong actions. Then she/he prays to God for forgiveness and guidance, and the process ends with the person doing charitable work.

Although there is a strong presence of religious thinking in the above-mentioned process of responding to a mental problem, for instance negative thoughts due to a life-threatening illness, like cancer, Islamic doctrine rejects supernatural or demonic explanations of illnesses and stresses. Illness is viewed as the product of an imbalance between the body's four cardinal saps, i.e., humores.[4]

Concerning the psychological problems caused by a crisis, such as being hit by cancer, it should be mentioned that Islam acknowledges the existence of mental ill health and therefore accepts the use of different kinds of psychotherapy and coping strategies. In this respect, it is important to mention that Islam distinguishes between psyche and soul, and in order to understand this, we need to look at the difference between Islamic and Western views on the relationship between body and mind.

The Western doctrine of the relationship between body and soul is principally derived from Descartes' doctrine (the so-called Cartesian duality). Descartes' philosophy starts from a clear cosmological dualism between body and mind. In such a division, all kinds of non-material elements are reduced to a single device. In addition, the difference between the soul and the psyche disappears. However, in Islam there is a clear difference between the soul (*ruh*) and the psyche (*nafs*). The recognition of such a difference means that the Islamic mindset, unlike the Western one, does not see any ontological dualism between body and soul.

According to Nasr (1975: 81), a well-known professor of Islamology, in Islam the revolt against God happens at the mental level, not at the bodily level. The flesh is only an instrument of the tendencies that occur within the psyche. It is the psyche that must be trained and disciplined, so as to be prepared to be united with the soul.

Although Islam differentiates between psychology and the soul, it sees no dualism between these two, because the soul is not the counterpart of the psyche. The soul embraces the psyche as well as the physical aspects of a human being. This helps us understand why the most intense contemplative life in Islam occurs within the framework of social life. In Islam, even worldly life is celestial. It is in this context that the healing effect of some spiritual actions is explained, for example, saying one's prayers or reciting verses from the Quran as coping methods.

In addition to the non-dualistic view of body and mind, Husain (1998: 285) points out another important issue in the treatment of a Muslim (or in coping with a serious illness) who has absolute faith in God's power in all matters. According to Muslim doctrine, nothing happens without the will of God, and this includes healthfulness and disease. For a Muslim, only God can provide a cure. One of God's names is "Al Shaafi," the Doctor. You accept the death of loved ones as God's will and, therefore, relatives do not usually consider healthcare personnel to be responsible for death. Suing a doctor for causing a patient's death is an unknown phenomenon in many Islamic countries. In our studies among Muslims (in Turkey and in Malaysia), we have observed this view of death and illness. The existence of a belief in destiny among our Muslim informants is a result of the absolute faith in God's power in all matters found in Islam (at least in some interpretations of it).

Regarding Islamic tradition and health, it is important to point out that Islam is not only a religion, but also a socio-political system that offers comprehensive methodological solutions to human beings' intellectual, spiritual and everyday problems. According to Muslims, God is the absolute transcendent, multi-skilled creator and nothing happens without His permission. Complete submission to His will and total confidence in His mercy give eternal peace. His laws aim at providing peace and security, as well as the possibility of creating a healthy, moral, safe and peaceful society. Diseases and misery can arise as Allah's tests for his subjects. Showing patience when problems arise heightens one's spiritual level. According to Muslims, Islamic traditions contain a highly developed healthcare system, which promotes mental health and prevents mental problems when facing a crisis. Among our Muslim informants, *sabr* (having patience) was used as a method for coping with cancer.

Husain (1998: 285) points out some factors healthcare personnel should consider when diagnosing and treating a Muslim. According to him, a Muslim patient engages in religious practices while using modern methods. These two approaches are not considered to be in opposition. In certain Muslim countries, some Muslims believe in the existence of supernatural beings, called *jin*, which can take different forms. Possession of a *jin* is a legitimate opportunity in the Muslim belief system.

In Chapter 5, we discussed the existence of such beliefs among Muslims in Malaysia. The use of acts of black magic as coping methods was found among Muslim informants in that country.

Obviously, the above points provide a generalized view of believing Muslims, and they hardly apply to a modern person who has internalized the norms and values of modern society, despite living in a Muslim country.

The influence of Buddhism

We have conducted our studies in Japan, China, South Korea, and Malaysia where the culture and people's ways of thinking have been shaped directly or indirectly by Buddhism. In addition, during recent decades in the Western world, some people's notions of body and soul have been influenced by Buddhist philosophy and its ways of thinking. Indeed, Buddhism has become one of the pillars of alternative medicine, alternative therapy, and wellness in the world in recent decades. Therefore, we considered it necessary to discuss Buddhism's view of health in this section. In an interesting text about Buddhist treatment of patients, Scotton writes about Buddhist medicine. He (Scotton 1998: 263) explains that in Buddhism there are "four basic principles" derived from the view of consciousness.

The first principle, *dukkha*, or suffering, means that existence is characterized by fundamental suffering. Hershock (2006: 40) explains dukkha as follows:

> Fundamental to the Buddha's public teaching was enhancing awareness of *dukkha* ("suffering" or, better still, "trouble") and the conditional pattern of its arising. ...In spite of the custom of referring to the practices recommended for alleviating and eventually eliminating *dukkha* as medicines, the Buddha's evident and unwavering strategy was to disclose and provide means of

dissolving the general patterns of interdependent conditions through which trouble and suffering arise.

The second basic principle, *anatta*, or non-selfishness, means that there is no separate existence in the phenomenal world. Buddha's analysis of consciousness concludes that a separate "self" can exist neither in any of the parts of consciousness nor in the sum of the parts of consciousness. All that can exist is a set of connection events, objects, emotions, and thoughts. Understanding that "reality" and "self" are only constant changes in a play of various mental and physical events is a necessary step toward liberation from suffering.

The third basic principle, *annieca*, or volatility, means that nothing lasts. Possessions, emotional states, relationships, even all of the planets have been created and their existence will cease. The only thing that varies is the degree of change. Relating happiness to such transient phenomena produces inevitable disappointment.

The fourth basic principle is *nirvana*, or liberation from suffering exists. It can be accomplished by freeing onself from the false feeling of a separate self and all that this feeling produces.

As Scotton (1998: 264) states, suffering, according to Buddhism, is caused by the dependency we feel in relation to things, as well as by our attraction to and loathing for different objects, creatures, ideas, and events. Our experience often affects us negatively; we want to resist and put an end to it. There will be no significant change if we do not flee, remain with our experience. We will once again be worried when everything ends, and in both cases we will suffer. Putting an end to suffering is only possible if we break the evil circle of belonging.

Buddhism differs significantly from the paradigm of dominant Western philosophy with regard to rational positivism. Buddhism presents a spiritual world where physical reality is ultimately a misrepresentation that seems to exist simply because it has been designed by our consciousness. What kind of reality do we design? We construct a material world that is the physical manifestation of previous experiences.

Such a worldview has clear implications for healing and coping, both physically and mentally. The path goes through a change of consciousness (ibid.). Of course, such a worldview, which is so different from the dominant view in the West, can result in a completely different set of priorities and behaviors than those we are used to. This applies in particular to those who advocate Buddhism, whom we call "Buddhist patients."

Some factors may affect both assessment and treatment of Buddhist patients. We have chosen some of these factors from a list presented by Scotton (1998: 266–267). In his experience, the following factors are important for Buddhist medicine:

1 A strong appreciation of the role of consciousness as a causative and healing remedy for dysfunction and disease. This factor can play an important role in treatment, as the doctor can engage the patient in using his/her ability to further understand and solve the problem. Because patients are already familiar

with psychological concepts, owing to their practice of Buddhism, the doctor can more easily highlight the psychological aspect needed for treatment.
2   An emphasis on the context of the psychological-spiritual-personal relation for the current problem. This factor can also affect the treatment and outcome. The psychiatrist should ask the patient about what he/she feels has caused the problem and listen to his/her description, which may be symbolic and/or literal.
3   The assumption that the Buddhist teacher is the patient's best guide to the ultimate essence of openness, because the study of psychic and spiritual outcomes is not treated separately in Buddhism, but perceived as indistinguishable. According to Buddhist medicine, such patient-doctor consultation improves treatment of and coping with serious illness in the best possible way.

To understand the importance of the above-mentioned aspects of Buddhist medicine, we should take into consideration one of the cornerstones of Buddhist teachings, i.e., the body-mind relation. In an interesting article, Ozawa De Silvia and Ozawa De Silvia (2011) explain that:

> The model of mind and body in Tibetan medical practice is based on Buddhist theory, and is neither dualistic in a Cartesian sense, nor monistic. Rather, it represents a genuine alternative to these positions by presenting mind/body interaction as a dynamic process that is situated within the context of the individual's relationships with others and the environment. Due to the distinctiveness, yet interdependence, of mind and body, the physician's task is to heal the patient's mind (blo-gso) as well as body.

Our study in countries where Buddhism has been an essential part of people's ways of thinking bears witness to the crucial role of the view of body-mind as it interrelates with coping with cancer. For instance, as mentioned before (Chapter 5), our informants in South Korea explained that they tried to maintain a balance between mind and body, and to remain in a positive state of mind. We found two patterns of coping related to the mind-body connection, calling the first one "peaceful mental attitude" and the second "positive life perspective."

The influence of Judaism

Providing psychological/spiritual care for patients facing a life-threatening illness is a difficult task, and this difficulty can be magnified when a person identifies as Jewish. The problem is that many believe that a person who identifies her-/himself as Jewish is an adherent of the Jewish religion. However, many Jews see themselves as ethnically or culturally Jewish rather than as connected to a religion or even as believing in God.

In this book, we have not discussed any cultural settings influenced by Judaism, but because we are attempting to explain the relation between religion, culture, and health in general in this chapter, in the following, we will offer some thoughts on the views on health found in Judaism. In doing this, we have mainly used Zedek's (1998) discussion on the main ideas about health and illness in Judaism.

There are several factors that should be taken into consideration when a patient identifies her-/himself as a Jew. Zedek (1998) points out that if the treatment concerns someone from the Orthodox Assembly, a person who is non-cooperative, it will facilitate treatment if assistance is obtained from an authority figure, usually a rabbi. This should be done to provide information that will enable cooperation or to easily obtain consent from the patient or family members. Orthodox Judaism assigns unusually great power to its leader; a rabbi's decision should be obeyed, at least theoretically, by the members of the assembly (ibid.). Such a view of a religious leader can pave the way for use of the religious coping method *Seeking Support from Clergy or Members,* where the patient searches for comfort and reassurance through the love and care of congregation members and clergy.

Another issue to be considered is the nature of the family constellation. Some sociologists have attributed to Jewish family life certain significant characteristics, such as a powerful care tradition. Zedek (1998) emphasizes that even if one could previously attribute such characteristics to a Jewish family, they seem less relevant today, when the influence of secular and materialistic culture on the lives of Jews is a fact.

Psychologists and counselors within psychiatry may, however, see Jews who agree with the attributes of a Jewish family. Such persons may show signs of denial, guilt, or shame regarding their emotional fragility. Being seriously ill and needing professional help may be perceived as an inconvenience for the individual and the family network.

Another point to consider is the role of the physician. Zedek draws our attention to a phenomenon, namely that, in Judaism, a physician is not only considered a specialist in medicine, but also as one who follows a higher calling. He who cures disease can be considered God's partner in "making the world perfect." However, it is not only the doctor who is responsible for helping a patient, but also the patient him-/herself who is responsible for taking care of his/her own illness and health. Men and women do not have the sole rights over their lives or their bodies. Therefore, they should be afraid and honor their body. They should eat and drink to provide good nutrition to the body and seek medical attention when they feel bad. Thus, the doctor has a commitment and authority in relation to the whole, and the patient is co-responsible for maintaining his/her health.

Another main principle in Judaism is that human life is of highest value. Therefore, to protect human life, the rules of the Sabbath, as well as other rules and laws, can be ignored. This refers to a religious rule that is called "pikuach nefesh" in Hebrew. According to this rule, it is not only permissible, but also necessary to violate other rules to save a person whose life is in danger, because a human life gets priority over rules.

Rosen (1999: 102) explains that because every moment of human life is of infinite value, it is forbidden in Jewish tradition to do something that may shorten a life, even by a very small amount of time. A person should not turn to a type of treatment that is known to be ineffective, because this could result in the shortening of life. Traditional Judaism does not distinguish between the prolongation of a healthy life and the prolongation of an unhealthy life (using artificial means).

This last point has become the cornerstone of the discussion among Jewish researchers and doctors concerning the use of alternative medicine. How doctors should relate to this is a question that has been widely discussed by doctors and psychologists over the past decade, especially with the increased use of some therapies and coping methods such as meditation, natural medicine, acupuncture, as well as religious practices to cure various diseases. In some countries, organized groups of doctors and psychologists have been formed that advocate the positive effect of the use of certain religious practices, such as praying. One of the well-organized groups is found among Jewish doctors and psychologists, but there are researchers and doctors who oppose such use of religious practices in medicine.

There are different reasons for the question of use of alternative medicine having become an intense topic of discussion among Jewish doctors and researchers. One reason may be that no other religion sees the repetition of the body as a duty in the way that Judaism does. Therefore, there is a strict ban on actions that shorten life. Other reasons may be that one's identity as a Jew is both ethnic and religious. Other religions largely limit religiosity to believers. However, one does not need to believe in God to call oneself Jewish. There are many atheists who self-identify as Jews and who respect Jewish culture and traditions.

Although some Jewish doctors and researchers advocate the use of prayer, amulets, and astrology, including alternative medicine, there are strong objections to such practices among Jewish doctors and their reasoning is based on Jewish tradition. According to these doctors, Judaism sanctions certain complementary therapies such as prayers and amulets as an addition to traditional medical therapy. They believe that the patient, according to Jewish tradition, should rely on and follow the scientific medical tradition. According to these doctors, trust in God's power and the use of prayer and other practices should happen as a private matter, but should not stand in the way or serve as an alternative to typical treatment. In other words, religious customs have nothing to do with medicine.'

Summing up: religion is an integral part of the culture. Culture, in turn, has influenced how religion is performed in every society; in this chapter, which focused on health and culture, it was therefore important to include a brief survey of the views of the dominant religions on health and illness.

Here, we described how Protestantism, Catholicism, Judaism, Islam, and Buddhism look at health and illness. The key pillars shaping ideas about health and illness in these religions have been presented. Of course, the presented views are general in nature and, therefore, cannot be applied directly to encounters with patients with the above-described religious backgrounds; each individual is unique and complex, and no one can be reduced to an ethnic, religious, or social group. However, having knowledge about the various elements of patients' ways of thinking can help us better understand how they perceive their own reality.

Trying to comprehend the coping method/methods each individual uses, however, requires that we focus on the trees, not the forest – on the individual, not the group. Here we are talking about different "individual" strategies used by those facing a life crisis, some by "sanctifying" certain objects or relations, some by struggling with their fate or their core values and norms, all in an attempt to cope with their crisis. Although these strategies are primarily individual, they are affected by the cultural settings in the context where an individual was socialized. In the following, we discuss this issue.

Sanctification in coping from a cultural perspective

Sanctification, sacred matters, and health issues

In the previous chapters, we have mentioned that some meaning-making coping methods used by our cancer patients, who were socialized in divergent cultural settings, were the result of sanctification, that is, giving special meaning to certain phenomena, which we call "sacred matters." In this final chapter, we return to this issue and try to discuss the sanctification of sacred matters more thoroughly, and to present our view of "sacred matters" and sanctification in coping based on the results of our studies.

Sanctification is an important phenomenon and should be of keen interest to those studying religious and spiritually oriented coping. Oddly enough, this phenomenon has not received a great deal of attention. One reason may be that sanctification does not directly apply to institutional religious involvement. Moreover, the sacred cannot easily be discerned in people's coping experience. One of the researchers who has paid considerable attention to the concept of sanctification and has developed it from different perspectives is Kenneth Pargament (Pargament & Mahoney, 2005; Pargament et al., 2014; Pargament et al., 2017).

We will, therefore, first introduce Pargament's discussion on sanctification and then put forward our own critique of some discussions on this subject, concluding with our own view. In introducing Pargament's view of sanctification, we mainly proceed from two important texts (Pargament & Mahoney, 2005).

Sanctification in a religious context

According to Pargament et al. (2005:179), "sanctification offers a powerful personal and social resource that people can tap throughout their lives; and the loss of the sacred can have devastating effects."

Considering sacred qualities as manifestations of God, the divine and the transcendent, sanctification can be defined "as a process through which aspects of life are perceived as having divine character and significance . . . a process of potential relevance not only for theists but nontheists as well" (Pargament & Mahoney 2005: 183). Here, sanctification is viewed as a "psychospiritual" construct. This is explained in the following manner:

It is spiritual because of its point of reference – sacred matters. It is psychological in two ways; first, it focuses on a perception of what is sacred. Second, the methods for studying sacred matters are social scientific rather than theological in nature.

(ibid.)

The authors try to not discuss sanctification from a theological perspective, but instead adopt a psychological one. This is why they ask the question: "Does the origin of what is sacred lie in God or in the human mind?" and provide the answer: "This question falls outside the scope of psychology. From a psychological perspective, we cannot determine whether God 'makes sacred' or people do" (ibid.).

Sanctification occurs not only in relation to theistic interpretations of various features of life, but also indirectly, implying that perceptions of divine character and significance can develop by investing in objects qualities that are associated with the divine (Pargament & Mahoney 2005: 185).

As concerns theistic sanctification, the authors mention that, according to religious education and tradition:

God's powers are manifest in many aspects of life . . . the God of most religious traditions is not removed from the workings of the world. The divine is said to be concerned with earthly as well as heavenly matters. Furthermore, the religions of the world encourage their members to see God as manifest in their lives. (Pargament & Mahoney 2005: 183, 185).

Concerning non-theistic sanctification, the authors maintain that "Sanctification can also occur indirectly; perceptions of divine character and significance can develop by investing objects with *qualities* that are associated with the divine" (ibid.). Included in these sacred qualities are attributes of transcendence (e.g., holy, heavenly), ultimate value and purpose (e.g., blessed, inspiring), and timelessness (e.g., everlasting, miraculous). Although it is possible for people to attribute sacred qualities to significant objects, in the form of a God or higher power, this means that any part of life can be perceived as sacred, the choice of the sacred is not arbitrary (ibid.) and several factors can affect it.

The sanctification process can affect coping, because sanctification may influence key dimensions of human functioning, including: (1) how people invest their resources; (2) the aspects of life people preserve and protect; (3) the emotions they experience; (4) the individual's sources of strength, satisfaction, and meaning; and (5) people's areas of heightened personal vulnerability (Pargament & Mahoney, 2005: 192).

When confronted with a difficult situation, people invest different available resources in an effort to cope. Sanctification may play an important role (negative or positive) here. Through sanctification of different objects – for instance, one's job, children, marriage, etc. – people redirect their attention during times of crisis.

Changing one's focus from the problem to the sacred object may offer a sense of security.

It is not unusual for people who are facing a crisis to make extraordinary efforts to preserve certain objects, phenomena, or aspects of life. In this connection, one preservation method is to sanctify these objects or parts of life. Becker (1998: 34) provides an example of a women sentenced to life imprisonment who invested an old chair with sacred qualities. Sanctification of the chair played an important role in bringing her comfort and security, helping her cope with her difficult situation in prison. The woman offered an explanation:

> With persistence and hard work I managed to get the chair sanded down, stained, and nailed back together, the chair was the beginning of the long, slow process of putting my life back together . . . It is difficult for me to describe the comfort and security my chair has brought me. Because of all the times I have prayed or meditated in it, it has become a sacred object. Throughout the years and all the changes they have brought, it is the one thing that has remained the same.
>
> (Becker 1998: 3, 4)

Pargament and Mahoney (2005) define the sacred as having a core and a ring. At the core of the sacred, we find concepts of God, the divine, higher powers, and transcendent reality. As Pargament et al. (2017: 2) explain:

> These concepts can take myriad forms ranging from monotheistic views of a personal God to polytheism to non-theistic perspectives on a transcendent reality, such as those articulated within Buddhism. From this point of view, people from diverse religious traditions – eastern and western – as well as those unaffiliated with any tradition can have a perspective on the sacred core.

According to authors (ibid.), these concepts are common across different traditions, even if no single element, such as theism, is present, although the core may be viewed differently. The authors emphasize that they "do not define the sacred solely by beliefs in God, higher powers, or transcendent reality." The sacred also encompasses a wider ring consisting of aspects of life (i.e., "objects") that take on deeper meaning and value through the process of sanctification (see Figure 6.1). As mentioned before, Pargament and Mahoney (2005: 183) regard sanctification as "a process through which aspects of life are perceived as having divine character and significance." As Figure 6.1 shows, the "'divine character and significance' encompasses not only theistic notions of the divine as a personal god(s), but also non-theistic views of the divine as a transcendent reality, and qualities that are often associated with theistic and non-theistic concepts of the divine" (Pargament et al. 2017: 3).

As the above discussion indicates, Pargament is trying to keep spirituality – as well as all endeavors in people's existential search for meaning or understanding of the life situation – within the realm of religiosity and transcendentally. It is precisely this point that we will comment on in the next section.

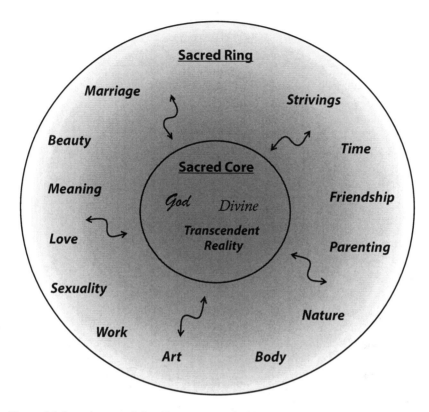

Figure 6.1 Sacred core and ring (Pargament et al., 2017: 3)

Comments on the view of the sacred in a religious context

In Chapter 2, we introduced Pargament's approach to religion and spirituality and earlier in this chapter his view on sanctification. In this section, we offer some comments on his approach to religion, spirituality, and sanctification. We believe it is important to put forward these comments because his approach has been critical in our project. Moreover, these comments are essential to understanding our own cultural approach to sanctification and sacred matters.

Comments on Pargament's definitions[5]

Let us restate the key issues in Pargament's approach to religion and spirituality, presented above.

1 Religion is *a search for significance in ways related to the sacred.*
2 Significance means *a wide range of things that may be important for the individual, institution, or culture.* It may concern the sense of satisfaction,

value, and importance that accompanies goal pursuit and attainment (subjective significance) or the goals people strive for in life (objective significance).
3. *The sacred refers to the holy*, and the core of the sacred consists of concepts of God, the divine, and transcendence. The sacred also includes objects that have been sanctified due to their association with, or representation of, the holy.
4. Sanctification is connected to aspects of life that may be perceived both *as manifestations of God and as embodiment of divine or transcendent qualities*. For this reason, sanctification is considered a process that may be relevant not only to theists, but also to non-theists.
5. Spirituality refers to *a search for the sacred*. Whereas religion includes the search for many sacred or non-sacred objects of significance, spirituality focuses explicitly on the search for the sacred.

By focusing on three terms – search, significance and sacred – Pargament offers new definitions of religion and spirituality. Although his definitions of these two terms broaden the realm of religiosity and spirituality beyond traditional concepts of God, they nonetheless remain within the realm of traditional approaches, in that they regard religion as a broader, more general construct than spirituality. Religion encompasses spirituality. Besides restricting spirituality to the realm of religion, Pargament's definitions also become problematic when we attempt to apply them to research on religion and health.

Pargament's definition of religion and the sacred, as he himself (Zinnbauer et al. 1999: 908) points out, contrasts with narrower and more polarized views on religious experience. It not only incorporates substantive and functional approaches into one approach, but also includes the positive and negative aspects of religious life. And although it distinguishes religion from spirituality, it does not regard them as polarized. People's personal and social experiences are also included. Religion involves not only the search for sacred ends (spirituality), but also the quest for secular ends using sacred means (Zinnbauer et al. 1999: 910). This is enabled by his broad definition of sanctification, which can embrace God, the divine as well as transcendent qualities, and is considered a process of potential relevance to both theists and non-theists. One problem with Pargament's definition of religion is that he does not clearly define what constitutes a religious pathway and what does not; nor does he clarify who is a religious person and who is not. This is because he, in his endeavor to overcome the problem of polarizing religion and spirituality – an endeavor we find interesting from a philosophical perspective – makes the definition of religion so broad that religion loses its divine characteristics. We will try to demonstrate this using an example from the study of Ahmadi (2006), which identified several cancer patients who did not believe in God or any other higher power, but who experienced a spiritual feeling, a unity of existence, when they were in natural landscapes. Note that if we accept Pargament's perspective on religion and the sacred, we must regard these atheists' search for significance through the sanctification of nature as a transcendent experience of the unity of existence, that is, as a religious pathway! According to Pargament, we should do so because we have here a case of "nontheistic sanctification," indicating that individuals can conceivably attribute sacred qualities to significant objects without espousing belief in God or a higher power (Pargament & Mahoney 2005: 185). Moreover, the fact that the object of significance is not directly related to God or the divine is not a problem, because it is related to a transcendent quality.

Staying with Pargament's perspective, not only are the pathways of our atheists – who admit to having had spiritual experiences and feelings – considered religious, but the atheists themselves can also be considered religious. This is because Pargament (Zinnbauer et al. 1999: 908) tells us that "when an individual seeks out a sacred destination in life, or takes a pathway that is somehow connected to the sacred, we describe that individual as religious." Our atheists have taken pathways that are in some way connected to the sacred – here thought to be a transcendent quality – which in this case consists of an experience of unity of existence through the sanctification of nature.

The question that arises here is whether an atheist's search for significance by means of the sanctification of nature makes him/her a religious person. If so, how can we distinguish a religious person from a non-theist or even from an atheist? This question is of more immediate importance and becomes more crucial in the context of empirical studies. For instance, if we wish to study the use of coping methods among different groups – such as religious individuals, non-theists and atheists – how should we categorize the atheists mentioned above? Do they belong to the "theist group," the "non-theist group," or the "atheist group"? Can we simply ignore how individuals see themselves – as a religious person or an atheist – and choose to categorize them according to our own definition? Certainly, there are often discrepancies between informants' and researchers' understandings of certain definitions, but definitions, although human constructions, cannot be arbitrary. They should not conflict with informants' own understanding of their affiliation with, e.g., a certain political, social, religious group. Moreover, definitions should be based on historical and social grounds (a given religion's history and social attributes).

In our view, regarding religion and spirituality as polarized is not merely a theoretical "problem." Moreover, this polarization reflects the spirit of our time, in that people no longer regard religion and spirituality as a unified phenomenon. Some studies (Zinnbauer et al., 1999; Scott, 1998) have supported this notion of polarization.

According to Pargament (Zinnbauer et al. 1999: 902), "religiousness and spirituality have acquired specific valences in popular and scientific writings." Here, he is referring to negative religiousness as opposed to positive spirituality (ibid.). He also reminds us that "Previously undifferentiated from religiousness, numerous forms of faith under the label 'spirituality' have risen in popularity from the 1980s to the present" (Zinnbauer & Pargament 2005: 24) and that these changes "have occurred against a background of decline in traditional religious institutions, an increase in individualized forms of faith expression, movement from an emphasis on belief towards direct experience of the sacred, and an American culture of religious pluralism" (ibid.). Thus, if the focus of research has changed from religion to spirituality, it is because, as Pargament points out, "Spirituality has also replaced religiousness in popular usage" (ibid.). Looking at the citations above, it is clear that people not only differentiate between religion and spirituality, but also self-identify as being either spiritually oriented or religiously oriented. Clearly, many people today take exception to what they understand as religion and seek other sources of "sacredness." Many associate religion with dogma, churches, priests, institutions, and political meddling. These people are seeking something else. We cannot, merely by changing how we define religion, change the historical background of religion or its social attributes. Moreover, we cannot change the fact that religion no longer attracts people to the same degree and that many people would rather not be identified as religious. This last point is very important, because if we are to carry out studies on religion and health, we must base our categorization of people into groups on how they view themselves. If a person self-identifies as a non-theist, we can hardly classify her/him as a theist just to suit our definitions.

Pargament can hardly disagree with this point. With reference to several studies, he emphasizes the following: "individuals have clear ideas about the meaning of these terms [religion and spirituality, author's note], are able to describe their beliefs in a reliable fashion, and are able to distinguish religiousness and spirituality from other constructs and phenomena" (Zinnbauer & Pargament 2005: 22).

Pargament is well aware of the risk researchers take when they fail to consider the various ways in which people relate themselves to what they find sacred and the ways in which they classify their philosophy of life. He (Zinnbauer & Pargament 2005: 30) states:

> On the other hand, should researchers define the terms in ways that are fully removed from popular uses, or in ways that narrowly exclude great sections of the religious and spiritual landscape, the legitimacy or relevance of the field may be questioned? The varieties of religious and spiritual experiences provide remarkable examples of human diversity. Universalist assumptions about the religiousness and spirituality of *all* people obscure important variations in the belief and practice of different people (Moberg 2002). At worst, they have the potential to insult or oppress minority groups.

The problem of Pargament's definition of religion and the sacred, discussed above, reflects the same problem he mentions in the preceding citation, that is, detaching definitions of terms from popular usages and excluding the various ways in which people express their spiritual feelings – practices that endanger the relevancy and legitimacy of the research field. This point is very important when we recall that in some countries, people who self-identify as spiritual but not religious, or state that they have experienced certain spiritual feelings but claim to be atheists, are not in the minority.

If our approach to studying the psychology and sociology of religion, especially in relation to health, is not theological in nature, but instead sociological or psychological, then we should take into account the changes experienced by people across the globe during the "postmodern era." We should accept that decreasing interest in attending church and participating in services as well as dissociating from religion and God is a sign of the growth of new approaches to the self and the other – new approaches that in turn have given rise to new understandings of what are called sacred values. According to Luckmann (1996), we are witnessing the development of "postmaterialist values" as the sacred values of our time, and this development goes hand in hand with individualization. Postmaterialist values are linked to present-day humankind's need for self-actualization. Pargament (Zinnbauer et al. 1999: 903) maintains that the tendency toward polarizing spirituality and religiosity is not the result of scholars' limited understanding of religion and spirituality, rather it mirrors the real changes occurring quite apart from scholars' definitions and ideas. Pargament (Zinnbauer & Pargament 2005: 27) emphasizes the following: "It is no coincidence that the popularity of spirituality has grown in a culture that values individualism, and risen during a historical period in which traditional authority and cultural norms were being rejected."

We agree the notions that the polarization between religion and spirituality is sometimes naïve and simplified and that the relationship between these two phenomena is much more complicated than: "spirituality is cool, and religion is uncool." However, we do find it difficult to start from Pargament's definition of religion in the research field of religion, spirituality and health without running the risk of neglecting informants' own understandings of their religious and spiritual feelings and lives.

The second problem we see with Pargament's discussion on sanctification is that it is not clear how he distinguishes between "manifestations of God," "embodiments of divine" and "transcendent qualities" when he stresses: "Sanctification may occur both directly and indirectly; that is, aspects of life may be perceived both as manifestations of God and as embodiments of divine or transcendent qualities" (Pargament & Mahoney 2005: 186). Because Pargament's definition of religion is linked to the concepts of the sacred and sanctification, it is critical to clarify what God, the divine and transcendent refer to. In our view, the first problem, i.e., defining religion too broadly, is partly due to the ambiguity surrounding what exactly is meant by "manifestations of God," "embodiment of divine," and "transcendent qualities."

Grasping Pargament's understanding of God, the divine, and the transcendence is important to comprehending not only his view of religion, but also his view of spirituality. Pargament defines spirituality as a search for the sacred, and the core of the sacred consists of the concepts of God, the divine, and transcendence.

On the one hand, as stated, Pargament defines spirituality as a search for the sacred. On the other, he emphasizes that the sacred refers to the holy and includes objects that come to be sanctified owing to their association with, or representation of, the holy. By connecting the sacred to the holy and by substituting the term "spiritual" with "divine" in his new definition of sanctification, Pargament ensures that the sacred will remain within the framework of religiosity and, thus, that spirituality will remain a part of religion. This allows Pargament to overcome the problem of polarizing these concepts, which we find in modern approaches. Nonetheless, we have some problems with Pargament's definition of spirituality.

If Pargament's definition of religion is too broad to allow us to distinguish between religion and non-religion and between a religious and a non-religious person, then his definition of spirituality is also too narrow to embrace many experiences non-theists or atheists describe as spiritual. In other words, in Pargament's definition, spirituality is still an integrated part of religion and its domain does not extend beyond the framework of religion. Consequently, pathways that do not refer to the holy or are not based on a belief in God or a higher power are still outside the realm of spirituality. This may cause serious problems in empirical studies when individuals self-identify as spiritual but not religious and claim to follow thus defined pathways.

Another problem is that Pargament's definition of spirituality does not consider one of the most important dimensions of spirituality: connection. In all spiritual pathways, even those focused on detachment from terrestrial life, the ultimate goal is connection with a transcendent source, a kind of unity. A definition that equates spirituality with a search for the sacred focuses on the means, but not the ends. As we saw earlier, in defining religion, Pargament proceeds from a "goal-related view of human nature." This is because he believes that, "people are proactive, goal-directed beings searching for whatever they hold to be of value in life. Every search consists of a pathway and a destination" (Pargament & Mahoney 2005: 181). If this holds, then why, in defining spirituality, is the most important goal – that of connection – left out? Pargament is well aware of the importance of connection in spiritual life. He (Zinnbauer & Pargament, 2005) refers to studies showing that informants tend to characterize religiousness in relation to formal/organizational religion, and spirituality in relation to nearness to God or feelings of interconnectedness with the world and living things. However, if we accept the notion that individuals' feelings of interconnectedness with the world and living things are spiritual in nature, then we must pose the question: Where is the "reference to the holy" here? Where is religion's place in this picture? Once again, as in the example above, we have a problem with atheists or non-theists who are searching for the unity of existence in nature. These people may well report feeling connected with the world and things in the absence of belief in God or any other holy source. If we consider these feelings to be holy experiences, then we, once again, have the problem of defining what constitutes religion and what does not.

In the discussion above, we have tried to demonstrate that Pargament's definitions of religion, spirituality, and sanctification, although rich and comprehensive, are problematic in that they draw a line between theists and non-theists as well as neglect the spirit of our time. As we see it, one of the reasons for this is that the studies on which Pargament and many other researches have based their definitions of religion and spirituality have been conducted in the United States, where the majority of people self-identify as religious and where, as Pargament (Zinnbauer & Pargament 2005: 28) mentions, even those who regard themselves as spiritual admit to being committed to a religion.

Our studies in different cultural settings, including non-religious cultures, have revealed that there are other secular theories, such as attribution theory

(Fölsterling, 2001), that can also be applied when studying coping in societies where religion does not strongly affect people's ways of thinking. Salander (2015) takes up this issue when explaining Frankl's perspective on meaning, according to which meaning is not of "divine," but of cognitive origin. From this perspective, if individuals are to avoid feelings of meaninglessness, they should find some kind of contrasting rational (meaning) that can play an essential role in restructuring their "worldview." These new experiences can then be assimilated, allowing life to become more comprehensible and predictable, and thus more trustful. Here we revisit a quote from Salander (2015: 18), who writes:

> In more secular terms, the process of giving a special meaning to objects may well be encompassed by Winnicott's (1971) intermediate area as well as attribution theory (Fölsterling, 2001). According to Winnicott and object-relational theory, people are, from early childhood to death, able to "play with reality" (Salander, 2012). The intermediate area is the mental area of human creation: in childhood in the doll's house or sandpit, in adulthood in the area of art and culture. It is the mental space between the internal world and external reality and it is thus both subjective and objective. Being human is being in between and thus being able to elaborate with facts, especially when confronted with unexpected negative facts such as a cancer disease.

Our view of sacred matters

Proceeding from the comments on viewing the sacred as a "divinity matter," we do not believe we should regard God, the divine, and the transcendent as the sacred core of all phenomena, which people "sanctify" when coping. Instead, we should differentiate between sacred objects that are theistic and those that are non-theistic. If we do so, we will have different "sacred rings," one with the outwardly transcendent as its sacred core (theistic sanctification), the other with the inwardly transcendent as its sacred core (non-theistic sanctification).

In this vein, we find the sacred ring below more appropriate for discussing non-theistic sanctification.

Our sacred core and ring can be found in the Figure 6.2 below. It should be mentioned that when talking about theistic and non-theistic sacred cores, our focus, like that of Pargament et al., "is not on the ontological reality of the sacred, but rather perceptions of the sacred." And the term object "is not restricted to interpersonal objects as is customary in object relations theory. Rather it is used more broadly to refer to any aspect of life" (Pargament & Mahoney, 2005: 25).

The above figure shows the sanctification of non-theistic coping resources found in our studies in different countries. They consist of different aspects of life and different objects that are imbued with non-theist sacred qualities created by individuals and become sacred resources.

In our studies, sanctification of nature is found among Swedish and Malaysian cancer patients (Chapter 3 and 5), sanctification of family and relationships among Chinese, Turkish, and Malaysian cancer patients (Chapters 3 and 5), sanctification

130 *The relationship between culture and health*

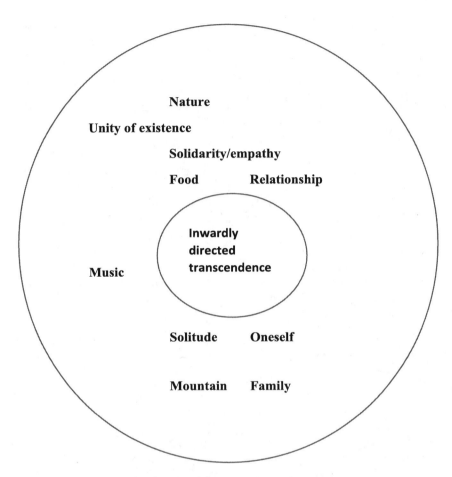

Figure 6.2 Alternative sacred core and ring

of mountains and food among South Korean cancer patients (Chapter 3), sanctification of music among Swedish and Chinese cancer patients (Chapters 3 and 4), and sanctification of oneself among Swedish, Turkish, and Malaysian cancer patients (Chapters 4 and 5). Feelings of empathy seemed to bring about the sanctification of suffering people among Swedish and Turkish cancer patients (Chapters 2 and 5), and sanctification of moments/positive solitude is found among Swedish cancer patients (Chapter 3).

Note that none of these "objects" is explicitly linked to God or a transcendent power, but this does not mean the people who sanctify these "objects" during the process of coping are not religious.

For example, one of the Swedish informants, who self-identified as an atheist, pointed out: "When I've been out in nature, first and foremost, I felt I was myself, that there was time for thoughts, it was peaceful, everything else disappeared. Whatever happens in the world for me or others, nature is still there, it keeps going. That is a feeling of security when everything else is chaos. The leaves fall off, new ones appear, somewhere there is a pulse that keeps going. The silence, it has become so apparent, when you want to get away from all the noise. It is a spiritual feeling if we can use this word without connecting it to God, this is what I feel in nature and it is like a powerful therapy." Here our atheist gives the sacred quality of timelessness to nature by pointing out that *whatever happens in the world for me or others, nature is still there, it keeps going.*

Sanctification and culture

Sanctification has an individual as well as a cultural face. Yet the sacred is conceived of differently across cultures. As Pargament et al. (2005: 187) point out:

> People differ in the aspects of life they hold sacred. These differences may be tied in part to an individual's particular religious identification. After all, members of religious traditions are taught to confer sacred status on different figures, present and past. They are also taught to sanctify other objects differently, such as physical objects, be they the sacred mountains of some Native American traditions, the idols and statues of Hinduism and Buddhism, or the various holy sites of Judaism, Christianity, and Islam. Within pluralistic, individualistic cultures we would expect important differences in sanctification among people more generally, irrespective of their religious affiliations.

Pargament and Mahoney (2005: 187) stress the role of religious institutions as one key source of education about sanctification. Besides these institutions, "organizations, communities, and the larger culture as a whole define what is and what is not sacred, what is to be revered and what is not" (ibid.). Our studies, presented in this book, also demonstrate the impact of religion and culture on the choice of sacred objects when coping with the stressors associated with cancer. Below, with the help of some examples, we will try to shed some light on this issue.

The fact that some Swedish informants perceived a sacred value in nature may be explained, as mentioned in Chapter 3, by recalling the prominent position of nature in Swedish ways of thinking and culture as well as that people living in Sweden are spiritual as opposed to religious and therefore more likely to describe even their religious lives in spiritual terms. We observe, therefore, two important tendencies among people in Sweden – seeking closeness with a supreme force and seeking a natural romanticism – both of which render nature a sacred object and accessible source for coping.

Sanctification of oneself is also a cultural orientation in Sweden. In analyzing the use of spiritual connection with oneself and meaning-making coping among Swedish cancer patients, we used Fromm's view of humanistic religion and notion that, in such an ideology, each individual achieves the highest degree of strength, not the highest degree of powerlessness, and that virtue is self-realization, not obedience (Fromm 1950: 37). Sanctification of oneself can then be seen as a result of the fact that Humanist religion has a strong prevalence in Sweden, where there also exists a relatively high degree of individualism.

Sanctification of solitude can be considered as sanctification of moments (Pargament et al., 2014; Lomax et al., 2011). Respecting other people's need for solitude is one of the cornerstones of Swedish culture, reflecting its strong tendency toward individualism (Baringa 1999: 5). As explained in Chapter 3, in an individual-oriented culture where solitude is valued, it is highly likely that people with a serious illness like cancer will not fear being alone with their thoughts and will sanctify moments of solitude, through which they find themselves.

Sanctification of family among cancer patients in China, Malaysia, and Turkey is probably a result of having been socialized in cultural settings where social relationships tend to be group-oriented.

The sanctification of mountains and food among cancer patients in South Korea can be also explained from a cultural perspective. We mentioned in Chapter 4 that Koreans think that human life came from nature and must return to nature when the body and mind malfunction, and thus they have strong convictions concerning the healing power of nature. It may well be beliefs in these ideas that lead cancer patients in South Korea to sanctify mountains and food when trying to cope with their illness.

Summing up: we have tried to show in this section that sacred matters are not only the products of religious beliefs, but also of cultural beliefs. As Pargament mentions (2017: 18), "Religions are not the sole source of beliefs and perceptions about the sacred. . . . Human understandings about sacredness are firmly rooted in collective life" (Durkheim 1915).

Our studies in different cultural setting show that cultures imprint their views of the sacred onto people facing a life-threatening crisis collectively and individually.

Religious struggles and culture

People who face difficult life events, such as life-threatening illness, may feel that they have been abandoned by God, begin to challenge trusting in God or begin to believe in supernatural powers, like black magic. Previous studies have framed some religious and spiritual (R/S) struggles as *negative religious coping* responses, such as blaming God, the Devil, or one's own sins for serious problems, or viewing problems as divine punishment. According to some researchers (Stauner et al., 2016; Wilt et al., 2017), R/S struggles that lead to negative coping strategies can have various health outcomes, such as more medical diagnoses, functional disabilities, depression, poorer cognitive functioning and subjective health, and negative effects on quality of life.

Wilt et al. (2016: 1) mention that R/S struggles involve tensions, conflicts, or anxieties regarding sacred matters (Exline, 2013; Pargament, 2007). These struggles might focus on the supernatural domain (God, the Devil), on other people, or on the self (doubts, moral conflicts, lack of meaning in life). Key points regarding R/S struggles are (Wilt et al., 2016: Exline, 2013): conflict, tension, and turmoil around sacred matters within oneself, with others, and with the supernatural; over the course of life, people can be shaken spiritually as well as physically, socially, and emotionally; people struggle with challenges in their lives to attain meaning.

According to Pargament (2017), the following types of R/S struggles are recognized: Supernatural, Divine, Demonic Intrapersonal, Moral, Doubt, Ultimate Meaning, and Interpersonal. When struggling, people may feel God has let them down, feel angry at God, feel as though God has abandoned them, feel as though God is punishing them, and question God's love for them (Exline et al., 2014; Wilt et al., 2017).

But an R/S struggle is not merely a personal matter; it is effected by the cultural setting in which the individual is socialized. Inozu et al. (2012) mention that obsessive belief characteristics can lead to subjectively recognizable R/S struggles, such as fears of God and sin, which vary across individuals and cultures. Studies indicate that religious struggles are common in theist countries. One study (Balboni et al., 2013) among advanced cancer patients in the United States shows that 58 percent experienced a spiritual struggle; 30 percent wondered why God allowed this to happen; 29 percent wondered whether they had been abandoned by God; 25 percent were angry at God; 25 percent questioned God's love for them, and 22 percent felt cancer was a punishment from God. In Egypt, 92 percent of patients with cancer reported believing God would help them with their illness (Kesselring et al., 1988). However, Sedlar et al. (forthcoming), studying atheists from three universities in the United States, found that the prevalence of R/S struggles was lower among this group than among believers. A team of researchers from universities in Oxford, Coventry, Royal Holloway University of London, Melbourne, and Otago conducted examinations of 100 studies on the topic published between 1961 and 2014, containing information on around 26,000 people worldwide. They (Jong et al., 2017) found that atheists struggle less with existential questions, especially anxiety over death. Fear of death was also lowest among atheists.

Stauner et al. (2016), citing Inozu, suggests that "The greater moral struggles among religious people may reflect tendencies of scrupulous cultures to express more concern about sin or of guilt-prone individuals to endorse more scrupulous beliefs" (Inozu et al., 2012).

Our studies, conducted in different cultural settings, show that cancer patients who are socialized in non-religious cultures tend not to believe their illness is a result of their own sinfulness or of God's anger. In these studies, we asked informants some questions about negative religious coping methods, which constitute an expression of "a less secure relationship with God, a tenuous and ominous view of the world, and a religious struggle in the search for significance" (Pargament et al. 1998: 712).

As explained in Chapter 3, only 3 percent of Swedish respondents answered that they thought God had abandoned them or felt anger toward God and that this had helped them feel better "to quite a large extent" when they felt stressed, sad, or depressed during or after their illness. A few (1 percent) responded "to a large extent." Nearly nine in ten (88 percent) answered "not at all" to the question about having been abandoned by God. Only 2 percent of respondents reported feeling that God had caused their health problems because of their actions or because they had not been sufficiently faithful. Asked whether they felt their own sinfulness was the reason for their illness, nine of ten (90 percent) responded "not at all."

In response to the question about whether evil power was the cause of their illness, only 1 percent of respondents chose a positive answer. Nineteen out of twenty (94 percent) responded "not at all." As the study shows, very few informants (1 to 3 percent) used any of the negative coping methods. There is no doubt that having been socialized in a culture that is non-religious and characterized by a high degree of rationalism has affected the informants in our Swedish study. Besides, as explained previously, the prevalent view of God in Swedish Protestantism is of a Creator God – one who has left humans to determine their own destinies and shape their own history.

In contrast, as we explained in Chapter 5, we have found belief in evil power among informants in Malaysia. They reported believing in black magic and therefore used the coping method of Demonic Reappraisal. Black magic or dark magic refers to the use of supernatural powers or magic for evil and selfish purposes. Malaysian folk religion advocated animistic and polytheistic beliefs. There are many in the Islamic-majority country of Malaysia who engage in shamanism and other supernatural rituals, despite the fact that such ideas and rituals are against Islamic teaching and considered to be s*hirk* (the sin of practicing idolatry or polytheism).

These examples highlight the crucial role of culture in the use of coping methods oriented toward R/S struggles. However, for some interviewees, the role of culture in coping may be even stronger than that of fundamental religious axioms. Believing in black magic and getting help with alternative treatment from shamans or the like show that cultural beliefs can be stronger than religious axioms.

Relation between religious, spiritual and secular meaning-making coping

In this book, we have focused on three domains of existential meaning-making coping methods: religious meaning-making methods, spiritual meaning-making methods, and secular meaning-making methods. Before summing up our discussion, we need to put forward our views on the connection between these three coping methods.

La Cour and Hvidt (2010: 1294) present a model of how the three domains (secular, spiritual, and religious) of existential meaning-making are related. In this model, these three domains have points of connection, i.e., the concepts and topics of each domain overlap to some extent, as shown in Figure 6.3. According to the authors, "Situating a given phenomenon in the figure will be dependent to some degree on conceptual and cultural context, rather than the phenomenon itself" (ibid.).

It would seem that this figure is based on the above-presented view of religion and spirituality advocated by Pargament, i.e., a definition of religion and spirituality that is problematic because it does not draw a line of demarcation between theists and non-theists and neglects the spirit of our time. As mentioned before, one reason

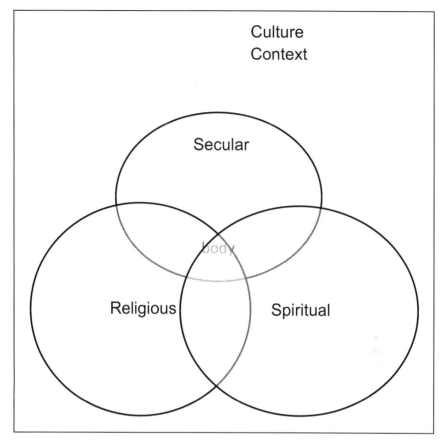

Figure 6.3 Relation of existential meaning-making domains (La Cour & Hvidt (2010: 1294)

for this problem is perhaps that, in the studies on which this definition is based, non-theists and atheists are not included and the cultural perspective is neglected.

With regard to the critical view we presented above, and based on our studies in both religious and non-religious societies, we suggest a new model of how the three domains (secular, spiritual, and religious) of existential meaning-making are related. In this model, as shown in Figure 6.2, the concepts and topics of the religious and spiritual domains overlap to some extent. The concepts and topics of spirituality and secular meaning-making coping also overlap, but there is no overlap between secular and religious concepts and topics. The reason for this is that, as mentioned before, our definition of religion is *a search for significance that unfolds within a traditional sacred context* (Ahmadi 2006: 72). We define spirituality *as a search for connectedness with a sacred source that is related or not related to God or any religious holy sources* (Ahmadi 2006: 72–73). Thus, secular

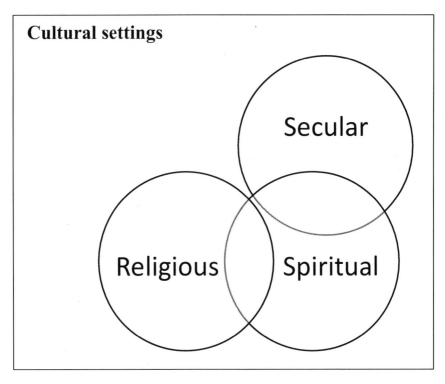

Figure 6.4 Alternative relation of existential meaning-making domains

meaning-making coping hardly has any point of connection with a traditional sacred context, but can overlap with a search for connectedness with a sacred source without relating to God or any traditional religious context. As mentioned before, sacred here is not defined in a religious context, but an inwardly sanctification context. This is illustrated in Figure 5.4 below.

Summary

Summing up: the strategies that people employ when they are stricken by disease, accidents, misfortune, etc., are cultural and historic constructions. As such, they are valid in concrete contexts and time periods. People in different societies have always used some methods, objects, belief systems – including faith in God or other supreme powers, religious sacraments, destiny, or other similar products of their own or others' imagination – to find relief from the anxiety and stress caused by various misfortunes. Some of the employed strategies can be characterized as passive acceptance and others as active resistance.

Regardless of the employed strategies or the secular or religious characteristics of these strategies, coping is about consoling. The coping methods individuals choose depend on where and when they live – and on what trends dominate their life context. In secular societies, religious or spiritual coping methods do not thrive to the same extent as they do in religious societies. Nevertheless, in secular societies, too, some people try to find a meaning in what is happening and to put it into a larger framework. However, the quest for meaning does not necessarily involve a belief in God or religion. Like spiritual and religious coping strategies, secular coping strategies are often employed to console the individual with the belief that she/he is part of a greater or supreme project – that she/he is a small cog in a bigger machine. The individual tries to look at her/his problems from above, from the perspective of a greater whole and see how small and unimportant she/he and her/his maladies are in relation to this whole.

As the studies underlying this book show quite clearly, nature may just as well function as the supreme entity, the whole or being in light of which the individual's own misfortunes lose, to some extent, their imposing definiteness and irreversibility. The insight that one's own life is transitory causes some people to look for the permanent, or at least something that is long-lasting. The forest, stones, trees, the soil itself and all the life that is captured in and around them comfort individuals with a permanency that goes beyond their personal crisis. This insight can console some and give strength to others in dealing with their situation.

Nevertheless, we should not forget that not all individuals who actively try to comfort and console themselves when stricken by a disease like cancer turn to an absolute or supreme being. Some try to achieve something they have always dreamed about while they still have time – a coping strategy that can be characterized as a conscious effort to neglect and forget the disease as much and as long as possible. Some people in secular societies with a relatively high level of economic prosperity adopt an extreme trust in scientific achievements and follow the most recent medical developments relevant to their disease, using money and medical technologies to resist their so-called fate, while others reach a level of transcendence at which they re-evaluate everything that has mattered to them earlier and try to make new priorities. Here even nature offers a possibility to individuals who are facing a crisis.

To what extent the secular or religious or spiritual coping methods can be chosen as a coping method depends on, among other things, the cultural context into which the individuals have been socialized. In other words, culture provides one's grounding in the search for meaning as well as in understanding and interpreting a stressful situation. In a stressful situation, the individual and culture are related to each other.

Our studies show clearly that, in secular societies, religion is not the only available resource in the individual's orientation system. Religion would seem to play an important role as a coping resource for those with limited options. In cultures with large non-religious resources and where religion is less a part of individuals' everyday life, it plays a minor role in the coping process. The tendency to "turn to religion in coping" is primarily a question of religion's position in the culture in which the individual has been socialized. In societies where religion is less prominent in the orientation system, and less relevant to life experiences, it loses its importance for coping, while other meaning-making coping methods related to nature or an inner "force" or positive solitude are the kinds of resources that provide meaning and comfort to individuals facing a serious crisis.

Culture can affect the coping process in four ways: first, the cultural context shapes the type of stress individuals are likely to experience. Second, culture may affect assessment of the stressfulness of a given event. Third, culture affects selection of the strategies individuals use in a given situation. Finally, culture provides the institutional mechanisms individuals may use when trying to cope with stressful situations.

The findings of our studies confirm the third way, i.e., "culture affects selection of the strategies that an individual uses in any given situation." Based on the results present in this book, hospital cancer therapists, social workers, psychologists, and patient navigators (crisis managers) can strengthen the fourth aspect, that is, they can promote the role of culture in providing institutional mechanisms that can help individuals cope with stressful situations. It is therefore crucial that these professionals, especially cancer therapists, turn more of their attention to the importance of meaning-making coping methods in different cultural settings.

Notes

1 Micro- and macrosociology can be seen as two different levels of analysis. Macrosociology involves analysis of either large-scale groups/societies, or of more abstract systems and social structures. Through macrosociology, we can see the whole and offer a better understanding of society, culture, groups and organizations. Microsociology, in contrast to macrosociology, focuses on the individual's daily interactions within a limited area. It is usually based on observation instead of statistics. It is also based on phenomenological philosophy and includes symbolic interactionism and ethnology.
2 Etiology is the doctrine of coordination or causality. The term comes from the Greek aitia, cause, and logia, teaching, and is used in philosophy, physics, psychology, and biology when discussing the causes of different phenomena. In medicine, terms are used specifically for reasons and underlying variables for diseases and pathological conditions.
3 Today, the technique of visualization is used as a tool in stress management and coping. It can be defined as a bodily and spiritual intervention aimed at relieving tension and promoting a relaxed and calm situation under stressful circumstances. The purpose of visualization is to incorporate the strength of consciousness, to assist in the healing of the body, to maintain health, or to relax through an inner communication that involves all the senses.
4 The word humor comes from the Latin humor, which means juice or fluid. Hippocrates, the father of medicine, born around 400 BC, developed humoral pathology, which means that human health depends on the body's four cardinal saps, or humores. These were blood-air, phlegm-water, yellow bile-fire, black bile-earth, all of which were balanced in a healthy person.
5 These comments have been discussed thoroughly in Ahmadi (2006).

References

Ahmadi F. (2006). *Culture, religion and spirituality in coping: The example of cancer patients in Sweden.* Uppsala: Acta Universitatis Upsaliensis.
Ahmadi, F. (Ed.). (2015). *Coping with cancer in Sweden: A search for meaning.* Acta Universitatis Upsaliensis. Studia sociologica Upsaliensia 63. Uppsala: Uppsala University.

Airhihenbuwa, C. O. (1995). *Health and culture beyond the Western paradigm*. London: Sage Publications.

Angel, R. J. & Thoits. P. (1987). The impact of culture on the cognitive contracture of illness. *Culture, Medicine, and Psychiatry* 11: 23–52.

Balboni, T.A, Balboni, M., Enzinger, A. C., Gallivan, K,, Paulk, M. E., Wright, A., Steinhauser, K., VanderWeele, T. J., & Prigerson, H. G. (2013). Provision of spiritual support to patients with advanced cancer by religious communities and associations with medical care at the end of life. *JAMA Intern Med*, 173(12): 1109–1117.

Barinaga, E. (1999). *Swedishness through Lagom. Can words tell us anything about a culture?* Research Paper Series 6: Centre for Advanced Studies in Leadership.

Becker, J. (1998). Readers write: My chair. *The Sun*, 33–34.

Durkheim, É. (1915). *The elementary forms of religious life*. New York: Free Press.

Eddy, M. B. (1875). *Science and health with key to the scriptures*. Boston, MA: Writings of Mary Baker Eddy.

El-Kadi, A. (2007). *What is Islamic medicine?*. Retrieved 9 January 2001 from http://www.islamset.com/hip/i_medcin/index.html.

Exline, J. J. (2013). Religious and spiritual struggles. In K. I. Pargament, J. J. Exline, & J. W. Jones. (Eds.). *APA handbook of psychology, religion and spirituality* (Vol. 1). Washington DC: American Psychological Association.

Exline, J. J., Pargament, K. I., Grubbs, J. B., & Yali, A. M. (2014). The religious and spiritual struggles scale: Development and initial validation. Psychology of Religion and Spirituality, 6(3): 208–222. DOI: http://dx.doi.org/10.1037/a0036465.

Freudenberg, N. (2000). Health and culture: Beyond the western paradigm – book review. *Health Education Research*, 15(4): 508–510.

Fromm, E. (1950). *Psychoanalysis and religion*. New Haven, CT: Yale University Press.

Fölsterling F. (2001). *Attribution – an introduction to theory, research and application*. Philadelphia: Psychology Press.

Gregory, S. P. & Baltimore, M. (2005). Cross-national correlations of quantifiable societal health with popular religiosity and secularism in the prosperous democracies. *Online Journal of Religion and Society* 7. Retrieved 1 September 200 from http://moses.creighton.edu/JRS/pdf/2005-11.pdf.

Hailparn, D. F & Hailparn, M. (1994). Treating the Catholic patient: Unique dynamics and implications for psychotherapy. *Journal of Contemporary Psychotherapy*, 2(4): 271–279.

Helman, C. G. (2000). *Culture, health and illness*. Oxford: Butterworth-Heinemann.

Hershock, P. D. (2006). *Buddhism in the public sphere: Reorienting global interdependence*. New York: Routledge.

Husain, S. A. (1998). Religion and health from the Muslim perspective. In Harold. G. Koenig (Ed.). *Religion and Mental Health*. New York: Academic Press.

Inozu, M., Clark, D. A., Karanci, A. N. (2012). Scrupulosity in Islam: A comparison of highly religious Turkish and Canadian samples. *Behavior Therapy*, 43(1): 190–202.

Jong, J., Ross, R. P, Simons, T., & Halberstadt 2017,, N., J. (2017). The religious correlates of death anxiety: a systematic review and meta-analysis. *Religion, Brain & Behavior.* Retrieved from http://www.tandfonline.com/doi/full/10.1080/21535 99X.2016.1238844.

Kehoe, N. C. (1998). Religion and mental health from the Catholic perspective. In H. G. Koenig. *Religion and mental health*. New York: Academic Press.

Kesselring, A., Dodd, M. J., Lindsey, A. M. & Strauss, A. L. 1986. Attitude of patients living in Switzerland about cancer and its treatment. *Cancer Nursing,* 9(2):77–85.

La Cour P. & Hvidt, N. C. (2010). Research on meaning-making and health in secular society: Secular, spiritual and religious existential orientations. *Social Science & Medicine*, 71: 292–1299.

Lomax, W. J., Kripal, J. J., & Pargament, K. I. et al. (2011). Perspectives on "sacred moments" in psychotherapy. *The American Journal of Psychiatry*, 168(1): 12–18.

Luckmann, T. (1996). The privatization of religion and morality. In P. Heelas, P., S. Lash, & P. Morris (Eds.), *Detraditionalization: Critical reflections on authority and identity* (pp. 72–88). Oxford: Blackwell.

Malony, H. W. (1998). Religion and mental health from the Protestant perspective. In I. Harold & G. Koeing, *Religion and mental health*. New York: Academic Press.

Moberg, O. (Ed.). (2002). *Research in the social scientific study ofrReligion* (Vol 1, pp. 133–152). Greenwich, CT: JAL Press.

Nasr, S. H. (1975). Sufism and the spiritual needs of contemporary man. In J. Needleman & D. Lewis, Dennis (Eds.), *Sacred tradition and present need*. New York: Viking Press.

Ozawa De Silva, C. & Brendan Richard Ozawa-De Silva Ozawa-De Silva, B. R. (2011). Mind/body theory and practice in Tibetan medicine and Buddhism. *Body & Society*, 17(1): 95–119.

Pargament, K. I. (1997). *The psychology of religion and coping: Theory, research, practice*. New York: Guilford Press.

Pargament, K. I., Lomax, J. W., McGee, J. S. & Fang, Q. (2014). Sacred moments in psychotherapy from the perspectives of Mental Health Providers and Clients: Prevalence, Predictors, and consequences. *Spirituality in Clinical Practice*, (4): 248–262.

Pargament, K. I. & Mahoney, A. (2005). Sacred matters: Sanctification as a vital topic for the psychology of religion. *The International Journal for the Psychology of Religion*, 15(3): 179–198.

Pargament, K. I., Omanb, D., Pomerleaua, J., & Mahoney, A. (2017). Some contributions of a psychological approach to the study of the sacred, *Religion*. Retrieved from http://www.tandfonline.com/doi/full/10.1080/0048721X.2017.1333205

Pargament, K. I., Smith, B. W., Koenig, H. G., & Perez, L. (1998). Patterns of positive and negative religious coping with major life stressors. Journal for the Scientific Study of Religion, 37(4): 710–724.

Rosen, F. 1999. Complementary therapies and traditional Judaism. *The Mount Sinai Journal of Medicine*, 2(66):102–105.

Rundström, B. (1997). *Invandrare i vård och omsorg. En fråga om bemötande av äldre*. Rapport till utredningen om bemötande av äldre. SOU Rapport 76.

Sahad, M. N. & Abdullah S. (2013). *Santau and Malay society: An analysis from the terspective of Islamic Aqidah*. Retrieved from http://jurnalmelayu.dbp.my/wordpress/wp content/uploads/2014/09/223–242-Santau.pdf.

Salander, P. (2015). Introduction: A critical discussion on the concept of spirituality in research on health, In F. Ahmadi (Ed.), *Coping with cancer in Sweden: A search for meaning*. Acta Universitatis Upsaliensis. Studia sociologica Upsaliensia 63. Uppsala: Uppsala University.

Scott, B. W. (1998). Treating Buddhist patients. In Harold G. Koeing (Ed.), *Religion and mental health*, New York: Academic Press.

Sedlar, A., Pargament, K. I., Exline, Julie J., Grubbs, J. B., & Bradley, D. F. (forthcoming). *Spiritually integrated psychotherapy: Understanding and addressing the sacred*. New York: Guilford Press.

Snow, L. F. (1978). Sorcerers, saints and charlatans: Black folk healers in urban America. *Culture, Medicine and Psychiatry*, 2: 69–106.

Stauner, N., Exline, J. J., & Pargament, K. I. (2016). Religious and spiritual struggles as concerns for health and well-being. *Horizonte*, 14(41): 48–75.

Thielman, S. B. (1998). Reflections on the role of religion in the history if psychology. In H. G. Koeing (Ed.), *Religion and mental health*. New York: Academic Press.

Wilt, J. A., Grubbs, J. B., Exline, J. J., & Pargament, K. I. (2016, January 21). Personality, religious and spiritual struggles, and well-being. *Psychology of Religion and Spirituality*. Retrieved from http://dx.doi.org/10.1037/rel0000054

Wilt, J. A., Pargament, K. I., & Exline, J. J. J. J. (2017). Trajectories of religious/spiritual struggles between years 1 and 2 of college: The predictive role of religious belief salience. *The International Journal for the Psychology of Religion,* 27(4): 172–187.

Winnicott, D. (1971). *Playing and reality*. London: Tavistock Publications.

Zedek, M. R. (1998). Religion and mental health from the Jewish perspective. In H. G. Koenig (Ed.), *Religion and mental health* (pp. 255–261). New York: Academic Press.

Zinnbauer, B. J. & Pargament, K. I. (2005). Religiousness and spirituality. In R. F. Paloutzian & C. L. Parks (Eds.), *Handbook of psychology and religion* (pp. 21–42). New York: The Guilford Press.

Zinnbauer, B. J. & Pargament, K. I., & Scott, A. B. 1999. The emerging meaning of religiousness and spirituality: Problems and prospects. *Journal for Personality*, 67(6): 889–919.

Index

active coping strategies 18
Active Religious Surrender 83, 87
Active Religious Surrounding 78–9, 91
Aflakseir, A. 90, 96
"Ah-dung-bah-dung" 62–3
Ahmadi, F. 23–4, 28, 40, 41, 52, 53, 56, 61, 66, 71, 124; religion, definition of 16
Airhihenbuwa, C. O. 105–7
alternative medicine 115
alternative therapy 115
altruism 80–1; in Swedish culture 41
anatta (principle) 116
angin 95
Ani, A. 92
animism 94, 95
annieca (principle) 116
anti-cancer medicine 103
anxiety 102
atheist group 54, 125
attribution theory 24, 128–9
avoidant coping strategies 18

Baltimore, M. 107–8
Barinaga, E. 39, 40–1
Becker, J. 122
"being a good person" 80–1
beliefs 1, 12, 102, 122, 136
Benevolent Religious Reappraisal 78, 90
Berger, P. L. 9
Bibby, R. W. 9
Bible 47, 109, 112
black magic 91, 95
body 114
body-mind-spirit relation 70
body-mind-spirit techniques 5, 70–1
bomoh 93, 95
Buddhism 2, 5, 89, 94, 115–17, 122, 131

Buddhist culture 2
Buddhist medicine 117

Cartesian duality 114
Catholic collectivization 111
Catholicism 111–13
Catholic psychology 111
Catholic teachings 112
Changzhen, Gong 69
China 70; civilization of 70; culture of 5; existential secular coping methods 66–70; inner peace 68–9; listening to music to ease pain 69–70; religious coping methods 65–6; study in 65
Chinese medicine 69
Chinese music 69
Chi-square test 84–6, 88
Christian culture 2
Christianity 2, 112; dominant view in 86; theological controversies in 85
Christian treatment methods 113
Coe, George 8
Coleman, P. G. 90, 96
Collaborative Religious Coping 79, 91
Comte, Auguste 40
Confucianism 63, 72
connectedness 135–6
consumerism 106
control 55
Cook, C. C. H. 12, 13–14
coping 110, 111–12; burdens of 20–1; characteristics of 4; components of 17; contextual approach to 2; definition of 17; impact of culture on 101; implications for 116; importance for 7; in nonreligious societies 28; oriented and existential 3; possibilities

for 4; resources of 20–1, 65; styles of 19–21
coping methods 1, 42, **43–4,** 136–7; culture on choice of 64; music as 70; nature-related 3; religious 2; research on 55; spiritual 2
coping strategies 2, 3, 17–19, 109; goals of 18; types of 18
cosmology 95
Craigie, F. C. 14
crime 107
cultural beliefs 96, 104
cultural importance 110
cultural setting 2; collectivist 2; feature in 104; individual 2
culture 1, 138; *vs.* health 101–9; of life 108; on meaning-making coping methods 4; non-religious 128–9; religious struggles and 132–6, *135, 136*; role in coping 1–2; sanctification and 131–2; of socialization 101; Swedish ways of 131

dark magic 91
death, cause of 1
Demonic Reappraisal 85–7, 91, 92, 96, 104
divinity matter 129
dominant cultural traits 3
dukkha (principle) 115–16

East Asia: coping study in China *see* China; coping study in South Korea *see* South Korea
educational theodicy 90
El-Kadi, A. 113
embodiments of divine 127
emotion-focused strategies 18
empathy/altruism 39–40; absence of 40; sense of 40; in Swedish culture 41
ethnic minorities 106
etiology 138n2
European Values Study Group (EVSSG) 57n3
everyday life 93, 94, 137; banality of 16; transcendent aspects of 24; in Turkey 5
"evil eye" 85–6; features of 104
existential coping methods 36–8, 50–2
existential meaning-making coping 15
existential meaning-making domains 134, *135, 136*
existential secular coping methods 61, 66–70, 80–2; in China 66–70; in Malaysia 92–3; in South Korea 62–5; in Turkey 80–2
"experiencing a strong spiritual feeling" 48

Facebook 89
family centeredness 67
family planning policy 73n4
family relationships 5, 66–8, 81–2
fasting 81, 97n2
fate 91, 137
fear of death 133
finding power inside oneself 80
Five Phases Music Therapy (FPMT) 69
Folkman, S. 17, 21–2
FPMT *see* Five Phases Music Therapy (FPMT)
Frankl's perspective on meaning 24, 129
Fromm, E. 22, 39, 80, 92, 131

gender-related dysfunction 108
"getting a spiritual feeling by helping others" 48
Gilsenan, M. 85
global changes 106
globalization 105–7
global trends 106
Glock's multidimensional measurement model of religion 10
"going to church" 45
Gregory, S. P. 107–8
Groebel, J. 81
Grouch, R. L. 47
group-oriented societies 104

Hall, G. Stanley 8
Handbook of Religion and Health (Koenig) 12
happiness 67, 110
healing: implications for 116; power of nature 62; process 69; therapy 41
health: contextual approach to 2; culture *vs.* 101–9; impact of culture on 102; individual responsibility for 103; shamanic view of 92
Health and Culture: Beyond the Western Paradigm (Airhihenbuwa) 105–6
healthcare systems 6
health promotion efforts 107
health research 1–2
Helman, C. G. 102–4
Hinde, R. A. 81

Hinduism 5, 89, 94, 96, 131
Hippocrates 138n4
Hobfoll, S. E. 17
Holahan, C. J. 18
Holistic Health 87
huji 73n2
human altruism 80–1
human diversity 126
human functioning: dimensions of 121
humanistic religion 80
Husain, Syed Arshad 113, 115
Hvidt, N. C. 134

illness 28, 31, 45–6, 49, 51, 69, 70, 78–80, 90; cause of 102–5; depression during 42; life-threatening 113, 114; meaning of 11; psychological effects of 18; by santau 105
Index of Religiousness 10
Indian/Hindu culture 5
individual identity 52
individual integrity 53
individualism 40
individual-oriented coping methods 103
individuals' orientation system 7
informants, information of 29
inner peace 70, 71
institutional religiosity 4
integrity 52
international trade 6
inwardly directed transcendence 13–15
Islam 89; forms of 89; influence of 113–15
Islamic culture 2
Islamic medicine 113
Islamic teachings 90

James, William 8
Jenkins, R. A. 15–16
Jews 118
Judaism: influence of 117–20; principle in 118; sanctions 119; traditional 119

Kehoe, Nancy Clare 111
Kenneth Pargament 120
Keramat 92–3
King, M. 10
Koenig, H. G. 12–13

La Cour, P. 134
Launier, R. 17
layman's theories 102, 105
Lazarus, R. S. 17, 21–2
liberals 111

life-threatening illness 113, 114
Little Emperor Syndrome 68
loneliness 64
Luckmann. T. 53, 127

macro-sociological perspectives 102–5
macrosociology 138n1
Mahoney, A. 41, 66, 122, 131
Malaysia 5, 6; *Active Religious Surrounding* 91; *Benevolent Religious Reappraisal* 90; *Collaborative Religious Coping* 91; culture and meaning-making coping in 93–7; demographic characteristics of participants **90**; *Demonic Reappraisal* 91; ethnic groups in 89; everyday life of 94; existential secular meaning-making coping methods 92–3; family relationships in 92; finding power inside oneself in 92; folk religion of 92–3; Islamization of 94–5; nature in 92–3; *Passive Religious Deferral* 91; *Pleading for Direct Intercession* 91; population of 89; *Punishing God Reappraisal* 90; religious coping methods 89–92; *Religious Purification* 91; *Seeking Support from Clergy or Congregation Members* 92; traditions in 93
Malony, H. W. 110–11
manifestations of God 127
meaning-making coping 2, 14, 21, 23, 25, 65, 101; culture on 4; notion of 3; strategies 3, 28; studies on 101
medicine: Buddhist 117; Chinese 69; Islamic 113; religious practices in 119; Tibetan 117
Meditation and Visualization 87
mental attitudes 63
mental health 110; Islamic strategy for 113; perceptions of 109; *see also* health
mentality 109
microorganisms 103
Mohamed, N.M. 92
Moos, R. H. 18
morality. 67
morbidity 104; accusation concerning 104; cause of 103; culture-based view of 102; perceptions of 109; supernatural explanations of 105
music of nature 50
music, religious 45
music therapy 69
Muslim belief system 115

Muslim countries: coping study in Malaysia see Malaysia; coping study in Turkey see Turkey

natural environment 103
natural religion 92
natural romanticism 52, 56; tendency toward 53–4
nature 49–50; prominent position of 51
nature-related coping methods 3
negative religious coping 46–8, 132
nirvana (principle) 116
non-religious cultures 128–9, 133
non-selfishness 116
non-theist group 47, 54, 125
non-theistic sanctification 121, 124–5

obedience 110
object-relational theory 24–5, 129
objects 130–1
one-child policy 68, 73n4, 73n5
orientation system 93
Orthodox Assembly 118
Orthodox Judaism 118
outwardly directed transcendence 11–13

Pargament, K. I. 15–16, 41, 54, 66, 112, 122, 131, 133; approach to religion and spirituality 123; definitions 123–4; discussion on sanctification 127; perspectives of 125; religion, definition of 16; theory of coping 17; theory of religious coping 21–2; view of sanctification 120
passive coping strategies 18
Passive Religious Deferral 78, 83, 87, 91
pawang 95
peaceful mental attitude 71, 117
physical health 108, 110; *see also* health
pikuach nefesh 118
Plato 108
Pleading for Direct Intercession 79, 84, 87, 91
Poole, R. 13
population: of cancer patients in Sweden 3; cultural characteristics of 6
positive life perspective coping method 63, 82, 117
positive solitude 39–40, 64
post-materialist values 53
pragmatism 56
predestination 91
pre-Islamic cultures 5

privacy 55–6
private religion 53
problem-solving strategies 18
Protestantism 109; influence of 109–11
psychological well-being 2
psychology 114
psychotherapy 114
public health educators 106
public health systems 102
Punishing God Reappraisal 78, 85, 87, 90

quality of life 67
Quran 91, 96, 113

Rahman, N. A. 92
rationalism 56
rational positivism 116
RCOPE *see* religious coping methods (RCOPE)
religion/religiousness 1, 7–15; approaches to 8–10; characteristic features of 109; "comeback" of 107; in coping 2; definition 123–4; definition of 3, 16, 126, 128, 135; Glock's multidimensional measurement model of 10; integration of 1; lack of interest in 4; positive impact of 108; psychology and sociology of 126; scope for 1; view of 134–5
religiosity 61, 63–4, 107, 122; changes in 66; definitions of 15–16; framework of 127; influence of 108; tendencies toward 42; *see also* religion/religiousness; religious coping
religious affiliation 42
religious and spiritual (R/S) struggles 132–6, *135, 136*; types of 133
religious attitudes 1
religious authority 54–5
religious coping 17, 23, 28, 54; dysfunctional forms of 22; functions of 22; methods of 21–5; Pargament theory of 21–2
religious coping methods (RCOPE) 2–6, 21, 23, 24, 29–36, 118, 137; advantages of 22; in Malaysia 90–2; methods 6, 29, 42; originators of 23; ranking of 47; in South Korea 61; in Turkey *see* Turkey
religious functions 23
religious meaning-making coping, 6
religious messages 112
religious music, listening to 45
religiousness, global indicators of 21

religious oriented coping 120
Religious Purification 79–80, 91
religious socialization 44
religious teaching 112
religious thinking, presence of 114
relying on oneself 54–6
research: religion and spirituality in 1; theoretical frameworks to 1
resilience, level of 63
Riesman, David 64
Roman Catholic Church 111
Rosen, F. 118–19
Rundström, B. 102

sacred core 122, *123*
sacred, definition 124
sacred matters 120–1
sacredness 126
sacred object 67
sacred rings 122, *123*, 129
sacred values 53
sadageh 81
Salander, P. 24, 129
salvation, emotional assurance of 110
sanctification 123–9; in coping 119–32; and culture 131–2; definition of 66–7, 124; of nature 124–5; Pargament's view of 120; process of 122; in religious context 120–3; view of 129–31, *130*
sanctification theory 24
sanctify 129
santau 95, 105
satan 86, 96, 97n5
SCOPE *see* spiritual coping (SCOPE)
Scotton 116
secularism 44
secular meaning-making coping methods 6, 87–8, 92–3
secular-rational rationality 4, 52
"secular" spiritual coping 24
secular spirituality 4
Seeking Support from Clergy/Congregation Members 80, 84, 92
Self-Directing Religious Coping 45, 47, 54, 55, 88
self-directing style 54
self-direction 55
self-identify 57n5, 126, 128
self-realization 53, 80
self-reliance 45
self-responsibility: level of 63
self-transcendence 13–14
Seoul, population of 64

sexuality 106
shamanism 5, 91, 92, 95, 96, 97n9, 134; impact of 92; spiritual and incorporate features of 61
Shi, L. Z. 67
sickness *see* illness
significance: definition 123–4
Skeat, W.W. 92
Sloan, Richard 13
social environment 104
social health: level of 107; *see also* health
socialization 2; culture of 101; in Sweden 45
social life of individuals 3
social relationships 64
social support 64
soul 114
South Korea: belief in healing power of nature 62; demographic characteristics of participants 60, **60–1**; existential secular coping methods 62–5; finding oneself in relationships with others 64–5; mind-body connection 62–3; religious coping methods 61; study in **60**, 60–1; traditional family of 72; transcendent power, relying on 63–4
spirits, variety of 95–6
spiritual beliefs 94
spiritual cleansing 91
Spiritual Connection 83, 87
spiritual connection with oneself 38–9
spiritual coping (SCOPE) 4, 6, 23, 24, 28, 41, 49, 70, 137
Spiritual Discontent 80, 84, 87
spiritual healing, effectiveness of 112
spiritual health 109–10
spirituality 8–15, 24, 28, 61; approaches to 10–11; changes in 66; in coping 2; definition of 3, 15–16, 124, 128, 135; degree of 61; influence of 108; integration of 1; lack of interest in 4; Pargament views on 15; popularity of 127; realm of 128; sense of 70; tendency toward 55; view of 134–5
spiritually oriented coping 48–50, 120
spiritual meaning-making coping, 6
spiritual music 41
spiritual rebirth 48
spiritual sanctification of nature 36–8
'spiritual' sense" 50
spiritual struggle 133
Starbuck, Edwin 8
stress individuals 101

styles of coping: anxious preoccupation 19; avoidance or denial 19; fatalism 19; fighting spirit 19; helplessness 19; hopelessness 19
subcultures 106
subjective well-being 61
Sunni code 89
Sunni imams 85
survival values 52
Sweden 3; history of 47; individualism of 40–1; population of cancer patients in 3; position of religion in 53; religious activities in 51–2; socialization in 45; welfare system in 103; *see also* swedish culture
Swedish cultural environment 28
Swedish culture 28–9, 109; existential coping methods 36–41; religious coping methods (RCOPE) 29–36; statistics 41–52; Swedish studies on coping from cultural perspective 52–6

theist group 45, 47, 54, 125
therapeutic methods 54
Thielman, S. B. 108
thinking: individualistic and collectivistic ways of 81; Swedish ways of 40–1, 131
"thinking about a spiritual force" 48
Tibetan medical practice 117
timelessness, sacred quality of 131
trade unions in Sweden 56n2
traditional Judaism 119
traditional rationality 52
transcendence 8–15; approaches to 11; attributes of 121; definition of 14; inwardly directed 13–15; outwardly directed 11–13
transcendent power, relying on 63–4
transcendent qualities 127
transcendent reality 122
Turkey 5, 6; *Active Religious Surrounding* 78–9; altruism 80–1; *Benevolent Religious Reappraisal* 78; culture 77, 93–7; demographic characteristics of participants **77**; description of sample **83**; everyday life of 94; existential secular coping methods 80–2; family relationships 81–2; finding power inside oneself 80; meaning-making coping in 93–7; *Passive Religious Deferral* 78; positive life perspectives 82; *Punishing God Reappraisal* 78; religious coping methods (RCOPE) 78–80, 82–9; searching for existential meaning 82; searching for meaning by contemplating philosophical issues 82; statistics in 82–3
Turkish culture 94

unification, spiritual sense of 53

visualization, technique of 138n3

Weber, Max 55
welfare system in Sweden 103
well-being 3–4, 28, 53–4, 61, 101; of individuals 108; Islamic strategy for 113; psychological 2
wellness 115
Winnicott 24–5, 129
Wong-McDonald, A. 47
World Values Study (WVS) 52, 84, 94, 97n4
WVS *see* World Value Study (WVS)

Young-Eisendrath, Polly 14

zakat 81, 97n3
Zedek, M. R. 118
Zein, Z. 84
Zimmerman, C. C. 82
Zinnbauer, B. J. 15, 16; religion, definition of 16